CEO LOGIC

How to Think and Act Like a Chief Executive

By

C. Ray Johnson

NEW AGE INTERNATIONAL PUBLISHERS
2006

Printed in India at V.K. Printer, Delhi
1 2 3 4 5 6 7 8 9 10

ISBN: 81-224-1726-4
Original Edition Price: $ 15.99
Indian Edition: Rs. 175.00
C-05-06-174

PUBLISHING FOR ONE WORLD
NEW AGE INTERNATIONAL (P) LIMITED, PUBLISHERS
(formerly Wiley Eastern Ltd.)
New Delhi • Bangalore • Chennai • Cochin • Guwahati • Hyderabad
Jalandhar • Kolkata • Lucknow • Mumbai • Ranchi
Visit us at www.newagepublishers.com

Acknowledgments

I owe a debt of gratitude to those many who encouraged me to document in book form the mentoring advice that I've used with clients and in my own career to think through the fundamental responsibilities of CEOs and top managers. My hope is that the wisdom of my own mentors shines through, and to them I offer my heartfelt thanks.

Many people helped to shape and produce this book, and to them I'd like to express my appreciation. My publisher, Ron Fry, and his capable staff, Stacey A. Farkas, Anne Brooks, and Mike Gaffney were enthusiastic about the book and responsive to my needs. My manuscript developer, Sheryl Fullerton, helped to shape the manuscript by offering professional advice on both form and substance; and freelance editor, Dana Bell, provided expert editing feedback and advice. And most of all, my deepest thanks go to my friends and associates, many of whom are acknowledged in the book.

Contents

Preface

The Foundations and Disciplines of Management

The management task is one of enormous challenges and, if done right, enormous rewards. But to meet the challenges of management in today's volatile marketplace, CEOs and managers at all levels need a new and complete mastery of both the foundations of solid management thinking and the practical application of the essential business disciplines. *CEO Logic* provides these guiding principles and proven tactics in the Foundations and Disciplines of Management.

Foundation 1: Business Philosophy

Learning to think like a CEO will improve the performance of managers at all levels. Develop a business philosophy consisting of fundamental business principles, your own personal management philosophy, and your insights into a particular business opportunity. Then convert these into core operating values. Use these core operating values to guide management decisions, actions, and resource allocations. The first rule of management is to select the right business. Develop and strengthen core competencies to enhance your competitive edge. You must do something better than your competitors, and that something must result in a unique, hard-to-copy, or at least distinctive benefit to your customers. Aim at satisfying customers and employees first, with a long-term goal of achieving profits.

Foundation 2: Strategy

The object of business strategy is to establish a competitive edge in the marketplace that will allow a company to prosper by offering a long-term better value to its customers. The strategic process involves matching the organization's internal resources to the external market. Strategy is the logic or rationale of a business that details both goals and methods of achievement. Through the process of formulating strategy, a CEO positions his or her company for success by making choices about customers to target, markets to enter, products to offer, risks to manage, vulnerabilities to defend, customer needs to satisfy, competencies used to fulfill those needs, and the organizational structure required to support those choices.

Discipline 1: Business Operations Planning

Validate strategies, allocate resources, and prepare for implementation. Project the actions required, resources needed, and results expected to carry out your strategy. Use planning to define and better understand the risks worth taking. Let management of these risks help you meet your goals. Develop formal programs to consider how you will really achieve your objectives. Use planning to determine viability, as a basis for evaluating potential solutions, and as a yardstick with which to measure future performance.

Discipline 2: People Management

The strength of a business resides in the minds of its people; manage accordingly. Human concerns are always an issue. Look closely at your people. Employers usually get the employees they deserve. Provide a viable business opportunity and hire the best. The teams with the best players have the highest winning percentages. Manage people as though they will be as they have been. Modify job assignments to utilize the strengths of managers. Organize the work to make their weaknesses irrelevant to their performance. Face up to mediocrity.

Discipline 3: Career Management

No business can continue to grow and prosper without nurturing its young managers. Help new managers to know themselves, to communicate effectively, and to make ethical decisions. Teach them about the organization, the politics and the philosophy of the business, and about the many advantages of mentors. But most of all, teach them about the work required to succeed. Require new managers to take personal control of their performance and their careers. If you teach them nothing else besides ethics, teach them to *get results*.

Discipline 4: Sales

Understand the difference in sales responsibilities for CEOs, sales managers, and salespeople. The *CEO* is responsible for every element in the marketing chain. The *sales manager* develops and disciplines the selling system, measures and manages sales efficiency, builds the sales team, defines the sales message, solves day-to-day problems, and motivates each salesperson toward optimum achievement. The *salesperson* delivers the sales message and sells. Develop a formal growth strategy and build a "selling machine" with the horsepower to meet your volume, margin, and market-share objectives.

Discipline 5: Numbers

The primary task of accounting is to help operating managers make better decisions. Equally important is its role in developing sound operating controls. The representations of traditional accounting, at best, offer some slight distortion of reality. At worst, they can be huge misrepresentations of the facts. Look to the fundamentals behind the numbers to discover the real truths about your business. Teach your accountants to make the numbers reflect reality and relate to management objectives.

Discipline 6: Banking

Bankers are often bad partners. Bankers offer one-sided deals that require you to accept 100 percent of the risk and the bank to accept none. Match your funding needs to the specific loan products offered by various lending institutions. To get their money, learn their rules and present bankers with "zero risk" opportunities.

Discipline 7: Cash Management

Cash is king. No cash, no company. End of story.

Discipline 8: Tough Times and Turnarounds

Survival displaces all other rules of management during tough times. Survivability depends on cash, credit, and product viability. See Discipline 7. Concentrate resources only on core opportunities. Minimize risk. Take the tried and proven path whenever possible. Radical change may be needed. Match the cure to the illness.

Discipline 9: Acquisitions

Don't buy it if you can't improve it. Compare the cost and viability of expansion by acquisition to that of internal development. Remember that distinctive or unique product or service benefits must be supported by hard-to-copy core competencies. In the long run, the acquired company's defendable core competencies, its funding structure, the strength of its ongoing management team, and your alternative operating strategy (in addition to the purchase price paid) will determine the future success of your acquisition. Develop a formal acquisition plan. Focus on current cash flow and future potential. Do not overpay.

Discipline 10: Leadership

Leadership is a matter of combining trained intellect, insightful intuition, and superior character, with character being the dominant factor. The secrets to leadership are passion, motivation, ethics, courage, communication, judgment, and insight. Passion supplies the energy, motivation attracts the followers, ethics generates trust from all constituencies, courage provides the backbone needed to make tough decisions, communication delivers the message, judgment supports good decision-making, and insight provides the capacity to select the right people, the right role for yourself, the right goal, and the right strategy.

Introduction

Difficulties mastered are opportunities won.
—Winston Churchill

When management gurus say that people are a company's most important asset, they are right. But they could refine that and say that *the strength of a business resides in the minds of its people.* The capacity to manage is based on a manager's ability to accurately perceive current circumstances, the foresight to consistently forecast future market needs, the capability to develop effective strategies, and competence in issues of implementation, such as the insight to select the right people for the right jobs. All of these capacities are predicated on *thinking* about the true purpose of human, physical, financial, technological, and even intangible resources in the right way. And that is true most of all for an organization's chief executive officer. The CEO holds the vision of the entire organization: everything from its business environment to its customers to its vulnerabilities and strengths to its cash position to its strategy, and beyond. To succeed in the role, the person in charge must *think like a CEO* about fundamental business principles and philosophy. He or she must develop and validate a personal vision of the organization, its future, and the planning and execution of its strategy. There's a certain discipline to thinking like a CEO, a discipline that is not inborn but that can be learned. And that's what *CEO Logic* is about. Even for those who aren't at the CEO level, learning this mind-set can improve personal performance. Any individual at any level in any kind of business can benefit from what this book teaches.

I have run a number of companies ranging in size from very small to one of the Fortune 500, but my purpose in this book is not simply to relate my own management philosophy or share my deeply held thoughts on the subject or even to tell you how *I* think. My primary goal is to provide an organized structure for thinking about business in an easy-to-understand format. The information provided in this book offers CEOs and businesspeople at all levels a chance to develop real power: Power to get out of tough situations, power to develop careers, power to make an organization perform, and the power to achieve true success. The secret to this power does not lie in style, presentation, organizational structure, or management technique alone. These are important tools, but they pale in significance to clear thinking, based on the disciplined application of fundamental business principles.

Let me offer a story to illustrate the power of clear thinking in professional management. In the early 1970s, I was involved in a business venture where we sold 5,000 motorcycles a year, each with a 100-percent full recourse financing—a type of retail financing that in effect requires the retailer to co-sign for the customer. This "co-signing" greatly facilitates finance approvals but adds a great deal of risk to the retailer. The terms of this arrangement were simple. If the customer did not pay, for any reason, we did!

We entered into recourse financing as part of an effort to rethink our overall marketing plan. This rethinking effort began when my old boss, Marvin Borr, figured we could sell more motorcycles if we could reduce the time from the customer's buying decision to the time we delivered the bike. There were a couple of major stumbling blocks to meeting this objective. The motorcycles took several hours to be serviced for initial use, and retail finance approvals sometimes took days.

All of our competitors accepted these conditions as unchangeable facts of life. Marv, who had mastered the ability to think like a CEO, felt there had to be a better way to address these issues. He believed that if we could just think about them in the right way, we'd find a solution. So he told me that he was sure that my management team and I could solve this problem and announced in public that, beginning in 30 days, all of our dealerships would be offering "one hour delivery." He began an advertising campaign that told everyone they could ride out on their new motorcycles within 60 minutes of their decision to buy one. Quick deliveries are fairly commonplace today, but they were unheard of in 1973.

We on the management team were stunned, but had no choice but to go to work on the task he had given us. Right after the announcement, Marv left for vacation, reinforcing the fact that the problem was ours. The last thing he told me before he left was, "Do it right and don't cost us any money."

As with many business problems, the solution turned out to be quite simple. First, we preserviced the motorcycles with everything but fuel and batteries. We pretested each bike by using an umbilical fuel tank and battery setup so that they could be made ready for delivery just by adding fuel, installing a precharged battery, and running through a final setup and safety checklist. Second, we worked out a "recourse financing" deal with our bank that raised the finance rate to pay for the potential of increased delinquencies but allowed us to make immediate on-site loan approvals ourselves. This forced us to become experts in credit management and skip-tracing, but that's another story. When Marv returned, the system was in place and running. Over the next five years, our business increased four-fold.

It was from this, and many other experiences like this one, that the concept of *CEO Logic* began. It started with these few basic rules of business problem-solving:

- Getting your management team to think like CEOs unleashes the strength and power that resides in their minds.
- The way you think about a problem has a big impact on your capacity to resolve the situation.

A totally committed work force gets the job done better

Complex problems are easier to manage when they are reduced to their basic elements.

In the case presented above, we learned that what seemed complex (one-hour deliveries), had only two elements (predelivery service and retail financing). The key was to figure out how to think about the task. Once we were committed to thinking about it in the right way, we could break the problem down, and the solutions then became obvious.

Successful CEOs have mastered the skills of directing their people's efforts toward the right issues, of gaining their total commitment, and of breaking complex business issues into their basic elements. *CEO Logic* offers a process that will help anyone with common sense and discipline to identify the simple decisions that underlie the complex particulars of any given business situation. This is the key to thinking like a CEO, and it can transform average managers into great performers.

This classic approach to business thinking is a practical philosophy developed, not in the halls of academe or at the feet of management gurus, but from 25 years of lessons learned from managing diverse public and private companies ranging from $5 million to $500 million in annual revenue.

The Organization of This Book

CEOs and managers looking to lead their organizations into the 21st century are stepping into positions of increased scope—and unprecedented risk. More than ever, they are forced to consider the soundness of the foundations on which their businesses are built. Part 1 defines the fundamental prerequisites for constructing business success. Chapter 1 discusses the three primary elements involved in developing a valid philosophy with which to guide business problem-solving and decision-making:

1. Mastery of Fundamental Business Principles
2. Personal Management Philosophy
3. Core Operating Values

Each element will be discussed fully in Chapter 1.

CEOs must also understand the importance of strategic thinking. Chapter 2 provides the logic and methodology for validating a CEO's vision of the future and for formulating specific operating strategies. The chapter discusses the theory and purpose of strategy, as well as specific steps to follow in strategy formulation. Included are the right strategic questions to ask and how to determine both valid goals and effective means to achieve them. The most important lessons in the chapter, however, are about how to position your company for success by making the right choices about products, markets, competitors, customers, organizational structure, and core competencies.

Part 1, then, provides the philosophy and foundation for thinking like a CEO, the habits of mind that underlie all effective management. But the fundamentals must also be applied and executed across the range of practical, day-to-day business issues. Parts 2 and 3 discuss the business regimen I call "disciplines"—so called because each discipline requires specific knowledge and considered application. Most fundamental thinking about business—whether about human, physical, financial, technological, or intangible resources—falls within one of 10 essential management disciplines. These are the key areas of business decision-making that all CEOs, entrepreneurs, and high-level managers must master in order to be successful in their careers:

- Discipline 1: Business Operations Planning
- Discipline 2: People Management
- Discipline 3: Career Management
- Discipline 4: Sales
- Discipline 5: Numbers
- Discipline 6: Banking
- Discipline 7: Cash Management
- Discipline 8: Tough Times and Turnarounds
- Discipline 9: Acquisitions
- Discipline 10: Leadership

Chapters 3 through 11 are about managing through the execution of nine of these 10 disciplines. Designed to be relevant to real people facing real and immediate challenges, each chapter provides specific applications of the business philosophy, vision, and strategy presented in the foundations. Chapters can be read in sequence or consulted independently. Together, the disciplines offer guidance for converting theory to results and provide a set of operating principles for businesspeople to use as decision-making criteria. Individually, they define success for each management discipline.

Part 4 addresses the more personal aspects of *CEO Logic*, including the 10th and final discipline: leadership. It is the most important of all management disciplines because it has the power to act as a multiplier for the other nine. It is about superior character, ethics, insight, intuition, and talent—with character being the dominant factor. The book concludes with two reflective chapters. Chapter 13 represents the wit and wisdom collected in the trenches of many years of experience in businesses ranging from startups to the Fortune 500. Chapter 14 returns to the concept of deriving simplicity from complexity, the habit of mind most central to the discipline of thinking like a CEO.

The lessons and methods of *CEO Logic* have emerged from my more than 25 years of management in a spectrum of public and private businesses. Each type of business I've worked in has contributed specific lessons. Retail provided experience in one-call selling, media advertising, handling customer complaints, and the extension and collection of credit. Manufacturing taught lessons in quality management, product development, asset utilization, performance measurements, production efficiency, and product warranty. Wholesale distribution offered the tools needed for telemarketing and inventory management, while service organizations communicated manpower utilization, scheduling, multicall selling, and more customer service. Real estate development established the groundwork for selecting the right business, managing banking relationships, and understanding the demands of market timing. Property management gave insights into picking the right partners and managing cash flow. The daily successes and failures of business have served to form the hands-on approach to business philosophy that you'll see in this book.

The stories, anecdotes, and personal profiles that I've used throughout *CEO Logic* are likewise drawn from the real-life experiences and wisdom of those with whom I've worked and shared "war stories" over the years. In certain cases, names and key details have been altered to protect the privacy of the individuals involved. Sometimes the examples offered combine circumstances and events from more than one real-life source. However, all stories and examples are drawn from actual business situations that I have observed, and are offered to enhance the reader's understanding of the fundamental concepts of *CEO Logic*. Fictional names, where used, are indicated in the text by an asterisk (*).

Let me add a note on the role models whom you'll meet frequently in the pages ahead. I present them in a particular way, for a particular reason. Most people in business understand and appreciate the obvious inspirational value a role model can provide. But general inspiration is not enough. To achieve full benefit, take your role models—and your own analytical abilities—more seriously. Try making a special effort to analyze and write down details of the behaviors, practices, and character traits that you admire in them. The practice of writing down your detailed thoughts about each role model, in each area of your life, is an important step in learning to truly emulate them. I've modeled this practice for you at various points in the book, in the hopes that you'll begin to take full advantage of the mentors in your own life.

Fundamentals tempered by time, experience, and good judgment are the real "secrets" behind thinking like a CEO. Let these fundamentals become your tools of the trade. Use these tools to help you think like a CEO, and open the path to enlightened leadership and enhanced performance. With your permission, these fundamental concepts and ideas will improve the way you think about business and set the stage for your extraordinary success.

Part 1

The Foundations

*C**EO Logic*** begins with clear thinking, based on the disciplined application of fundamental business principles. Part 1: The Foundations teaches these fundamentals, the essential groundwork required for constructing success in any business: *how to develop a valid business philosophy and how to apply that philosophy strategically.*

Chapter 1 offers insights into fundamental business principles, catalysts for developing individual personal management philosophies, and guidance for preparing core operating values for a specific business. Chapter 2 addresses the critical and strategic issues of core competencies and competitive edge.

Together, these chapters lay the groundwork for the clear thinking that is the hallmark of *CEO Logic*. Begin here to build the foundation for your own success.

Part I

The Foundations

Chapter 1

Thinking Like a Chief Executive Officer

Out of intense complexities, intense simplicities emerge.
—Winston Churchill

CEOs are the proclaimed heroes of the business world. They make the big decisions, they make the big saves, they earn the million-dollar salaries. Everyone tries to learn their secrets in order to replicate their success in the game of business. But too often the focus is on what they are *doing*—how they are reengineering a company in trouble, leading a successful reinvention of a company's image or executing a daring acquisition. Doing, of course, is essential—the ability to take the right risks and follow through on strategy is part of what all successful top managers do. But something else is missing, the something that is the *real* secret to all those CEOs' impressive accomplishments. That something is the *thought* that drives the action. No one leading an organization can do it well unless the fundamentals have been thought through—only then can he move ahead to implement them in creative, innovative, and effective ways.

This systematic clear thinking about the fundamentals is what *CEO Logic* is all about. Top managers, of course, immediately see the value in learning to think like a CEO. But ambitious businesspeople at all levels are also realizing that their own success depends on their ability to think strategically and incisively, the way the best CEOs do. For most of the past century, business success has been driven by manufacturing productivity. As a new century approaches, however, the business environment is rapidly and radically changing. In the future, business success will depend more and more on the capacity to acquire and leverage knowledge. And it is the clear thinking of the CEO that is defining the new standards of what we need to know to remain competitive in the world of business.

The Philosophical Foundations of *CEO Logic*

What, then, are the challenges facing CEOs that force them to a higher level of thinking? The key issues that CEOs and senior managers confront every day are often very different in scope and consequence from those they faced in lesser assignments. Instead of having the middle manager's responsibility for playing by established rules and meeting predetermined targets, the CEO has both the opportunity and the obligation to determine the nature of fundamental operating systems, company culture, parameters of the business, and the structure of the organization. This freedom to increase the scope and risk of decisions forces top management to think differently about business. Operating without the safeguards that come with lower positions and largely determining their own authority levels and operating parameters, CEOs have to develop for themselves the concepts and principles that will be reliable foundations for their management decisions. If they fail to do this, so will their businesses fail. But even those at different levels of responsibility in an organization will find that a well-thought-out philosophical foundation will guide their decisions and actions to new levels of success.

For anyone, at any level, a comprehensive and valid business philosophy begins with at least three primary elements:

1. *Mastery of Fundamental Business Principles:* Market realities regarding management, competition, and economics that determine the general business environment.
2. *Personal Management Philosophy:* Your own core ideology that reflects your beliefs and values regarding management style, organizational structure and goals, policy, people, character, and operating methodology.
3. *Core Operating Values:* A defined set of operating practices, consistent with your personal management philosophy and the fundamental business principles that you believe are necessary to be successful in a specific business in a specific industry.

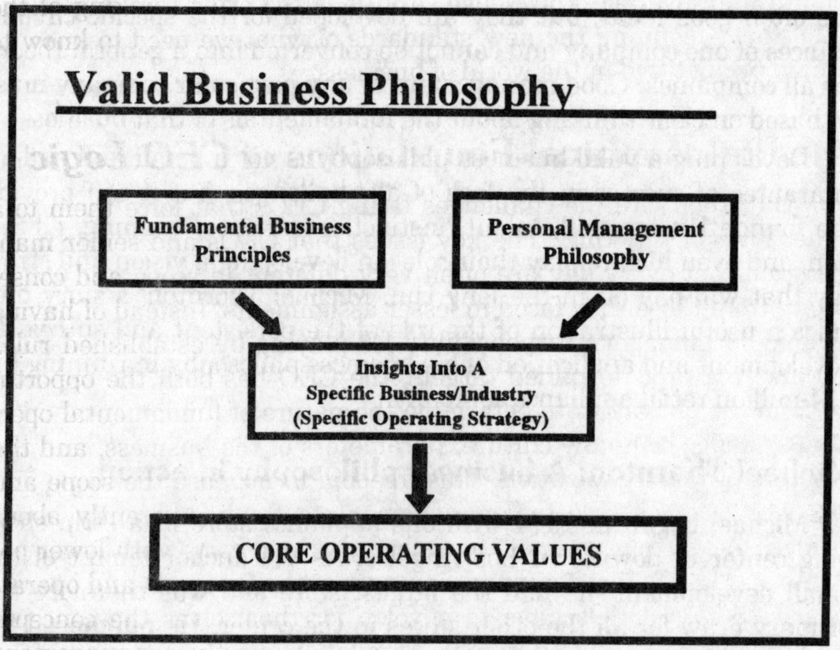

The goal of developing a valid business philosophy is to take the theoretical and practical elements of fundamental business principles (inescapable market realities that govern and drive all businesses) and your personal management philosophy (your own core ideology) and apply them to a specific business opportunity in order to arrive at a set of core operating values (practical company guidelines). In effect, by establishing core operating values, you are developing a "mini-business philosophy" that applies to the opportunities, problems, resources, and competition in your specific business.

Articulating your business philosophy helps to clarify the road to success, regardless of your position. Experienced CEOs know there is no packaged "best way to manage," and so should you. There are only valid operating principles that can serve as a foundation to guide a company and its management team. During these times of change and uncertainty, business is always complex, difficult, unpredictable, challenging, and competitive. A CEO soon learns that there are no secrets or shortcuts to effective management. The trendy management programs with catchy names developed by clever consultants are often good ideas, but they are developed for the specific circumstances of one company and cannot be converted into a general theory for all companies. Good management of any particular company must be based on clear thinking about the fundamentals of that business.

Developing a valid business philosophy is not a be-all and end-all guarantee of success in the face of all challenges, but it can provide the foundation for skill, talent, instinct, experience, training, education, and even luck to play their roles in developing a vision and strategy that will pay off in the long run. Michael Thornton*'s story provides a useful illustration of the role of the persistent and successful development and application of his business philosophy in running his $14-million retail appliance company.

Michael Thornton: A business philosophy in action

Michael began in 1974 with one appliance store in a strip shopping center in downtown Los Angeles. As the anchor tenant of the small development, he had the largest store and was therefore the primary draw for all the other stores in the center. He purchased his products at competitive costs, priced them fairly, and ran a low-overhead operation. He developed a selling system that moved products but also allowed his customers to feel comfortable during the process. Michael and his company became known for honesty, value, and hometown service.

When Michael expanded his operation, he attempted to duplicate his original concept. Eventually he opened 11 stores in mostly urban locations. Business was good for a while. But his success brought competitive challenges. First, other appliance chains expanded into his territory. That hurt margins. Then he faced competitive challenges from specialists who competed in only one or two facets of his business. That hurt volume. At this point, Michael realized that just being an honest, fair, and somewhat crafty businessman was not enough. He needed to improve his competitive strategy.

Michael's first competitive move was to increase his advertising in order to generate more and better-qualified store traffic. His competitors countered by increasing their own advertising or by moving to malls. His second move was to further improve his advertising by touting independent product tests and using celebrity testimonials.

His competitors mirrored his actions. Then he relocated from urban strip centers to suburban malls and concentrated his locations to get the most out of his advertising efforts. His competitors followed him to suburban malls, eliminated their own advertising, and used their window and store displays to convert general mall traffic to appliance store traffic. The elimination of advertising costs actually gave them a cost advantage over Michael's stores, and his margins deteriorated further. Michael's next move—to narrow his focus by specializing in TVs and stereos—worked for a while, but soon a number of his competitors followed. He realized once again that something was missing from his operating strategy.

What had gone wrong? Michael Thornton was still honest, still gave value, still ran a low-overhead organization, and was working harder than ever. He blamed his problems primarily on his inability to accurately predict his competitors' counter moves. To some degree, that was correct. But his main mistake was in failing to recognize that he was violating a fundamental business principle: *Unique or distinctive customer benefits must be generated and supported by hard-to-copy core competencies.*

Michael's original concept for his business worked until it was copied. His improved advertising had the potential to become a core competency, but it was never fully developed. In addition, his move to suburban mall locations was inconsistent with his increased advertising strategy. Higher square-footage costs of suburban mall store leases only make sense when the store can take full advantage of the mall-generated traffic. Michael's increased advertising probably helped his in-mall competitors as much as it helped his own stores. Concentrating on TVs and stereos, likewise, was not grounded in a core competency, and was therefore easily countered.

Michael finally realized that he needed to develop a valid business philosophy. To guide his business decisions, he needed a set of core operating values that was consistent with market-dictated fundamental business principles as well as his own personal management philosophy. His old strategy was consistent with his personal ideology and view of the industry, but violated certain undeniable business truths. Without core competencies and high entry barriers, his competitors could (and therefore would) easily copy his strategic moves.

After rethinking his core operating values, Michael's final move was to abandon his mall locations for large single-point destination stores. He kept his focus on TVs and stereos, as well as his hometown, friendly selling system and his strategy of concentrated locations. In addition, he put more effort into improving his advertising. These strategies worked. Because Michael had first pick of the few available sites for his large destination stores, it was difficult for his competitors to copy that move. The relocation from malls lowered his facility costs as a percent of sales, so he could use the additional margin to fund his increased advertising. Michael's in-mall competitors either could not find similar destination locations or could not afford to respond. His stores became known for large-store competitive prices with hometown friendly service. He had established a competitive strategy that would allow him to fully leverage his core competencies of "hometown selling" and "advertising for cost-effective store traffic." His competitive moves were consistent with his valid business philosophy. And by creating high entry barriers for competitors, he was developing and leveraging his core competencies while protecting his strategic position.

The moral of Michael's story is not about a specific successful strategy. In fact, my guess is that Michael will face additional challenges from the superstore chains that compete in his product lines. *The lesson to be learned is about the importance of developing a valid business philosophy to guide fundamental management decisions.*

Element 1: Identifying fundamental business principles

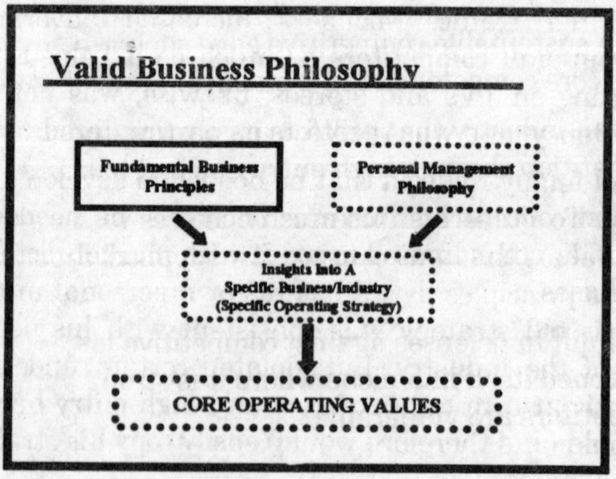

There are certain inescapable market realities that dictate the parameters of both the general business environment and the particular competitive environment of your business. Learning to keep these always in your sights will be your starting task.

The seven steps that follow will guide you as you begin to apply the fundamental principles of business management to the particulars of your own business challenges. Clarify your thinking about these fundamentals and you will be on sound footing for the mastery of *CEO Logic*.

7 Steps to Thinking Like a CEO

In its most fundamental form, thinking like a CEO means having the perspective to step back, analyze, and understand the business you're in, your core competencies, the wise and selective use of resources, the critical issues you face, the ways you'll measure the performance of individuals and the organization, and the role of key managers. Using the seven steps that follow will guide you in thinking about these fundamentals of the management process in a way that will help you excel in your role and achieve the business results you desire.

Step 1: Have you selected the right business?

Your first responsibility as CEO or senior manager is to make sure you're in the "right business." The right business:

- Has a sustainable competitive edge supported by one or more core competencies in a stable or growing market.
- Is in an industry that protects its participants from casual competition through high entry and exit barriers.
- Neither concentrates too much business with any one customer nor is limited to too few suppliers for critical purchases.
- Has built in defenses against competitive forces or has positioned itself in a niche where it is strong and competitors are vulnerable.

These elements allow a company to satisfy its customers at a price that creates an acceptable return on investment. In today's successful businesses, great people, good strategies, guaranteed customer satisfaction, and even some of the off-the-shelf management programs such as re-engineering, are important elements. But if you pick the wrong business, good companies and great people will fail. Select an industry in decline and even the best strategies will be meaningless. Target customers who cannot afford to buy, and customer satisfaction will be irrelevant. Pick a business where suppliers or buyers have too much power and your re-engineering effort will fail. Even teamwork and empowerment cannot overcome a bad business selection.

At one time, I worked with a very bright and enterprising CEO who was also the owner of a medium-sized business that was primarily involved in real estate development. At the time Renee Sebastian* inherited this business from her father, the company owned small developments in five states. They developed property and managed construction for single-family residences, multifamily housing, retail properties, and commercial office buildings.

Their business was marginally profitable, growing in revenue but declining in cash flow. Renee had worked in the business for many years and was highly skilled at construction management, but her problem seemed to be in knowing how to think about the business she was in. What should she be monitoring and controlling? Should she be growing or downsizing? Did she need to focus on increasing revenues or reducing costs? She came to me with these and many more questions.

Our first step in addressing her problems was to analyze the existing business, the available resources, and the markets in which she was operating. We found that she and her management team were particularly good at designing, developing, and marketing entry-level, single-family homes in California but had no special expertise in commercial real estate or in multifamily housing development. In addition, it became evident that the Southern California marketplace was a much stronger venue than her out-of-state markets and that her own management expertise—and that of her senior management team—was much more effective in that market than in remote locations in other states.

Through analyzing strengths and weaknesses in the company's core abilities to compete, available resources, past performance, and forecasted market conditions, we decided to:

- Limit Renee's focus to the development of entry-level, single-family housing in Southern California.
- Build-out or sell-out all other existing developments.
- Support the "entry-level" decision by focusing on price-point and key selling features. If, for example, entry-level homes were selling at $129,000 in a given marketplace, the company would only develop a particular property if it could offer the key selling features (such as tile roofs, cathedral ceilings, or designer windows), make an acceptable return (based on a formula that considered the cost of the land purchase, development, building, marketing, and financing, plus a target profit), and still meet the $129,000 retail price-point. If it could not make its target costs and profit, it did not buy the property.

In addition to those early decisions, Renee later decided to offer more competitive retail financing, which she developed through alliances with local lenders. She even eventually established her own mortgage company. Renee's valid and focused business selection allowed her to stay ahead of the market with land options and purchases consistent with the selling trends.

In the long run, Renee's decisions *not* to develop multifamily housing, *not* to do business out of state, *not* to pursue commercial development, and *not* to offer high-end custom homes contributed to her success as much as did her decisions about what she *would* do. The process we went through in helping Renee define her business and focus her resources taught her much more about how to think like a CEO—and that became the key to her success.

Where's your sustainable competitive edge? The most critical element in selecting the right business is a sustainable competitive edge. *No sustainable competitive edge, no sustainable profits. End of story.* Many business experts feel that 75 percent of business results are directly related to industry selection and timing. If you entered the California real estate market in the 1970s or early 1980s, others are now probably addressing you as "Ambassador." If you made that same decision in 1988, your mail is probably having a hard time finding you. Management and capital can do a lot, but they cannot make up for selecting the wrong business.

Competitive edge may come from your company's ability to offer its product at a lower price or to differentiate it in some compelling way. It may take the form of a unique design feature or a special service. But that advantage must above all grow out of what your company is especially good at—its core competency. Core competency may reside in a special capacity, a distinctive approach to the business, or a unique access to resources.

The CEO's task is to leverage one or more of these core competencies into an advantage in the marketplace. You have to lead the way by increasing investment in the capability, supporting it, nurturing it, and keeping the organization focused on it. You need to make sure, to whatever extent possible, that your competitors cannot easily duplicate that advantage. If, for example, your research and development group generates profitable, patented products that are central to your business, that R&D capability is at the heart of your core competency and is the key to your competitive advantage. As CEO or part of the senior management team, it is your responsibility to constantly measure the efficacy of the R&D department in an effort to continually find ways to enhance its capabilities so that you can gain an advantage over your competitors.

Competitive advantage may also be created by changing the way your company does business. Starbucks Coffee, for example, created a new sales and distribution channel for its coffee when it began selling out of its own cafes rather than through independent grocery stores. They also reconfigured the product from whole or ground beans to drinks, such as mocha or latte. Dell Computers and Gateway Computers modularized their products so that customers could "custom design" a computer to their specific needs and order it directly from them, thus bypassing the cost of computer resellers. The "superstore" concept of Home Depot, Office Depot, and Circuit City, among others, has also changed the way business is done in their respective industries. Their new concepts for distribution and their warehouse approach to retailing have spawned a whole new industry, appropriately known as "category killers," so-called because no other store in their vicinity can compete with their product lines.

Specialization can also create competitive advantage. ADP and Paychex focus only on the narrow issue of processing payroll. The automotive service industry has also divided its approach to business by segments (for example, tune-up, oil change, transmission repair, windshield replacement). All of these businesses have used distinct competitive approaches to select the right foundation for growth and prosperity. In each case, the strategy has been to use a special competency to offer a unique or distinctive benefit to the customer while simultaneously setting up a barrier to competitors.

Consider these other factors when thinking about core competency and competitive advantage:

- *Entry and exit barriers.* Industries, such as consulting, that encourage severe competition by virtue of low entry and/or exit barriers often produce low-return enterprises.
- *Changes in government regulation.* Regulations, such as those affecting life insurance sales, nuclear power plants, or real estate syndication, may drastically reduce profit potential.
- *Market saturation.* Too many players, as in the recreational vehicle or mobile home business, can create tough competition in flat markets, where all revenue increases must be generated at the expense of a competitor's market share.
- *Product obsolescence and competition.* New technologies, such as typewriters faced from word processors, can not only limit or change demand but can also affect the inherent viability of a business.
- *Threats from substitution.* New products, such as artificial sweeteners for sugar or aluminum for steel, can change an industry almost overnight.

Learning to select the right business is the first step to thinking like a CEO. It deserves careful consideration and analysis, because a mistake in the selection process could prove fatal to your business.

Have you selected the right business?

- What are the opportunities and vulnerabilities of a business in your industry?

- What are your plans to deal with these opportunities and vulnerabilities?
- What barriers are in place to protect you from aggressive competitors?

What is affecting your core competency and competitive edge?

- What do you do well that results in unique or distinctive benefits that your customers are willing to pay for?
- What is your competitive edge? What are you doing to strengthen it?
- What threats are likely to come from existing competitors, customers, employees, or suppliers?
- What is the risk of new entries into the market?
- What is the potential threat from substitute products?
- How will the company be affected by likely or pending government regulations?
- How will a change in financial markets or your cost of capital affect your plans?
- What significant business or market conditions are likely to change in the foreseeable future?

Step 2: What elements drive results?

What are those few success factors that separate the winners from the losers in your industry? What disciplines or activities directly impact volume, margin, cash flow, and return on investment? What elements in your business determine customer or employee satisfaction? A direct marketing firm may be driven by its ability to generate cost-effective leads. A manufacturing concern may drive results by its capacity to design desirable products or its ability to react quickly to changes in the marketplace. A distribution firm may find its success in its inventory control capability, its ability to control margin, or its productive and cost-effective selling system. Issues such as low cost, high quality, timely shipments, ability to accurately read the market, inventory availability, or cost-effective sourcing of materials may drive results in your business. The key is to identify these "drivers" and turn them into core competencies. Failure to do so can prove very costly.

I once consulted with a successful chain of retail stores founded in the 1980s that had achieved impressive success by placing their outlets in large, upscale malls and catering to the needs of solid, middle-class customers. As they grew, Jeff Edwards*, the founder and CEO, had changed his vision of his business. He developed a strategy for moving out of the malls and creating what he called "destination superstores" that would attract a larger, more qualified, and less price-sensitive customer base. As Jeff began to implement that strategy, he also adopted a series of new management concepts designed to increase teamwork and empowerment among his staff. His primary strategy was going well, but other aspects of the business were not. It appeared that margins were falling as overall sales numbers weakened. Jeff called me in to discuss what he might do differently to get his company back on track.

As we analyzed this company and Jeff's efforts as CEO, two things became clear. First, his superstore strategy was fundamentally sound, but the organization itself had forgotten that it was first and foremost in the *retail selling* business. It was not in the business of expanding its stores or empowering employees—although those were important and admirable goals. Its primary business was selling products to retail customers, and the effectiveness of his retail selling effort determined the level of his success. Jeff had neglected to maintain focus on his selling system. Initial attention to customers as they entered the store was weak, salespeople were not qualifying the customer's needs and ability to pay, presentations were focused only on product knowledge, and no one was asking closing questions consistently enough to get the sales that would fuel the rest of his expansion strategy.

Second, Jeff misdirected his own efforts by dedicating 100 percent of his attention to implementing his strategy to move out of malls and into his superstores. This left no time to manage in-store sales and operations. His priorities were not aligned with the kinds of things that he had always done to create success. Since the selling system was the primary business element that needed attention, it was clear that Jeff could provide his own solution. For many years he had used a state-of-the-art selling system, which he personally developed to drive the success of his company. It was, according to my way of thinking, a case of lost focus. It was as if Jeff owned a race car and had been tweaking the body, upgrading his drivers, and buying new tires, but not focusing on how to make his engine more powerful. In this case, retail selling was the "engine" that powered his business, and Jeff Edwards had the ability to turn it into a core competency. *The important lesson here is to never forget which elements drive your success, power your business, and determine what business you are in.*

What elements of your business drive results?

- What are the key differences between winners and losers in your industry?
- Which factors in your business most affect volume, margin, return on investment, cash flow, and customer satisfaction?
- Which department manager(s) would you least want to lose to a competitor?
- Who or what in your company directly makes you the most money?

Step 3: Are the right people in the right positions?

If a CEO's most important responsibilities are to make sure the organization is in the right business and to stay focused on the "engine" that drives it, then the next key step is to make sure the right people are in the right management slots. Like other aspects of being a successful CEO, the first step to making good people decisions is to know how to *think* about them. Following are a few tips that I've found invaluable over the years.

Begin by sizing up candidates as people. Determine whether they are good people before you determine whether they are good managers. The value of integrity and character cannot be overstressed. Find out how they have handled difficult, delicate, and/or awkward situations in the past. Ask questions to determine how they feel about people and their communities. Ask about their friends and their hobbies. A look at these issues of character will ensure that you build your team on a solid foundation.

Look for success in the candidate's employment history. Find out whether this person has had real success in at least some aspect of his or her life. It's unlikely that a candidate has been waiting forever for this exact job to kick-start his or her success.

Evaluate the candidate's level of enthusiasm. Once the candidate understands the company's competitive advantages, the nature and responsibilities of the position, and the personal opportunities for growth and advancement, he must respond with enthusiasm about joining the company. The candidate should want the job, and should say so. *No enthusiasm, no job offer.*

Avoid buying the candidate. Too often, companies will offer to pay far in excess of market value for candidates whom they consider to have especially good credentials or experience. The temptation is to try to buy or bribe these so-called "good" candidates in order to convince them to join the team. And that's usually a mistake. Money should be part of the equation, but not the only or even the primary factor in the candidate's decision. Individuals should join an enterprise because they sense a great opportunity and feel their skills and talents fit the situation. They should be comfortable with the personal chemistry they feel in the interview and believe superior performance will be rewarded. If they are joining the company only for the short-term pay increase, they may not be prepared for the hard work required for them to contribute and to succeed. In addition, they are more liable to leave the company for the next short-term pay increase (no doubt from a competitor). As a general policy, I recommend not beating the candidate's current salary by a large margin to entice him to join your organization.

Are the right people in the right position in your organization?

- Do the managers in charge have the right strengths for the job?
- Are all of your managers consistently generating results?
- Do any of the current managers require replacement or upgrading? What is your training plan?

Step 4: Are you addressing the right issues?

Peter Drucker, in his book *Management: Tasks, Responsibilities, Practices,* said it best: "It is more important to be digging the hole in the right place than to be digging the hole right." The "right issues" are those few that, when addressed effectively, result in the greatest improvement in performance for the company. The CEO and the senior management team, with the broadest and most strategic sense of the company, are the ones who must determine what the right issues are and know how to think about and stay focused on them.

The difference between working on the right issues and working on doing things right is the difference between effectiveness and efficiency. Effectiveness is getting the right task completed successfully. Efficiency is getting the task accomplished using a minimum of resources. Using an analogy, you might say that effectiveness is like rowing a boat in the right direction, while efficiency is just rowing the boat at top speed using a minimum of effort. When you're rowing in the right direction, you make more progress. *There is nothing so wasteful as doing with great efficiency that which does not have to be done at all.*

Many businesses fail because the CEO and senior management team are addressing the wrong issues. If the company needs alliances with suppliers and improved product development in order to lower costs and satisfy its customers, but instead spends its resources on sales and marketing, it will not matter how well it does in sales or marketing. Eventually, the real problems will surface and set the company back. The process of selecting the right issues begins with a top management team capable of perceiving the problem correctly.

Criteria for selecting issues to address generally revolve around quantity, quality, cost, investments, and intangibles, such as reputation or employee morale. If more than one is involved, one will usually take precedence over the others. When, for example, Mazda began selling its cars with a Wankel (or rotary) engine, it had excellent advertising, strong technical support services, and an impressive distribution system of dealerships. Mazda was producing, shipping, and selling a more-than-adequate quantity. Their costs and investments seemed in line, and their early reputation was excellent as they rode the wave of enthusiasm for Japanese cars generated by Toyota and Nissan. But when the Wankel engine's lack of market acceptance became apparent, Mazda began to fail miserably. The company, however, continued to focus on distribution, rather than on correcting the product's deficiencies. They were focusing too many of the company's resources on the wrong issues. On a smaller scale, that is like a struggling restaurant trying to counteract its problems with bad-tasting food through better advertising. If the focus on advertising is successful, all it will do is encourage more customers to try the bad food.

Are you paying attention to the critical issues and correct priorities?

- Have you identified the key issues that have the greatest potential to generate profit?
- What significant unanticipated events or surprises have you experienced? What can you do to avoid similar occurrences in the future?

Step 5: How are you measuring performance, progress, and yourself?

In order to know whether you're focusing on the right issues, as CEO and/or senior management, you must make sure you have timely, accurate, relevant, and understandable methods of measurement. Without good measurement, it's difficult to think clearly and proactively about issues. A few tips are worth keeping in mind.

What you measure is what you will manage. If you say you want performance, whether in productivity, increased volume, greater accuracy, or improved quality, but you measure and give promotions or raises based on loyalty, you will get loyalty, not improved performance.

Pay attention to how you measure. Many years ago, Firestone Tires measured tire rejects at its factories by "percent good," for example, 98 percent good. That method worked well for some time, but when producing hundreds of thousands of tires, 2 percent "bad" is a lot of tires. Switching to measuring "the number of rejects per 10 thousand tires produced" changed everyone's perspective on the manufacturing process by shifting the focus to matters pertaining to quality. Improvements in quality generated both lower operating costs and greater customer satisfaction, both of which became key factors in Firestone's many quality successes.

Focus on the "true purpose" of each major resource. Knowing true purpose makes it easier to refine the measurements of performance in using a particular resource. With Firestone, for example, it was not enough just to measure performance. It had to be measured in such a way that it created enough of an impact to cause managers and workers alike to change their behavior, that is, to reduce the number of rejects. The true purpose of this measurement was to create improvements in quality by changing everyone's behavior. Thinking of this measurement as a management tool and resource helped Firestone to determine its best use.

How are you measuring performance? The other component of measurement is a performance feedback system that regularly, consistently, and clearly communicates project status to those who are accountable. Measurement without effective communication to the people doing the work is just not productive. And unless the feedback is regular and predictable, it won't be effective in making an impact on those who are responsible for performance.

One caution: With computers, it is easy to develop cumbersome and complex measurement systems that seem to capture every bit of information about every activity. But don't confuse raw data with useful information. Measuring too much is as dangerous as measuring too little. Focus your measurements by narrowing their scope and limiting your presentations to the important performance issues. In addition to the more typical performance measurements relating to volume, margin, customer satisfaction, and employee relations, different industries may require others. Service companies, for example, may want to add measurements of manpower utilization, while manufacturing companies may want to focus on cost-of-quality measurements or capacity to meet the production schedule, and distribution companies may be concerned about their performance as measured by percent of stock-outs or time between order and delivery. Keep in mind that the true purpose of most measurement feedback is to generate an informed response from those who are responsible for doing the work.

Sometimes getting the attention of those who are accountable for the work takes skill and boldness. For example, in one small manufacturing company where I consulted, a new general manager, Rob Harper*, was assigned to run the organization. Rob found that Don Yoder*, the current production manager, had achieved excellent results in every way—from cost and quality to expenses to maintenance to staff morale—except in meeting the production schedule. He just could not seem to get the finished units ready in time for dealer pick-up. Discussions, memos, and statistical reports did not materially change the situation. Don understood that the company's primary customers (the dealers who sold their product to consumers) were upset, but he proclaimed that managing cost and quality caused the chronic lateness.

One day, after Don left to go home, Rob and the staff constructed a 20- x 40-foot "wall" about 40 feet from Don's office. They painted a large graph on it showing the last two weeks' daily production deliveries compared to plan. Green was used to show on-time deliveries and red was used to reflect late deliveries. They extended the graph so that it would be able to show daily shipments for the next six weeks.

The next day, Don was furious. He went into Rob's office threatening to quit. When Don calmed down, he reluctantly accepted the situation. Everyone in the factory was going to see the delivery results. Rob agreed that after 30 days of on-time shipments, the graph would be dismantled. Forty-two days later, the graph was down and late shipments were a thing of the past.

This story is not a perfect example of leadership and management. Most would question Rob's strategy of confronting Don in front of his subordinates. It does, however, show the potential of measurement feedback. The moral of this story is not about confrontation. It is about getting the attention of those accountable for the work. *Performance measurement without impact is wasted effort.*

Do you have the right performance measurements in place?

- Are accurate and timely performance measurements in place?
- Do those accountable know how they are doing and can they perceive even small increases or decreases in their performance? Are they measuring their own performance?
- Are measurements focused on critical issues?
- Are you in a position to satisfy customers and employees while still making money?

Step 6: Are you delegating strategy and its execution?

Delegation is not only an important skill, but also a key indicator of whether or not you are thinking like a CEO. If everything else is in place—the right people, the right focus, and the right measurements—your managers should then be able to put together correct strategies and action plans on their own.

As CEO, there is, of course, almost always a role for you, even in departmental issues. In particular, your thoughts are often needed to make sure that managers are getting started in the right direction. Although you will want to remain accessible and visible to the workforce, you cannot allow yourself to become 100 percent obsessed with departmental decisions. To put it plainly, as CEO you have other responsibilities. Your continuous and constant involvement in one department can distort your perspective on the overall company and can stifle good people by giving them no room to operate. If you can't resist the temptation to stay involved in the development and execution of day-to-day strategy in a particular division or department for more than 90 days, then I suggest you get someone else to run your company. Running a key department in a large organization is never a part-time job, no matter how extensive your experience.

The one exception to this rule is CEOs in very small businesses that are planning to stay very small. Very small businesses often require everyone, including the CEO, to wear several hats. These CEOs may need to be product developers and shop supervisors, as well as the sales force. That, however, will not work once the company expands. Then the CEO's role is to provide the overall perspective—and that requires a full-time effort.

Learning to delegate in a growing company can naturally be a problem, especially if the CEO founded and has played a central role in the organization. In one service company where I consulted, the CEO, Philip Jenkins*, called me in to discuss his customer relations problems. It seemed that his relationship with key customers had been weakening for several years. Philip was particularly concerned because he had always taken personal responsibility for this part of his business. He told me that he had founded the company based on the promise to always be easily accessible to customers and always to exceed their expectations. And, he said, he was working harder than ever at this part of the job.

Philip could not understand why his company's customer relations performance had deteriorated in spite of his personal attention and the fact that his overall customer service strategy had not changed. As we continued to discuss the company's history, the problem became quite obvious. When the company was small, Philip's personal involvement was the key to its excellent reputation with customers.

As the company expanded from three to 18 offices and from one to six states, Philip could not be as accessible to each customer. He neither delegated the responsibility for customer service nor set up systems to empower his people to handle it. In addition, in some states, he did not have the right personnel in place. Once we defined the problem, we were able to devise a new customer service plan. Philip saw that he needed to hire the right people, train them in what he knew about customer service, and delegate the customer service responsibility. He also set up performance measurement and feedback systems, empowered his people with authority and operating parameters, and held those responsible for doing the work accountable for satisfying the customers. Philip's strategy that had worked so well in the early stages failed as the company expanded. In the end, he learned a tough and costly lesson about effective delegation—and about how to think like a CEO.

Are strategy and its execution being delegated to key managers?

- Have you delegated the right degree of authority to your operating managers?
- Are the right resources available to them?
- Do your people truly understand the tasks to be accomplished, the quality standards that apply, and the deadlines associated with them?

Step 7: Measure your progress by focusing on results

Regularly monitoring actual against planned performance with key managers on critical issues keeps you as CEO and your organization focused on results. That doesn't mean ignoring the little things that also come to your attention. I worked for a manager who said, "Take care of the little things and the big things will take care of themselves." He was right not to let "the little things" slip by and to promote attention to detail. But it is also important to keep most of your time and resources focused on the big things—such as customer satisfaction, employee relations, growth opportunities, cash flow, and margins of profitability—that will keep you competitive.

Recently I worked with one of the executives in my own company on this very problem. Deborah Minor* wanted to balance the need to address small cost overruns and minor bureaucratic rule-breaking with the bigger issue of obtaining additional business. In her division, she correctly noted that increased volume would be the primary key to her success and that no amount of cost-cutting or rule-following could materially improve her bottom line. Deborah's solution was to delegate the minor issues to first-line supervisors, while keeping the majority of her management team focused on the major issues relating to acquiring new business.

I've seen similar situations in many other companies, where top management (unlike Deborah Minor) has failed to stay focused on the big issues that are central to their success. One CEO of a $41 million company, for example, asked for my help in reversing his loss of market share. Carl Austin* had built his very successful distribution company based on strong alliances with key suppliers. His suppliers' role was to manufacture quality products on a cost-effective basis. His role was to inventory the product, market and sell it to end-users, and stay abreast of needed product improvements that the marketplace demanded. Carl had done well on inventory and marketing and selling but had not done so well in keeping up with product changes based on market feedback. His company's success over the last few years had made his management team so complacent that they had all failed to stay in touch with the end-users of the product, and, as a consequence, had also failed to provide needed product improvement recommendations. Lack of attention to this one key issue led to their loss of market share.

Formal meetings with predetermined schedules and organized agendas help keep everyone focused on how their efforts are measuring up to desired results. When managers have to prepare a formal presentation, it forces them to step back from the details to gain the perspective they need to appraise their overall progress. When these review sessions are not formally scheduled, performance monitoring and the resulting adjustments in strategy often get delayed or even ignored. This emphasis on focusing on results may seem almost too basic to mention. But too many companies have unconsciously drifted away from the practice of regularly analyzing and discussing results. How many times during conversations with associates about business have you said, "We used to do that. I wonder how that got away from us?" If you use a regular, predetermined review plan, your organization will not have to continually relearn that which it already knows.

Are you measuring your progress by focusing on results?

- Have you helped management stay on track by regularly reviewing plans and progress?
- Which departments or divisions are on-plan and which are off-plan?
- Are current operations in line with your overall vision for the company?
- Do your plans have the horsepower to get the job done? If you are effective at executing your plans, will the results of your planned efforts make the company or department successful?

Fundamental Business Principles: Getting Started

Use this starter list to begin your process of identifying those principles that you believe drive and govern all businesses—including your own. As you read this book, add those principles that will become part of your own valid business philosophy.

Fundamental business principles starter list

- No sustainable (hard-to-copy) core competency, no sustainable competitive edge.
- No sustainable competitive edge, no sustainable profits.
- Individuals and/or organizations with negotiating power will use it to their own advantage.
- Low exit/entry barriers and high profits invite competition.
- There are always potential threats from substitution and new entrants into the market.
- Your return must exceed your cost of capital.
- Positive economic performance, more and more satisfied customers, and eventual liquidity are the tests for a successful strategy.
- Priorities: Customers, employees, growth, and profitability.
- There is no such thing as an endless boom market—manage accordingly.

- Resources must be focused to be effective.
- You manage what you measure.
- People will be as they have been.
- The business must be structured to succeed with ordinary people.
- Work on the right things before working on doing things right.
- Continuous improvement is a necessity.
- There must be good consequences for good performance and bad consequences for bad performance.
- Good people are more important than good systems.
- The key to worker commitment is worker involvement.
- People who feel good about themselves will perform better.
- Thinking through the true purpose of resources is critical to the management of those resources.
- All management is personal.

Element 2: Documenting your personal management philosophy

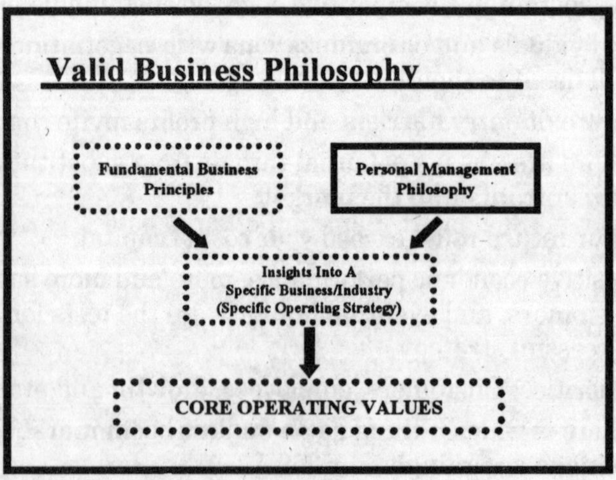

Mastering the fundamentals of sound business principles is central to your success, but that understanding must be accompanied by a thoughtfully considered personal management philosophy. The intentional process of analyzing your personal assumptions, values, and beliefs about business will make you the kind of business leader whose operations are based on conscious principles rather than vaguely defined beliefs and old habits. As CEO, you must be the one who determines moral and ethical standards and codes of conduct based on your personal beliefs. You alone decide the eventual purpose of the organization. In analyzing your own motivations and passions, you'll come to know yourself better and be in a better position to determine the most effective role for you to play in your company. Whether your primary goal for the business is to build equity, generate cash flow, increase reported earnings, provide employment for family and friends, or to offer not-for-profit service to the community, you will decide. And your personal management philosophy must guide your actions and your values.

Some CEOs are best as motivators, some as inventors, some as salespeople, some as strategists, and others as managers. Regardless of where you are most comfortable or proficient, all CEOs need a sense of urgency to excel and a wariness of complacency. You need to be able to think through important issues to provide firm guidance and to communicate and sell your vision in a way that overcomes the natural resistance to change. Clear targets, operating models consistent with strategies, and firm deadlines all fall in the domain of top management. An effective CEO finds leaders within to initiate change and assigns managers within to anchor this change in everyday practices. Whether you lead the pack or organize and facilitate from within, you must have a clear grasp of your own most effective management style.

The process also involves looking at your perceptions of the roles your senior management team and others should play in the organization. An effective analysis reveals your views on what you think works and what does not, and your beliefs on the best way to interact with others, the kind of people who impress you, and the kind who do not. It shows the way you prefer to work with customers, employees, shareholders, suppliers, competitors, and peers. And it gives perspective to your feelings regarding work ethic, character, expectations, compensation, recognition, and fair play. In short, conscious analysis will help you define the kind of people you like to work with and the way that you plan to do business.

Your analysis and development of your personal management philosophy will be most powerful for your organization if you write it down so others can see it. It will make the philosophy more concrete and facilitate your selection of team members and strategies that will work for you. In addition, it can help you communicate and link vision, strategy, and implementation. Successful companies reflect their leaders' core ideology and beliefs. Taking the time to articulate your personal management philosophy will pay off in both peace of mind and bottom-line performance.

A Personal Management Philosophy

Here is my own perspective on the 10 most important elements of my personal management philosophy:

1. The strength of a business resides in the minds of its people. Manage accordingly.
2. Clear thinking is the basis for effective management. Fill your company with clear thinkers.
3. Integrity is a requirement. Operate with trust, honesty, and candor.
4. Engage, perceive, think, and adapt (not necessarily in that order). Face challenges aggressively.
5. Customers and employees must be satisfied. Under-promise and over-deliver.
6. Systems are necessary, but the right people are more important than the right systems. Do not tolerate mediocrity and never lose a good performer because of money.
7. Good management involves continuous improvement on the right issues. Set clear priorities and attack the status quo.
8. Price is always an issue. Know your costs.
9. Good performance is the only basis for company politics. Hire, promote, and give raises only to good performers.

10. Bureaucracy is the enemy. Centralize the paper, but decentralize the power and the people.

Following are a few specific thoughts relating to the development of your own personal management philosophy. In the "know who you are" example later in this chapter, you will find an illustration of how one successful CEO integrated his personal management philosophy into his core operating values.

Know what you are "dumb" at

Dave Yoho, international businessman and consultant, calls knowing what you are dumb at "cognitive ignorance." By that he means being aware of that which you do not know. A bigger danger is "noncognitive ignorance"—when you don't know what you don't know. Will Rogers said, "It's not what we don't know that causes trouble. It's what we know that ain't so." There may be no greater error in management than not taking the time to analyze your own capabilities and experience to determine where your knowledge is weak or your skills are lacking.

Sometimes success breeds arrogance and false pride that can result in lost money and bad decisions. It is easy to come out of a successful project and plunge fearlessly into the next one. A little fear or apprehension is a good thing, especially if it causes you to step back and take a true inventory of your real strengths and weaknesses. Know what you are good at and do it. Know when to seek help or coaching to help you with what you're "dumb" at.

Some years ago I worked with an extremely capable division president in the recreational vehicle industry who had used his skills to build great success. Brad Evans* was an organized management thinker and a strong motivator of people with a reputation within the company and in the industry as one of the most effective hands-on leaders in the business. And he was formidable in his ability to analyze markets and financial issues. But Brad had one great flaw: He did not know what he did not know. He believed that because he was so effective as a leader and manager in *most* aspects of his business, that he was, therefore, capable in *all* aspects of his business. And that was not true. Despite his many strengths, Brad did not have a feel for design and couldn't translate market demands into salable products. His other qualities contributed to his success—and to the arrogance that made him oblivious to his weakness in judging design. That arrogance led to unattractive products, which of course eventually led to low sales volume and reduced profits.

Fortunately, Brad recognized his shortcomings before his division failed entirely. And the solution was quite simple: He needed to delegate product design to someone with good taste who could translate market demands into attractive and salable recreational vehicles. Once he did so, his division was back on a successful track.

Know who you are—and who you are not—as a person and a company

Jack Jones, CEO of Greystone Management Group and a Los Angeles real estate specialist, always professes to be a novice at management strategy and business philosophy. Nothing could be further from the truth. Over the course of 25 years, Jack and his dad have built a sizable real estate empire in the greater Los Angeles area. Trained and educated as aerospace engineers, they both somehow decided that real estate was the future for the Jones family.

Without much formal business training, Jack went on to develop what I consider to be a classic management philosophy that has withstood the test of time. In fact, it has withstood more than the test of mere time. Earthquakes, fires, riots, mudslides, and depressions in the California real estate market all have tested the Jones' strategy more than once. It is still thriving today.

With prodding, Jack admits that their strategy is as follows:

- Use their special knowledge of Los Angeles area niche markets to make bargain purchases of existing properties.
- Purchase only existing apartment properties within an hour's drive of their headquarters.
- Offer a price based on current cash flow so that each property pays for itself. Never pay a price so high that investors do not get an immediate return.
- Invest for capital appreciation *and* cash flow.
- Build strong relationships (with brokers, finders, and lenders), as well as a reputation for being easy to work with and a closer of deals.

- Finance conservatively, recognizing that financing affects the margin of safety. (Jack and his family usually put up half the money needed and often split the initial debt and equity conservatively.)
- Take care of investors' money like it was your own. (This was easy since the Jones' money was right beside their investors' money.)
- Focus the whole management company work force on rate, occupancy, and net operating income.
- Hire and use local people, not necessarily from the real estate industry, as resident managers for leasing, resident selection, maintenance, and security.
- Make the resident managers kings and queens of the company. Make sure everyone else in the company from accountants to supervisors is there to help the resident managers be successful.
- Be patient with people, deal with them with integrity, respect their individuality, and trust them to perform.
- Buy only what you know how to operate.
- Know when and what to buy and when not to buy.

One of the smartest moves I ever saw Jack make was really a non-move; he decided *not* to buy any properties during the time we now know was the hyper-speculation period leading up to the Los Angeles real estate depression in the late 1980s. This decision may seem obvious now, but few others in the marketplace picked up on it at the time. Jack followed his program of only buying existing properties at a price that would allow for an immediate return to his investors. When opportunities dried up, he quit buying. This "non-philosophy" really paid off for Jack and his investors.

Jack leads by sticking to his so-called non-philosophy. My sense is that this non-philosophy has become a terrific tool for his people. For a man who says he knows little about business philosophy and management strategy, his non-philosophy looks a lot like what most experts would call core operating values. Jack knows who he is and who he is not. This accurate self-evaluation has created the foundation for much of his great success.

Element 3: Establishing core operating values

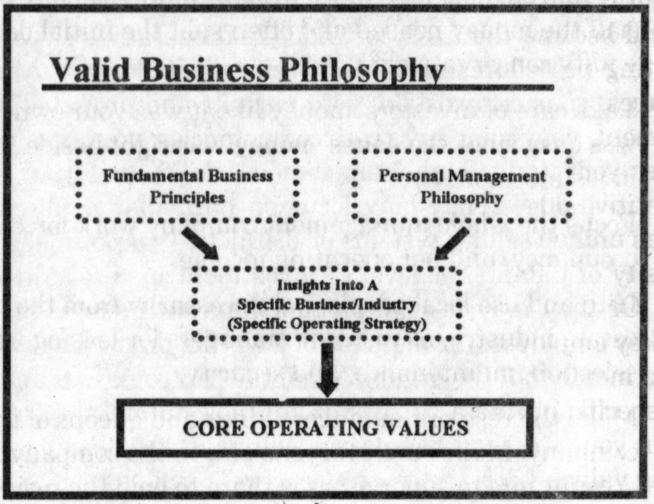

The final step in developing a valid business philosophy is to apply your fundamental business principles and personal management philosophy insights to a specific business opportunity. The purpose of this final exercise is to convert the theoretical to the practical. The result will be to develop usable operating guidelines—your core operating values—based on real opportunities and real threats for a real business. To be effective, core operating values need to be consistent with and combine elements from your personal management philosophy, your particular insight into a specific operating strategy, and the fundamental business principles that govern and drive all businesses.

Every individual business operates from a set of core operating values, whether explicit or implicit. Most CEOs of small and medium-sized enterprises have neither fully analyzed, fully discussed, nor fully documented these values. They apparently have not learned the lesson or do not see the need to use clearly articulated core operating values to define the way in which their companies plan to do business. When carefully thought through, core operating values communicate a philosophy, define a company culture, and create guidelines for everyone in the organization. They embody specific worthwhile and desirable ways to compete in a specific business within a specific industry.

Core operating values reflect your vision and strategy as CEO for your company. The individual elements of your core operating values will become the basis for individual operating procedures. These operating procedures must be specifically tailored to your available resources, your competition, your current and projected economic environment, your company's core competencies, your personal style and values, your individual management skills; and your insight into competitive edge. They may focus on particular performance issues, such as unique selling systems or distinctive marketing programs, the necessity of patents, or level of investment in research and development. Or they may involve partnerships with suppliers, ways to attract key employees, or methods of lowering production costs. As CEO, or as a member of the organization, the central issues of how to make your specific business successful and how to maintain a competitive edge in your specific marketplace will be at the heart of your core operating values.

An example from a real company may help clarify what core operating values are and how they contribute to business success. For many years I have worked with Mark Ortiz*, the CEO and owner of a very successful, growing, and prosperous distribution company with $29 million in revenues. As we have worked together, we have defined and refined his core operating values as follows:

- Continuously and personally analyze the marketplace to determine the right products, pricing, and service.
- Contract with quality manufacturers and suppliers who are able to respond to market-dictated product changes on short notice.
- Treat suppliers as partners.
- Limit the concentration of business to 5 percent of total for any one customer.
- Keep overhead low.
- Work only with people you like and respect.
- Allow people their idiosyncrasies and their personal time needs, as long as they perform.
- Only distribute products with a defendable competitive edge and a clearly defined economic reason to exist.

- Make key employees owners.
- Avoid labor-intensive aspects of business.
- Your word is your bond—there is only one level of integrity.

Mark Ortiz has documented his core operating values and shared them with everyone in his organization. They serve as decision-making criteria for people at all levels and communicate the essence of his philosophy of what success is for his company—and how it is achieved. Although these core operating values are, from his point of view, the only acceptable approach to Mark's business, they may not be valid or appropriate for another company, perhaps not even for one in the same industry. Core operating values are driven by specific resources and opportunities, as well as by top management's personal evaluation of the best way to conduct the business. For that reason, they are variable and individual; however, given their fundamental importance, it is critical for top management to know what they are and to make their core operating values explicit for all members of the organization.

Core operating values must:

- Define all critical success factors for a specific business in a specific market, at a specific time.
- Be consistent with market-dictated fundamental business principles.
- Reflect the actual resources available.
- Correspond to the CEO's personal management philosophy and capabilities.
- Deal with current and projected market conditions.
- Offer valid criteria for systematic analysis and decision-making.
- Be aimed at true market opportunities.
- Be durable enough to withstand attack.
- Provide guidance for major policies.
- Above all, define the business, develop distinctive competencies, and strengthen competitive advantages.

A good way to begin documenting your core operating values as CEO is to analyze your company's past successes and failures. Look at the reasoning behind and the consequences of decisions you have made. Sometimes it is helpful to ask a friend or associate to serve as a sounding board or facilitator to help with this process. Focus on those core operating values that represent your most deeply held beliefs of what is necessary to be successful in your company and your industry. "Politically correct" mission statements may be good public relations, but they are not substitutes for core operating values, because they provide no real day-to-day guidance. The questions that follow may be helpful to you in documenting the core operating values for you and your company.

What Are Your Core Operating Values?

These questions will bring you closer to the answer.

- What have you done well/poorly in the past that most contributed to your successes/failures?
- Why do customers buy from you? From your competitors?
- Who has succeeded and who has failed in your industry and why?
- What makes participants in your industry vulnerable?
- Which departments are most important to your success?
- How do you measure the company's performance daily, monthly, yearly, and for the long run?
- How important are suppliers to your success?
- How do you manage quality, cost, quantity, and investments?
- How do you manage intangible resources, such as employee and supplier loyalty or reputation, among key customers?
- Which relationships inside the company are most important to your success? Outside the company?
- What is the biggest distinction between your products or services and those of your competitors?
- What has changed in the past and what is changing now in the industry?

Valid Business Philosophy = Recipe for Success

Business and management philosophies exist in every organization. Some are explicit, some implicit. Senior management's day-to-day decisions about resource allocation or employee assignments will eventually reflect the company's true belief system. The question, however, is not whether decisions and resource allocations are based on a *particular* approach. The question is whether the pattern of decisions and resource allocations is based on a *valid* approach, that is, one that is reasoned and rational, with an aim toward satisfying customers and an eventual goal of positive economic performance.

A sound business philosophy inspires good people to aggressively seek and achieve valid, and sometimes even noble, causes. It is critical in coordinating essential activities, developing a framework for corporate governance, and competing in this "survival of the fittest" marketplace.

I get the impression in my work that many managers (especially managers of small and medium-sized enterprises) consider business philosophy to be just so much academic theory. They get to work early each day, work hard, and let their in-basket, drop-by appointments, and incoming phone calls schedule their day. They feel that they have a general sense of the business and believe they can make good decisions on the run. They are primarily reactive rather than proactive and preach a philosophy of action over analysis. Does all of that sound admirable? It is—to a point. *The problem is that action without vision is just as ill-fated as vision without action.* A valid business philosophy can provide the confidence you need to follow your passions, and passions are what drive business success.

The CEO's passion for a particular idea provides the energy that converts philosophy into action. A business philosophy may face pressures to compromise in order to generate short-term performance. There may be nonbelievers who will challenge the vision. There may even be demands for change among competing factions within the company. A CEO's passionate belief in a well-developed personal and business philosophy is a necessary anchor that stabilizes the organization and keeps it focused.

Competitive forces and the underlying economics of business are constantly changing. Technology, the marketplace, financial markets, distribution logistics, customer attitudes, and employee expectations are never static. *Organizations are governed by inescapable market forces—many of which inevitably generate predictable patterns of results.* High-success businesses with low entry barriers will breed competition that erodes margins. Customers, suppliers, or employees with superior bargaining power will eventually use it to their advantage. Distinctive customer benefits offered but not generated and supported by a company's core competencies will soon be copied. Developing a valid business philosophy means creating a foundation of ideas and concepts to use as guiding criteria for decision-making and action. The primary purpose of your core operating values is to make visible to everyone in the company that which is often hidden—the specific path to success for your company. Core operating values, in combination with the other two primary elements of your business philosophy, are the underlying principles that guide you in establishing policies, actions, and your specific operating model. Most critically, they will allow you to validate your vision.

A company must always be changing and improving to distinguish itself from its rivals. The only proof of a valid business philosophy is in the company's ever-increasing, more and more satisfied customer base, and in its sustained economic performance. If you are not pleased with the results you and your company achieve, perhaps it's time to take a fresh look at your business philosophy. You'll also want to think about your specific operating strategy, which is the subject of Chapter 2.

Chapter 2

Planning Strategy and Making Decisions

The problems of victory are more agreeable than those of defeat, but they are no less difficult.
—Winston Churchill

Planning strategy and making decisions are the CEO's major tasks. In recent years, we have witnessed the so-called "pizza wars." The early battles focused on convenient location, restaurant design, food quality, and price. Then came Domino's. Domino's changed the nature of the fight. They introduced delivery as a new and important battleground. Many of their competitors responded by offering their own delivery service, which seems an obvious counter-strategy, but it hasn't worked. Domino's delivers its pizzas hot within 30 minutes, while their competitors are struggling on both counts. What have the others missed? Is it just a case of needing to find a better way to keep the pizzas hot, or to work out more efficient delivery systems, or is there more?

Some of the problem may be related to the differences in how Domino's and its competitors are structuring their businesses. Domino's is not just a pizza restaurant that delivers. It is what might be called a pizza restaurant without a restaurant—at least the dining room portion of the restaurant. It has outlets that serve one purpose: to make pizzas for delivery. It doesn't have the structure or the fixed costs of a dining area. No tables, no booths, no dining room building, no dining room rent, no dining room utilities, no dining room servers, no anything relating to a dining area. In the restaurant business, the more substantial the dining area, the higher the fixed costs—costs that continue regardless of how many customers are served. Food prices generally must be raised to offset costs that are incurred but not covered by enough revenue during slow days. Domino's has, in effect, converted these fixed dining room costs to variable delivery costs that increase or decrease with volume. Their costs only increase as business goes up. The result is that a slow day is less costly to Domino's than to a full-service restaurant.

Domino's traditional restaurant competitors are also finding it hard to match them in timely delivery. They have neither the money nor the staff to handle deliveries efficiently because the marketplace will not allow them to include the cost of both delivery and dining room service in the price of their products. Customers in the dining room are not willing to pay for the cost of delivery, and home delivery customers are not willing to pay for dining room costs. And that puts a squeeze on the operating budget, which affects service. Attempting to staff both a dining room and a delivery service with the same people causes compromises in both areas.

The reality is that traditional restaurants are not structured to respond to both markets. The in-restaurant and in-home pizza customers have different needs. I suspect that the traditional full-service restaurants will eventually be forced to open "delivery only" outlets separate from their restaurant dining rooms in order to compete effectively with Domino's.

The moral of this story is not about pizza or about delivery versus dining room service. It is about creating a core competency—in this case pizza delivery—that is hard for competitors to copy. Domino's leveraged the potential benefits of this core competency by aligning its operating systems (in particular, the no-dining-room aspect) with its overall strategy. By creating this particular barrier to competition, Domino's protected its strategic position. Leveraging a core competency into a market edge is what strategic thinking is all about.

The central strategic question is: "Why should a prospective customer purchase my product or service over others available in the marketplace?" If you as CEO have a hard time answering that question, your company may have a problem. That's where strategic planning and decision-making come in, but they're not the traditional planning and decision-making that we've often been taught.

Playing the Business Game Using *CEO Logic*

Most off-the-shelf management programs that address issues like quality, culture change, customer satisfaction, or employee empowerment presuppose that you can anticipate all major business opportunities and problems. So they focus on helping you anticipate and deal proactively with what they see as predictable situations. They offer strategies and tactics as if business were a board game with fixed rules, limited moves for each player, a fixed beginning and end, and a preset number of participants. Too bad this is not reality.

In the real world, the game of business is played quite differently:

- The three main players (customers, companies, and existing competitors) have a virtually unlimited number of moves.
- Each player's move has the potential to affect every other player as much as it affects the one who made it.
- The board, that is, the business environment (the economy, industry traditions, and factors such as government regulations), is also a player and is allowed to change without notice.
- Some, all, or no rules can change during the game.
- The beginning and ending points are poorly defined and are always changing.
- New participants can enter the game without notice at any time.

Stories of the unpredictable nature of business are common—and sometimes enlightening. When the steel can manufacturers, for example, were just beginning to understand the container game, along came a new player in the form of aluminum cans. When the sugar industry started to shake out winners from losers, along came a new player—artificial sweeteners. These are not aberrations; they are the realities of how the game of business is played.

Understanding that the game of business is unpredictable does not mean that strategy and sound decision-making are futile. CEOs must formulate strategy and see that it is carried out in their organizations.

But they should never forget that there are too many moving parts in any industry to be able to anticipate everything that can happen. Proactive initiatives and strategies are needed as an opening gambit, but your game plan must be flexible enough to allow your organization to react to actual events and outcomes.

The fundamental business principles, personal management philosophy, and core operating values that were discussed in Chapter 1 are crucial to dealing successfully with a constantly changing business environment. CEOs and top management use those foundations to adapt ideas and solutions to fit new contexts and situations as they arise. They are aggressively *proactive* about that which can be anticipated, and appropriately *reactive* to whatever occurs unexpectedly. They understand that the main difference between proactive and reactive management is timing. Situations that can be anticipated allow more time to assess the problems, evaluate their causes, analyze available resources, and construct plans and strategies. Unexpected situations require the same problem-solving process, but timely execution is critical. Thinking like a CEO means learning both these moves as you master the game of business.

Strategy and the CEO's Vision

The transition to top management calls for unleashed passion for great ideas, expanded decision-making scope, a clearly articulated value system, and an all-encompassing view of strategy—all of which lead to new business and personal priorities. *Passion drives vision.* And clear vision is the basis of our capacity to navigate that sea of opportunities and problems that we call business. In becoming a CEO, you don't lose your original passions for customers, products, processes, or markets. But those passions must be transformed and harnessed to enable you to impart your vision of the future to your organization, to communicate the core operating values you espouse, and to establish your priorities. The scope of operations is expanded from focusing on short-term departmental results to balancing the concerns of customers, relationships with employees, planning and coordination for future growth, concerns with market viability, and the necessities of managing for both long- and short-term profit and cash flow.

I recently became aware of a striking example of how vision combined with sound business principles can create a successful enterprise. A CEO, Robert Halifax*, wanted to create a chain of Mexican restaurants that would dominate the region. His passion for creating healthy, great-tasting food was the driving force behind his vision, and his strategy was based on a few select core operating values:

- No products would be offered that were not made from healthy ingredients (for example, no refried beans, no MSG, nothing cooked in animal fat, and no preservatives).
- Menu prices would be competitive but not the lowest in the business. His prices would be high enough to allow the restaurants to serve high quality, healthy food.
- Service would be competitive but not the fastest, because no meals would be prepared in advance.
- Each facility would be well-designed, clean, and neat, with low overhead costs.
- Locations would be concentrated in one general market in order to maximize advertising dollars.

This company has gone on to expand and achieve the regional dominance and prosperity the founder saw in his vision. This CEO's passion for healthy food was present in almost every decision his management team made. His passion was reflected in several ways: By his decision not to offer certain popular but nonhealthy menu items; by his personal attention to recipes, cooking utensils, and cleanliness; and by his determination not to expand beyond his ability to personally oversee the operation. His ability to communicate his vision clearly and persuasively made it possible for his management team to expand the business profitability while he realized his dreams.

Vision can be defined as a realistic, appealing, and focused picture of the future that identifies both a goal and a general strategy for achieving that goal. Vision is essential when a CEO or senior manager looks at which markets to enter and which to avoid. A CEO must answer the questions: Where are we now? How will we do business based on our values? What is our core ideology that supports our business philosophy? Where are we going? When will we get there? How will we leverage our strengths to enhance our ability to compete in the marketplace? A vision, to be effective, must meet four challenges:

1. It must clearly define an important future goal, or at least a major direction for the company.
2. It must be exciting or enticing enough to provide the motivation for people to follow that direction.
3. It must be articulated with sufficient clarity and commitment to provide guidance and coordination for disparate groups.
4. It must outline a general strategy for achieving the goal.

A statement of your vision can be as brief as *national prominence through regional dominance* or it can be stated with more detail in order to include charter issues, such as specific products, markets, industries, distribution channels, price points, description of business type, or even style of doing business. In the example above, *national prominence* defines a future goal for the company. It provides a standard of measurement and establishes a direction for everyone. *Regional dominance* implies a general strategy and a specific approach to achieving this goal. Together, *national prominence through regional dominance* serves as an excellent example of a "battle cry" that can be used to excite and motivate the work force.

A clear vision of the future, sold persuasively by a CEO who believes in it passionately, provides a major part of the guiding criteria for developing a specific operating strategy. Not only will it define direction, but a clear vision can become the unifying force within a business. It is the necessary predecessor to strategy formulation.

The CEO's Role in Formulating Strategy

The strategic process involves matching the organization's internal resources and capabilities to the external market. Through this "matching" process, a company identifies both its goals and how it will achieve them. That allows it to establish a competitive edge in the marketplace that will allow the company to prosper by offering a better value to customers. Through the process of formulating strategy, a company makes choices about customers to target, needs to satisfy, markets to enter, products to offer, risks to manage, vulnerabilities to defend, core competencies to strengthen, and organizational structure to establish. Decisions not to pursue these are equally important. A strategy without customer-definable trade-offs is easier to replicate. Low-cost strategies, like the one used by Southwest Airlines, are made stronger, not weaker, by its service trade-offs—like no food service, no use of agents, and no seat assignments. The existence of these and other service trade-offs not only serve to lower overall costs but also make it much harder for competitors to match Southwest's total offering without disrupting their own "normal" services. Formulating strategy, in short, creates the operating plan for what an organization will and will not do and how it will and will not do it.

There is some question among management experts about whether it is best to begin formulating strategy by focusing externally on the marketplace and its dynamics or internally on the organization to identify ways to strengthen and leverage core competencies. To me, this a false dichotomy. An organization needs to do both: It must analyze its competitive environment in order to position or reposition itself to take advantage of perceived market opportunities *and* it must assess its own capabilities to look for a market fit. It does not matter which part of the analysis comes first.

If you are in search of detailed argumentations for these varying analyses, the extensive management literature on strategy provides valuable insights into the process and its purposes. The rigorous academic and analytical approach of Harvard's Michael Porter, author of *Competitive Strategy,* provides a good foundation for thinking about competitive strategy through his presentation of the "five forces" (customers, suppliers, substitutes, rivals, and new entrants) and his three ways to compete (cost, differentiation, and focus). In his book *Competitive Advantage,* he has also written extensively about other important strategic issues, such as the limitations of operational effectiveness and the necessity of creating fit between the many activities of a company. The recent focus on core competencies by Gary Hamel and C.K. Prahalad in their book *Competing for the Future* adds significantly to that foundation. Their definition of core competencies as "the skills that enable a firm to deliver a fundamental customer benefit" is both accurate and succinct. Kenichi Ohmai's view of strategy, presented in *The Mind of the Strategist,* causes us to take a more practical look at competitive forces in the marketplace. His statement that a good business strategy "is one by which a company can gain significant ground on its competitors at an acceptable cost to itself," provides a valuable lesson. His realistic view of strategy focuses very clearly on the three main players—the customer, the company, and the competition—each making moves and affecting the game. There is even considerable benefit in understanding the more creative, human, spontaneous, and intuitive view of strategy offered by the somewhat controversial Canadian Henry Mintzberg, in his book *The Rise and Fall of Strategic Planning*. And no meaningful discussion of management and strategy could be held without looking at the work of Peter Drucker. In particular, I like his work on the four elements of his "valid theory of business" (reality in assumptions; "fit" between decisions and mission, core competencies, and the environment; communication of strategy; and continuous testing of strategies) as presented in *Managing in a Time of Great Change.*

These management thinkers offer much food for thought to anyone interested in thinking about strategy like a CEO. *CEO Logic,* however, suggests an immediately practicable method for formulating sound strategy. While Chapter 1's concentration on fundamental business principles, personal management philosophy, and core operating values was designed to describe a general theory of business, this chapter outlines a practical framework for converting that philosophy into results through looking at specific choices on strategic elements such as products, markets, customers, and organizational structure. We begin with a nine-step model of strategy formulation that provides an overview of the process of making decisions about means and ends, about where to go, and how to get there.

The 9 Steps of Strategy Formulation

Strategy formulation is primarily about choices, but making those choices is easier when you have a proven process for thinking them through. The nine steps of strategy formulation will guide you in thinking about the best ways for your company to add value, meet your customers' needs, and make money. They offer a basis for you to develop and carry out plans to compete in the marketplace while you pursue opportunities, defend against threats, strengthen and leverage core competencies, react to change, and outmaneuver your competitors. As we review each of the nine steps, I'll include an example to show how a CEO I recently worked with (at a company I'll call Stratomax*) formulated strategy for his organization.

Step 1: Review and analyze the current and historical competitive status of your company. Look at your recent and past successes and failures in products, processes, geographic areas, market segments, customers, and competitors.

Stratomax: This $20-million service company has been growing steadily and profitably for six years and has been able to dominate in three regional markets. Right now, it is strong in its original market, but under attack in the other two. Its single product is a service, which it provides to customers significantly larger than itself.

Step 2: Analyze resources and capabilities. Take inventory of your firm's unique resources, including intangibles and tangibles—everything from proprietary technology to patented products or services to high quality reputation. Look closely at your core competencies, such as creative research and development, specific access to materials or markets, or low-cost sourcing or manufacturing.

Stratomax: The core competencies of this company are twofold. First, its measurement and control of costs is better than that of its competitors. Second, it has developed a cost-effective selling system that competitors have not yet been able to duplicate. The company's day-to-day operating strategy (i.e., hiring, scheduling, compensating, staffing, pricing, MIS, accounting, and risk management) are consistent with and totally supportive of its two core competencies.

Step 3: Analyze the competitive environment. Who is strong and who is weak? How do the strong exercise their power? What is the size of each market segment? What are the industry entry and exit barriers and what are the opportunities for substitution? Who competes on price, who competes on product or service differences, and who are the niche players?

Stratomax: The competition is made up of two types of businesses: those (about 10 companies) that are similar in size and make-up and others (about a dozen) that are much smaller. Each of the similar-sized companies has developed some degree of regional dominance due primarily to being there first. The smaller competitors are too small to be a significant threat at this time. Most (perhaps 85 percent) of the type of service that Stratomax supplies is still performed in-house by potential customers. (This in-house work is universally noncompetitive with the outsourced work, for a variety of structural reasons.)

Step 4: Assess the risks, threats, and vulnerabilities. How will customers, suppliers, and competitors respond to your actions? What are the inherent liabilities associated with doing business in your industry? What other threats do you face, such as disruptions caused by unions, bankers, or investors?

Stratomax faces the following risks, threats, and vulnerabilities:

1. The company's customers are hundreds of times larger and hold most of the negotiating leverage.
2. 50 percent of the industry follows a low-bid process.
3. Customers talk about the importance of quality and service, but make most contract awards based on price.
4. There is the potential of substantial liability for one-time incorrect service performance. A big claim might materially affect insurance rates that could only partially be passed on to customers.
5. The human resource (hiring and training) programs, technological upgrades, and quality assurance programs needed within Stratomax to improve future performance and to meet the next round of customer expectations are too expensive for one company to bear.

Step 5: Determine the primary force that drives success in your business and industry. The forces that drive success could be cost, technology, new product development, reputation or image, size or market share, ease of product use, access to distribution channels, manufacturing capacity, reliability, or any other dimension of perceived value.

Stratomax: The current driving force in the industry is price (cost from Stratomax's perspective). As the customers become more and more sophisticated at outsourcing the service, the technology and quality required to deliver the service will become more and more important.

Step 6: Test the reality of your assumptions. In *Managing in a Time of Great Change,* Peter Drucker advises that you audit and verify your perceptions as they relate to your mission, core competencies, and competitive environment. It's good advice.

Stratomax: Audits have been done by Stratomax personnel to verify the company's assumptions. Revenue per employee comparisons have been made to test the company's efficiency claims. Dun and Bradstreet reports, interviews with former employees of competitors, and analyses of public information have been used to verify other assumptions.

Step 7: Determine your mission. Define and refine your true objectives. Detail exactly what you intend to achieve. Avoid the vague and often obscure mission statements that nearly all companies have developed to placate and impress their various constituencies. These meaningless public relations statements are often ignored by all except the author, and should be limited to corporate greeting cards and employee bulletin boards. Limit your mission statement to bold but achievable targets.

Stratomax: Its primary mission is national prominence through acquisition and regional dominance. The company's secondary mission is to mitigate the risks, threats, and vulnerabilities outlined in Step 4.

Step 8: Formulate your strategy. Tie the means to the mission. List five or six ideas that detail how you will achieve your goals. Avoid vague statements like, "We will be the best," or "We will work with a great individuality." Be specific and practical.

Stratomax: The strategy for achieving its primary mission of national prominence through regional dominance is to form a holding company to acquire its major competitors. Each acquisition will be used to establish a foundation or foothold in a particular region. From this foundation, the company will attempt to expand dramatically by going after the substantial "in-house" business within each respective region. The secondary mission of mitigating risk will be achieved by using the larger revenue base of the expanded company to offset the future high cost of training and technology and the potential for one-time liability costs. The new holding company will contract for technology and training, which will allow each subsidiary to share and use those programs and upgrades, while only paying for part of the costs. In addition, the holding company will purchase insurance for all units to lessen the impact of any one claim. Each business unit will be incorporated separately to contain any potential one-time liability problems. The parent company will initially centralize cost control in order to bring its superior methods to each subsidiary. It will also roll out its cost-effective selling system to all subsidiaries. Finally, the original company will analyze all subsidiaries for positive operating practices to use throughout the corporation.

Step 9: Engage, execute, communicate, perceive, react, and modify. Strategy formulation is seldom finished. The destination often changes during the journey. At this point, as CEO, your perceptions, creativity, and intuition may be more important than the formal strategy-making process. Developing a strategy that works is not a purely analytical process; it is as much an art as it is a science. There is no formula or central unifying concept that guarantees success, only general principles to guide your decisions, actions, and resource allocations. Measure the results of your strategy often, continuously communicate your strategy to everyone involved, concentrate on detailed execution, and prepare yourself for unanticipated events.

Stratomax: The strategy is in the early stages of implementation. The CEO of the company is engaged in the process and realizes that modifications will be made as events change. At this point, acquisition targets have been analyzed and identified, private placement (fund-raising) documents have been prepared, and an investment banking firm has been hired. The next 24 months will either validate or invalidate the strategy.

The CEO's Guide to Strategy

The strategic issues you as CEO must be clear about include:

- Where are you—and your competition—now?
- What factors distinguish winners from losers in your marketplace?
- How can you reduce the bargaining power of customers and suppliers?

- How do you increase barriers to existing competitors and potential new entrants?
- What have you learned in the last year, three years, five years?
- What threats and vulnerabilities do you face? Which do your competitors face?
- How do you create value? How do your competitors?
- What is your cost position? That of your competitors?
- What are your core competencies?
- What distinctive or unique benefits do your core competencies deliver to your customers?
- What new benefits should you be considering?
- Who are your customers?
- Why do customers buy from you? From your competitors?
- How do customers know about you? About your competitors?
- What drives your current market?
- What will drive your future market?
- If you left your company today, how would you compete against it?
- How are your markets defined?
- How will your products change? Your competitors' products?
- What related markets are you choosing not to serve and why?
- What resources are available to you? To your customers?
- Describe the three most important contributions senior management can make to the organization.
- Where do you want to take your company (goals)?
- Describe a best case and worst case scenario covering the next three to five years.
- How will you achieve your goals?

Thinking Like a CEO—About Strategy

In addition to using a sound model for formulating strategy, it's also important to be aware of some general underlying practical principles about the way strategy works. These principles form a foundation for thinking like a CEO who has mastered the art and science of strategy.

There is never enough

There are never enough resources, no matter the size of the company, the wealth of the individual, or the scope of the project. Whether you're Intel or Microsoft, the major contractor behind an airport expansion, or the owner of a coffee shop, resources (human, physical, financial, technological, or intangible, such as reputation and goodwill) are always limited—and it's up to top management to develop strategies that will allocate them with care.

Many of our federal budget problems are caused by decisions made incrementally, rather than as a result of setting priorities for the allocation of limited resources. CEOs and top management must always be aware that their incremental judgments regarding how much good a particular project will do might be misleading. *The bottom line in making a strategic decision about a resource is determining how much good it will do (in relation to its cost) compared to all other projects being considered.* It is not enough, for example, to determine whether an effort to devote more resources to engineering would improve products or increase productivity. That is only one step in the decision-making process. The real issue lies in comparing the cost and benefits of this program against all competing programs and setting strategic priorities accordingly. Test each project for its fit and operational alignment with your overall strategy. Remember that a strategy defines the negative decisions of what you will not do or will not offer as much as it identifies the positives. This is what effective, tough-minded management is all about.

Kill one bird with many stones

Focus is the key to getting things done with limited resources. Slam the palm of your hand on a table with 20 pounds of pressure, then do it again holding an ice pick in your closed fist. Twenty pounds focused on the tip of an ice pick will do some damage, but 20 pounds dispersed across the surface of your hand will only hurt your hand. The same is true with every resource. Effective strategies accept and incorporate focus into their plans. The more assignments you give to an individual, the less effective he or she will be in any one of those assignments. The more ways you spend and spread your money, the less impact your money will have. Ask yourself this question: Will it do more good to give a thousand dollars to one charity or one dollar to a thousand charities?

If you regularly follow the admonition to "kill two birds with one stone," you will consistently come home out of stones and with no birds. It is nearly impossible to overestimate the damage done when a company's resources and top management's efforts are spread too thin.

This power of focus is illustrated by the changes that Brad Wilson* of Bluestone Distribution Corporation made in his company. When Brad saw that several of his divisions were losing money, he investigated and found that, over time, the division managers had been given more and more responsibilities following a strategy of decentralization and empowerment. Division bookkeeping, payroll, cash management, ordering of supplies, human resource records, and design and production of promotional materials had all been added to their operating duties. Brad concluded that the division managers were spending too much time on administration and not enough time on selling and shipping. His new strategy canned the "empowerment" program, moved the administration (mostly paperwork) back to corporate, and refocused his team on selling and shipping. Within three months they were back on track.

Balance and rank decision-making criteria

Any important business strategy needs to be examined and evaluated in light of its effect on customer satisfaction, employee satisfaction, opportunities for future growth, and profitability—*in that order*. As a member of top management, you must weigh this hierarchy of criteria when setting priorities, balance them against each other, and align them with your overall strategy to sustain your company's competitive edge.

Answering the demands of this decision-making hierarchy takes on different forms in different companies. To achieve high customer satisfaction and a competitive edge, one company may need to zero in on product development and supplier alliances. Another may have to concentrate on direct selling and low-cost production to achieve the same results. Customer satisfaction alone can take many forms. Success depends on top management's ability to identify which issues are central within complex situations.

Although the hierarchy among the criteria is important, all criteria must be balanced in making a final determination. When strategies focus on profits first, companies are often forced to bear the long-term consequences of losing their competitive standing in the marketplace. Other strategies focus only on customers and never address the issue of making money.

Linda Matthews*, founder of a nationwide franchise company in the early 1980s, built her organization up to 163 locations in 14 states. She was awarded "entrepreneur of the year" by an industry magazine and was touted as "ahead of her time" in several business journals. She had a passion for her business and deep concern for the welfare of her franchisees. But she was not making any money. Every time she ended a period with positive cash flow, she invested it in support programs for her franchisees. Eventually, her 100-percent focus on franchise owners and 0-percent focus on profits forced Linda to sell the business. The strategy of the new owners reduced the amount of resources committed to franchisee programs, made a reasonable return, and saved the business.

Put volume before profitability

In most businesses, you need to hit a critical level of volume before you become profitable. You cannot save your way into profitability. You cannot, for example, hit the labor percentage targets in a restaurant without a definable minimum number of customers. At some point, you will get down to one cook and one server, but then the volume will be too low for you to make your food cost or to cover your overhead. Unless you have found a no-overhead, no-investment business with contract employees paid 100 percent on commission, your strategy needs to deliver volume before you can have a chance at profits.

Many managers look first to improving efficiency as a primary management strategy. Efficiency, whether in the form of cost reduction or productivity enhancement, is enticing because it appears to be more "mechanical" and tangible and thus more within the manager's control. The ingredients of growth (such as product development, customer satisfaction, advertising and merchandising, or selling procedures and techniques) involve participation by others, such as customers and thus seem harder to manage and less obvious or objective. Since CEOs and senior managers may fall short of the level of confidence they need to implement the right decisions, they may be subject to pressures that can keep them from shifting their focus from efficiency to volume improvement. But they would be wrong to capitulate. In most businesses, there is no way to create profit without achieving volume. Formulate your strategies accordingly.

Operational effectiveness is not by itself a strategy

Management initiatives, such as "benchmarking," that attempt to identify the best practices in an industry are quite useful. Programs to reduce cycle-times or to increase productivity are necessary elements in any plan to compete. These management applications, however, often have a limited life span and do not directly relate to providing a long-term, distinctive, or unique benefit to your customers. Each of these programs to achieve operational effectiveness is also available to your competitors. Therefore, if you are successful with them, others will follow. Marry these kinds of programs with the leveraging of core competencies to form an overall strategy that produces a distinctive and hard-to-copy offering. Be careful in chasing any program (like benchmarking) that has the potential to make you more like your competitors. In the long run, you are only paid for your differences.

Trust your intuition

While it's important to consider the four criteria of priority-setting (customers, employees, growth, and profitability) and to gather information, facts, and opinions in an organized and scientific manner, the final strategic decisions must also "feel right." As a top manager, you must use your intuition as well as your head in any decision. Intuition is not magic; it is a by-product of knowledge and experience. Experienced managers who have done their homework can usually trust their gut feelings. Whenever you hear yourself saying that you have decided to go a certain way but are doing so "against your better judgment," stop and give the decision more time. Talk to friends and associates. Tell them the pros and cons as you see them. Relaying your thoughts to others may help confirm your intuition and make you more comfortable with the strategy your gut tells you to take.

In 1980, Bob Wasieko, division president of a high-end motor home company, told me his thoughts on product development. The particular decision he was pondering concerned the interior design of his most expensive motorcoach. Improved sales volume of this unit was a key to his strategy. His designers and market analysts made several specific recommendations, but Bob was still uncomfortable with the choices offered to him. During a factory review, he showed me some solid walnut cabinet doors that were left over from a high-end unit that had been discontinued some years earlier. Bob got the idea to use those walnut cabinet doors as the foundation for the interior design of his high-end motorcoach. He also decided to use a similar version in solid oak in a new medium-priced model. Both units were a great success. In fact, the upgraded cabinets in the mid-priced unit set the standard for the industry. Bob's sense of the situation told him his other product design alternatives were not right. By listening to his intuition, he made a significant step in turning his division around.

Can your strategy get the whole job done?

As a top manager evaluating the viability of proposed strategies, calculate the potential for results by following this simple exercise: Assume that each step in the plan will be 100-percent successful. Then, ask yourself whether the plan provides enough improvement to meet the overall targets.

Many managers have developed strategies that sounded great but lacked the horsepower to do the whole job and meet the company's objectives. For example, if one element of your strategy has to do with reducing high labor costs and the recommended remedy is to reduce overtime, it's important to know whether eliminating the overtime would have the potential to completely solve the problem. If eliminating all of the overtime would still leave you with excessive labor costs, the overtime was not the only problem.

Good managers do not offer window-dressing solutions (ones that look good but don't have the desired impact). They match strategies and resources to the size of the problem. It often pays big dividends to take the time to validate the potential effectiveness of strategies and their related action plans.

Keep an eye on the back door

When contemplating a strategy pertaining to a new product, business partnership, or major project, look closely at the costs and consequences of abandoning it. No one makes 100-percent correct decisions. Even when you reduce the risk of failure through prototyping, test marketing, and trial runs, it still pays to know in advance what it will cost if you fail. Top managers sometimes bypass failure analysis during their strategy formulation process to avoid the potential for demotivation or criticism. A positive "can do" approach may lead you to ignore the possibility of failure. As a general rule, however, don't place the bet unless you can afford to lose the money—and you will not know if you can afford to lose the money until you analyze the potential costs of failure.

Robert Terry* specializes in developing airport real estate—specifically, building and leasing hangars for small airplanes. In the beginning, his strategy was to build special-purpose tee-hangars designed primarily for small airplanes. The interlocking shape minimized cost while providing ample room to store an airplane. After the small airplane industry slump of the late 80s, he moved into building rectangular hangars that can still store airplanes but can also be used for general storage. The cost is a little higher and the margins for general storage are a little lower, but the general storage option provides a good "back door" strategy when he needs it.

Leverage your core competency

We emphasized the importance of core competency in Chapter 1, as a business fundamental, but it also pays to keep it central in formulating and following through on strategy. As was mentioned earlier, strategy is usually aimed at one or more of the following three objectives:

1. Exploiting opportunities.
2. Defending against threats.
3. Strengthening and leveraging core competencies.

As with the case of the Domino's "pizza wars," the capacity to leverage your core competencies is directly related to your ability to achieve a competitive edge in the marketplace. The more hard-to-copy your core competencies, the more sustainable your competitive edge, and therefore, the more sustainable your profits.

Plan for continuous improvement

Continuous improvement by itself is not a strategy, but all effective strategies recognize that there is no such thing as the status quo. If things are not getting better, they are getting worse. The CEO and top management must respond by understanding that improvement is a requirement, not an option, and that all strategic goals need to be directed toward it. The old adage, "If it ain't broke, don't fix it," promotes stagnation, lack of improvement, and eventual deterioration. The retail storefront will deteriorate without a program in place to keep it up-to-date. Accounts receivable collections will start to slow without a system to monitor and expedite late payments. Customer satisfaction will wither and die without regular—if not constant—attention. It takes a dedicated strategy and well-directed resources to compensate for the natural tendency toward deterioration.

Continuous improvement is the hallmark of almost every quality improvement plan. Everyone from Peter Drucker to Philip Crosby to W. Edwards Deming has supported this concept. So why is it so difficult to implement? Why is there such a tendency for so many top managers to "leave well enough alone?" The answer is that improvement requires change, which is often uncomfortable. It takes committed leadership to deal with people and organizations that are uncomfortable because of the change required of them. Too often, leaders simply mouth the rhetoric of continuously improving performance without putting their words into action. It is foolish, however, to keep doing the same things while expecting different results. A true commitment to excellence requires a tough-minded focus on the changes needed for improvement, and an intolerance for poor strategy and weak execution. If your current strategies and standards do not demand continuous improvement, then those strategies and standards are not acceptable.

Like everything else in business, strategic management is an endless process of improvement. It is a journey with a clear direction but no final destination, and it must strive toward improvement every day. If you can make an improvement on an important issue each day, you will meet with success. Any size improvement (large or small) will do, as long as it affects a key issue. One improvement each working day is 250 a year. If you can convince just three others in your business to do the same, that's 1,000 a year. A thousand improvements of any magnitude per year on important issues will have a big impact.

Understand the importance of systems—and ordinary people

Most organizations are made up of ordinary people, not superstars. Even though it's great to have superstars, it's not realistic to expect that you can build a whole company with them. In the long run, only the team approach works. All systems and projects have to be broken down into bite-sized chunks so that an average worker with a good effort and proper direction can perform the tasks successfully. All strategies must reflect this reality.

Henry Ford said, "The purpose of an organization is to create extraordinary products with ordinary people." I think that pretty much says it all. Another way of looking at this issue is to recognize that *85 percent of chronic business problems are due to the systems in place, not the people involved.* When ordinary, caring people fail regularly at a particular task, it probably has more to do with a faulty system than a faulty person. Develop your strategies accordingly.

This axiom is somehow easier for managers to accept when the tasks in question are mechanical rather than managerial. When a manager looks at a mechanical task, such as a machining process, the idea that a chronic variance is probably in the machine is believable. After all, you cannot expect a machinist to work with .0001 inches tolerance if the machine is not calibrated to do so. But that same manager might not want to believe that an ongoing management problem or a persistent administrative breakdown may be caused by inadequately designed systems. When the overall sales quota is missed for the sixth month in a row, it is still easier to blame the sales force than to attack the forecast, pricing, selling system, or product design. But chronic problems are generally related to bad systems. The search for strategic solutions begins with analyzing, evaluating, and validating the system.

Learn continuously about critical business issues

Strategy formulation requires a special focus on the critical issues of your business. If your business sells contract labor, then you cannot know too much about labor utilization. If you have a distribution company, then you cannot know too much about inventory turnover, obsolescence, margins, new products, and lead times. If you are in the apartment rental business, you cannot know too much about acquisition price, rate, and occupancy. The problem is always too little information, so learn and acquire all that you can to increase your understanding.

If managing a particular issue is absolutely vital to the success of your business, read about it, measure it, talk about it, and strategize on it. Write memos about it, ask for advice on it, hold meetings about it, and then measure it again. You cannot focus too much on a strategic issue vital to the success of your company.

Keep corporate staff lean

Whenever I am asked about the proper size for corporate administration, I always say, "Two: you and me—and I'm not so sure about you." Avoid strategies that rely on corporate staff personnel to achieve results on line functions. Corporate staff cannot compensate for other weaknesses in the organization, its structure, or its people. For example, if you have a strong corporate sales manager, you may tend to think he or she can cover for weak field sales managers. But that doesn't work. None of the field jobs is a part-time job, and the so-called corporate "experts" never seem to have all of the information they need to make good decisions on local issues. Design your strategies to let local managers make their own decisions, and keep a minimum corporate staff focused on its own tasks.

The following example makes this very point. I was called in to help turn around a recently purchased furniture manufacturing company. Their products were good, their markets were viable, and, except for the previous 18 months, the company had had a history of competing effectively in the industry. Corporate staff was strong, but division and department management was weak. The one-step strategic solution was obvious: Put the corporate managers back to work. Give them "real jobs" and use them to replace weak division and departmental managers.

The resulting reduction in corporate expense and increase in division performance eliminated the losses and put the company back on the path to prosperity. It's too bad all turnarounds are not this straightforward. It does show how important it is to create a strategy that keeps your corporate staff lean and puts your best people out where the real work is being done.

CEOs always like to surround themselves with highly talented and qualified people. That's good, if all those people have real jobs with real revenues from real customers and real profit and loss responsibilities. If that doesn't describe the situation, design a strategy that will give real jobs to these talented folks.

Decentralize first

Effective strategies centralize the paperwork and support administration but decentralize the power and the people. Although there are often undeniable advantages to centralization, particularly in cost savings and control, it's generally better to bring decisions down to the lowest level possible. Corporate administration always has priorities that are different from those of its divisions. Divisions can focus solely on satisfying their customers, while corporate often has its own set of problems and opportunities. Formulate your strategies to let the people in the field do their own work by allowing them to make their own decisions.

Sometimes a particular function, such as risk management or human resources, must be centralized because each individual division cannot yet afford its own. When this is unavoidable, then do so, but also put in a "sunset" provision—decide how often and when you will review the decision, with the intention of moving control of the resource out to the division as soon as it is economically feasible.

Beware of campaigns

When Charles Stanley* was promoted from controller to president, his first strategic move was to bring in two sets of outside consultants to facilitate employee communications and to initiate cost reduction programs. His management team did not entirely understand his logic. Many thought that perhaps Charles figured he would need to improve employee communications after he made employee cutbacks. The company's senior management team did not see the consultant's programs as an integral part of their overall strategy—

just another in a long string of programs. In the previous 14 months, they'd had programs on mission statements, employee empowerment, and team management. None of it was sticking. Charles was falling into the same trap as his predecessor in his attempts to manage primarily by campaign. A strategy consisting only of campaigns has no substance.

Campaigns for cost reduction, product improvement, quality improvement, customer service, and the like are fine when you use them to punctuate or draw short-term attention to a particular critical aspect of operations. But campaigns alone will not replace fundamental management strategies like the ones we talk about in this book. You cannot manage an issue such as quality or customer service by campaign only. Campaigns are inherently temporary affairs. When I find a company that has a large number of so-called management improvement campaigns in its strategic plan, I immediately look to see if the CEO really knows the business. Good business and good strategy are built on sound judgment, good people, hard work, valid business principles, and excellent values. The "fad management" approach confuses the work force and rarely addresses the right issues. Almost everyone can spot a manager who is managing based on the last book he or she read.

Put just one person in charge

Good strategic decisions can sometimes be arrived at by committees, but implementation and execution are best carried out by one person. Better yet, let the committee analyze the problem, gather the facts, validate the opinions, and offer alternatives, and then allow one manager to make the decision and be responsible for carrying it out.

As a CEO or top manager, you have to respect other points of view, especially contradictory ones. Differing perspectives can offer valuable insights into strategy formulation. No one perspective is always right. It is said that democracies produce the best decisions but dictators are best at carrying them out. Perhaps that is why we have a democracy for our government but not for our military.

Strategy always exists—and it always matters

It is often undocumented, vague, or set by default. But it is always there. Strategy is implicit in the decisions, resource allocations, performance measurements, reward systems, and actions of a company. Without a well-communicated strategy, there will be insufficient guidelines for day-to-day decisions. There will be no framework for coordinating the efforts of disparate groups, performance measurements will vary from department to department, and correct priorities will not be set.

A well-formulated strategy informs everyone where they are now, where they are going, and how they will get there. It also provides a methodology for validating both goals and how you will achieve them. Strategic thinking changes the way you perceive your company. You will no longer look at your business as a portfolio of products and services. When looked at strategically, it will appear as a portfolio of core competencies being leveraged to deliver unique or distinctive benefits to customers. In tough times, strategy provides a basis for rethinking a company's concept and using that new concept as a basis for achieving market leadership. Chapter 1 provided a philosophical foundation for top management thinking. Chapter 2's discussion of strategy will take you further down the road to thinking like a CEO by helping you to convert that philosophy to results. The remaining chapters will complete the journey.

Part 2

Management Organization and Execution: Disciplines

The philosophical foundation you learned to construct in Part 1 has given you an overall framework for thinking like an effective CEO about the broad challenges of business. Now your task is to learn to apply and execute the fundamentals across the entire range of practical, everyday regimens of business—the 10 disciplines of management. *CEO Logic* guides you through this task by defining the true purpose of each specific management resource in order to focus it on the right strategic target.

Chapters 3 through 7 are about management execution of the most widely practiced business disciplines: business planning, people management, career management, sales, and the numbers. Each chapter applies the principles of Part 1 to a particular management discipline, allowing managers to effectively convert theory to results.

Chapter 3

Business Operations Planning: Define the Risks Worth Taking

Large views always triumph over small ideas.
—Winston Churchill

Joe Markowitz*, CEO of Markson Retailers, was discussing the need for formal business operating plans at a meeting with a group of his peers at an industry function. Joe said, "I understand the business, I know what's right for our organization, and I make decisions accordingly as I go along. This is the way we've always done it and we have been successful. It's my opinion that formal operating plans would only mean more administrative bureaucracy for me and my company." A question was raised by one of Joe's associates: "How can you make decisions about your new retail store concept without forecasting the cost and return? Are you absolutely sure of all your assumptions? Aren't you afraid of over- or under-committing resources to this project?" Before Joe could answer, another question was posed: "Don't you feel concerned that this major new strategy might put your whole company at risk?" Joe replied, "I know my business and my industry inside and out, and I've always trusted my intuition." The meeting closed with no further discussion on the matter. Joe's attitude about formal operating plans may be typical of many entrepreneurs but it is not consistent with the vast majority of successful CEOs and business managers. Indiana University basketball coach, Bobby Knight, was quoted in Steve Alford's book *Playing for Knight* as saying, "The will to succeed is important but what is more important is the will to prepare."

Operations planning completes the planning process that starts with business philosophy, vision, strategy, and mission. It is the vehicle that allows for the application of logic to work. Its focus is on strategy validation, resource allocation, and implementation. Operating plans enable CEOs to convert vision and strategy into actions and results.

Operations planning answers a range of essential questions about the nature of your business today, feasibility of your goals detailing where you want to be in a certain time frame, the actions required to get there, and the resources needed. Top managers use operations planning to validate their strategies and assumptions, to evaluate potential solutions and the consequences of decisions already made, and as a yardstick with which to measure future performance.

The Whats and Whys of Planning

Although many people in an organization participate in creating the plan, everyone does so at a different level. Top management usually addresses the largest, global issues. Senior management, along with all other operating managers, generally are responsible for the rest. Everyone should be encouraged to question and provide comment on the entire plan, because that will not only improve the plan, but will also build a broader base of commitment to it.

The operating plan allows a business to:

- Describe and communicate company philosophy and mission, and in doing so, identify specific values, targets, and objectives.
- Validate major concepts and strategies.
- Review and test critical operating and economic assumptions.
- Analyze the details of significant risks, obstacles, and opportunities, and describe how they will be addressed and/or capitalized upon.
- Analyze pros and cons of major available alternatives.
- Evaluate the likely impact of potential major internal or external events (such as key retirements, acquisitions, new government regulation, recession, divestitures, currency issues, competitive threats) and develop contingency plans.

- Establish priorities and time frames both for the short and long term.
- Develop and refine decision-making criteria.
- Identify, allocate, and coordinate resources in a strategic way.
- Determine the optimum management and organizational structure.
- Analyze cash flow and capitalization issues.
- Develop financial and operating controls.
- Allocate major responsibilities and develop short-term tactical action plans.
- Represent and communicate operating expectations in quantitative terms: unit and revenue plans, and financial statements (i.e., profit and loss, balance sheet, and cash flow).
- Educate, motivate, and gain the commitment of staff and management.
- Provide a method to measure current and future performance and progress.

What's in a plan?

The following is a typical operating plan format designed to incorporate both operations planning issues discussed in this chapter and strategic issues from Chapter 2:

1. *Executive Summary.* A synopsis of the plan, no more than two pages in length.
2. *Company Philosophy.* Describes what the business does—and does not do—and how it does it.
3. *Mission.* Describes the basic purpose and main focus of the business or project in order to clearly define the target.
4. *Basic Planning Assumptions.* Provides details on major economic and operating assumptions such as industry outlook, regional economics, or the availability of critical resources.

5. *Definition of Business, Industry, Markets, and Products.* Outlines each of these as well as the participants in and demographics and economics of your particular business.
6. *Current Status of Business.* Assesses the organization's marketplace position, profitability, reputation, return on investment, supplier relationships, and employee relationships.
7. *Strategy.* Describes the operating decisions and company objectives relating to assignments of major resources and the leveraging of core competencies as applied to major problems and opportunities. Outlines how the organization will establish a competitive edge and be placed in a position to succeed.
8. *Action Plan.* Lays out the day-to-day details of tactics: Who, what, when, where, and how much will be needed to accomplish the overall plan.
9. *Long-Range Direction, Scope, and Objectives.* Defines long-term strategic success, such as dominance of a market or industry, becoming number one in quality in a given product line, or reducing cost by half.
10. *Benchmarks and Milestones.* Subdivides exactly what is to be accomplished into measurable sub-goals, and provides a method to measure interim progress.
11. *Debt Analysis.* Provides the details of each existing and forecasted loan, including amounts, rates, terms, covenants, and fees.
12. *Financial Plan.* Provides a quantitative representation of operating expectations, including a unit sales and revenue plan followed by projected financial statements for profit and loss, balance sheet, and cash flow.

This format reflects only a generic plan. Not all business plans will be structured precisely in this way because each situation will have its own special needs. But following this format can ensure that managers stay focused on the essentials of what will strengthen the business and help it to realize its objectives.

Short- and long-term planning

As a top manager, you need both short- and long-term plans, because both serve different but complementary purposes. Short-term plans and updates (90 days to one year) are used primarily to run the company's operations. Their time frames reflect the realistic lead times required to make operating changes. They also need to reflect the company's ability to know what is truly coming in the marketplace. If plans are based on too short a time frame, there will not be enough time to change resources or programs. Detailed forecasts that extend far into the future are equally ineffective, since they can be no more than guesses.

Long-range plans (longer than one year) are used primarily for determining capital and credit requirements, resource capacities, and strategic issues concerning decisions about resource allocations, core competencies and competitive edge, and overall company direction. They are less detailed because they are designed to guide the larger issues that concern the organization. Businesses generally need well-detailed and defined short-range goals but require only direction and scope in their long-range planning. Firm and specifically defined long-range goals are unnecessary, unless they are established to support the long-range consequences of decisions that have already been made. In devising long-term plans, the time frames should correspond to the commitments of major resources. If the minimum commitment for a particular acquisition is five years, then it is important to plan and forecast five years insofar as possible before making the purchase. If you are planning to enter a new market that has large entry and exit barriers, take a much longer look at what will become your company's future responsibilities.

As a top manager, you're the one charged with understanding and planning for the consequences of the decisions you make. Every decision has a tail on it, sometimes short and sometimes long. When you decide to make an acquisition involving a six-year payback with no opportunity to sell off the asset prior to six years, then your six-year plan becomes a six-year commitment, not just a six-year forecast. Your management team must now actually commit to making this plan happen and not just to viewing the planning document as a best-efforts prediction.

"Chance favors the prepared mind": Risk analysis

Just as Louis Pasteur pointed out in this famous quotation, preparation is essential. And operations planning is a type of preparation that allows a business to analyze and evaluate potential risks. Remember that, in effect, a business gets paid for taking certain calculated risks. *The purpose of planning is not to eliminate all risk but to determine which risks you are willing to take.* The key is to understand the degree and nature of the risks in order to develop the capacity to manage them with an acceptable degree of certainty. Risk has two key aspects:

1. Chance: The likelihood of success or failure.
2. Magnitude: The degree or size of potential gain or loss.

Top managers benefit from thinking about risk in terms of these two distinctive but interrelated dimensions. You may decide to accept a greater chance, or likelihood of failure, if the magnitude of the potential gain is high, and/or the amount of the potential loss is low. You may also accept or reject a risk based on your perceived capacity to manage it.

A commodities trader, for example, may be willing to accept certain transaction and receivables risks but may not want to bear an inventory or market risk. A distributor may be willing to accept both receivables and inventory risks but may want to limit manufacturing and warranty exposure. Certain manufacturers are willing to accept production, receivables, inventory, and warranty risks but choose to sell through distributors in order to avoid the end-user marketing risk. Risk—when understood—can be a friend to business. If you're thinking like a CEO, you understand that a unique capacity to manage a certain risk is often exactly the reason a business is paid. In any event, risk management and planning go hand in hand.

The following story illustrates the relationship between risk and opportunity. In the early 1980s, the Arizona real estate market was booming, especially in single-family, entry-level homes.

Bud Therion* had had a long and successful career working for others in real estate development and sales. As he looked at the booming market for single-family, entry-level homes in Phoenix, he thought there might be significant opportunity there for him to start his own business. His main resources were his time, skills, and reputation. He had saved a small nest egg, but did not want to put it at risk. His goals were to be master of his own business, minimize the risk of failure, leverage his skills and reputation, and improve his standard of living. When he analyzed the major elements of the real estate development process, they looked something like this:

- Locate a potential site.
- Analyze site potential in detail (look for highest and best use).
- Tie up the land with an option or purchase.
- Address the political issues of zoning and usage.
- Engineer a specific site plan.
- Develop roads, lots, and infrastructure (utilities and amenities).
- Design and construct houses.
- Market and finance houses to the public.
- Provide after sale service (warranty).

Bud realized that each step of the development process came with its own risks, rewards, and required resources. He compared the risks he was capable of managing with the risks associated with each step. He also looked at the risks that traditional developers were willing or unwilling to accept. Because small- and medium-sized developers were primarily oriented to construction, they were often not prepared to handle the time-consuming political aspects of zoning and site approvals. In addition, the time delay from site location to site-plan approval increased market timing risks for these same developers. He determined that many developers would pay extra for ready-to-develop land parcels that came complete with zoning and specific site-plan approvals. This immediate availability would reduce their risk of missing the market due to excessive time lags.

Once Bud had identified the risks he was capable of managing and therefore willing to take, he sought and found a partner willing to take the financial risk in optioning or acquiring properties. Bud would take care of locating a site, analyzing its potential, and addressing zoning and site approval; the partner would provide the funds for buying or optioning the land, and the developer could then proceed with developing the project and building the houses. All three parties—Bud, the financial partner, and the developer—would be compensated for the risk they assumed and managed. Each could avoid or at least minimize the risks he found most objectionable. Each would be rewarded according to the risks and investments he undertook.

The Planning Process

Think like a CEO and follow this three-step approach to preparing for your plan. First, develop a planning format. Many companies have trouble with planning because their managers do not understand the process. Select a format for your plan (there are many books available on the subject, or use the one presented earlier in this chapter) and follow it.

Second, establish firm time frames and deadlines for planning. Planning is often put off because there appears to be no urgency.

Third, determine the purpose of the plan before starting the planning process. Be careful to limit the scope of the plan to its purpose. A structured approach to planning will provide more useable information.

Plan big, then small

As the leaders of the planning process, CEOs and top managers usually begin by looking at the larger issues: major initiatives, market shares, annual volumes, and annual returns. Once you have examined these larger issues and have calculated such items as year-to-year revenues for the whole company, the process can then move on to projecting individual product line revenues. Watch out for "incrementalism." For example, one company I know asked all salespeople to provide incremental customer-by-customer sales forecasts for the upcoming year that would then be rolled up into a total increase in volume for the new year over the last year. On the surface, this seemed like an acceptable idea. In reality, this company sold big-ticket items with unit prices in the $10,000 to $70,000 range, and many customers had only purchased a few units each in the previous year. The sales force was, of course, encouraged to be positive. So, if a customer had purchased only two or three units the year before, surely they could buy four or five units the next year. When the final totals were tabulated, the next year's business was forecasted to improve a whopping 96 percent, even though the industry market was projected to be flat or slightly down, and the company had no real plans, products, or programs to increase market share.

A lot can be done with positive attitude, but it is not possible to gain huge market share increases without allocating the resources to achieve them. Counting on an incremental sales forecast like the one above is more wishful thinking than planning. The same goes for margins and returns. Huge efficiency improvements or substantial cost reductions are not possible without corresponding changes in the methods, procedures, and/or resources devoted to accomplishing them.

Start with short-term baseline plans

Short-term baseline plans cover profit and loss, balance sheet, and cash flow issues. They assume no new business, no lost business, no new efficiencies, and no lost efficiencies other than what is known and guaranteed at the time of the planning. They reflect only operating or strategic decisions that have already been made. They are designed to help you see what will happen if you maintain current efficiency levels and do not apply or withdraw additional resources to or from your operation. They become the base documents to which contingency plans for projects or consequences can be added. They prevent guessing about future events for which timing and likelihood are doubtful or unknown. Short-term baseline plans are a good foundation for planning that can deter management from the tendency to add expenses and assets prematurely.

Follow with contingency plans

Contingency plans detail the effects that major events or projects that might reasonably happen will have on profit and loss, cash flow, and the balance sheet. They can be analyzed and examined both incrementally and in combination with baseline plans. And they should be added to quarterly updates of the baseline plans as soon as each particular contingency issue becomes inevitable. This allows you to have better control over the timing of additional expenses and/or assets. Contingency plans also help in making the strategic decisions required to strengthen the competitive position of your company.

For example, suppose you were operating a $30-million company and were planning two $5-million acquisitions over the next 14 months. Suppose further, that your internal growth rate was 20 percent per year and was expected to continue at the same rate. How do you plan and forecast for the upcoming year?

You would separate each element with baseline and contingency plans. Each potential acquisition would be forecasted separately and added to your baseline plan only as each came to fruition. Each major element (such as a major new contract) relating to your internal development would be treated in the same way. This approach can also be used for "what if" contingencies, such as loss of a major account or entry of a new competitor. Your baseline plan would include only that increase that was already achieved at the year-end just previous to the planning period. This process takes away much of the guesswork in planning and provides clearer guidelines for operating managers.

Focus on substance, not form

When it comes to planning, managers may at times focus too much on technique and presentation at the expense of substance. An example is all of the fuss about exit strategies. All successful and positive exit strategies involve economic performance and eventual liquidity. Some exit strategy issues, such as legal structure and accounting form, must be addressed early on, but if the company achieves economic performance, it can take advantage of most exit strategies.

Attack the variances

Performance analyses based on planned versus actual results are the basis for most performance measurement. As such, these analyses are at the heart of management effectiveness. Top management must take the initiative to discuss planned versus actual performance regularly with other managers and to respond quickly and decisively. Once you have specifically identified the variance in dollars, percentages, and time frame, you can then figure out what caused it, and who or what allowed or generated the performance deviation. Then you can decide whether the variance was good or bad, discuss that with those involved, establish a corrective action plan, and project future results. If you can get to the source of planned versus actual variances, the solutions will be within your grasp.

Know your audience

The business plans discussed so far have been directed at developing the criteria and foundations for management decision-making. There are, of course, other forms of business plans. Plans developed for investors or bankers require a different focus than those for managers. Bankers want to be shown that there is "zero risk." They want to know that their money will be paid back in full and on time (see Chapter 7). Investors primarily want to understand the risks and opportunities associated with potential returns on their investment. Think like a CEO by targeting your plans to your audience, making sure that your plans meet their specific needs.

A few cautions

1. Use it or lose it. An operating plan must be dynamic in order to be useful. Quarterly updates keep a plan fresh and relevant. If you don't update your plan, you may fall into the common trap of creating a great plan that lies in a desk drawer until next year's planning session. Keep the plan in front of you for the duration of the plan, and make changes as circumstances dictate.

2. Understand the hidden messages in resource allocations. Although the decisions about allocating resources seem to be just that—business decisions—they also disclose a company's priorities. Allocations let everyone know which departments and individuals have the company's blessing or signal decisions that have been made that affect individuals and their behavior. In one swimming pool equipment manufacturing organization, turnover in sales staff seemed almost out of control. Some of their best salespeople were leaving, but they could not figure out why. They held meetings with the sales reps to explain the company's commitment to them, they redecorated the sales office, and even put substantial money into sales contests. When none of these moves worked, the company brought in an outside consultant. He analyzed the problem and found that most of the turnover was in one part of the sales force that sold a particular product line. When he looked further, he found that this product line was slated to be eliminated at the end of the year. Advertising had been cut back, inventory levels had been reduced, and promotional literature was not replaced when it ran out. The sales force noticed the lack of support before it was announced, interpreted its meaning, and made their own plans to leave before they were let go. Management had intended to tell the reps that there would be a new product line for them once decisions were finalized, but the sales force had no way of knowing that. From what they could see, the change in allocation of resources telegraphed management's intention to make a change. And they assumed it wouldn't be to their benefit.

3. Commitment is the key. Think through the true purpose of your efforts, select the issues critical to your success, develop powerful strategies, design effective action plans, and write them down. Then, execute your plans with conviction and enthusiasm.

My long-time friend and associate, Robert (Bob) Wasieko, is the best I have ever met at executing a plan with total commitment. Bob is a high energy, sales-oriented management professional. He successfully managed a $100-million manufacturing and sales division for me. He is a quick study on any subject and a great communicator. Often his public speaking presentations generate standing ovations. He is driven by a huge desire to succeed. He is loyal to his people and his organization and has great personal stamina. His optimism and enthusiasm enable Bob to withstand great adversity without being thrown off track. He is a time management wizard. I have never seen anyone better organized or who uses his time more efficiently. His greatest strength, however, is his ability to develop and commit to a plan.

Some years ago, Bob was faced with the task of turning around a major but troubled division of a much larger corporation. Several people in the company had already tried and failed at this very same task. Bob had the support of his immediate senior manager, but was challenged on many other fronts. Other senior managers, peer division managers, and many members of his own team were skeptical of his chances for success. Bob analyzed the threats and opportunities facing him, developed a detailed plan of operations, and stayed his course. He followed his plans despite the outside criticism and lack of support. I have no doubt that his ability to deliver tremendous energy to a plan is a primary factor in Bob's great success with this division. Bob Wasieko is an expert at thinking, planning, and committing like a CEO.

Final Thoughts on Business Operations Planning

Top management has a special responsibility to the planning process. While other members of an organization must be involved in the plan, senior management starts the process and determines its scope and direction. *Top management, with input from many sources, is the keeper of the vision. It has the primary obligation to make sure the organization builds and strengthens its core competencies in order to protect and sustain its competitive edge.* And the business operating plan is a strategic tool and the final step in making sure this obligation is met.

Top management also has the responsibility to bring others into the process at the appropriate time and level. Each person in the organization must understand and agree with his or her particular role in the final plan. Each one must be convinced of its viability and be persuaded to engage wholeheartedly in the effort. Each one must be helped to develop the pride and the passion that top management feels. Each one must be inspired to perform and encouraged to cooperate. Each one must understand that the planning process is not just a cold analytical exercise in numerical projections but is about people. Each one must come to know that his or her own success, as well as the success of many others, depends greatly on the effectiveness of the planning effort. Each one must also know that actual performance will be measured against the plan and that recognition of his or her achievements is guaranteed. Only top management can drive this knowledge and commitment throughout the organization.

Three companies were competing in the same industry. Company A looked to minimize risk, reflecting its view of a volatile industry. Company B felt the need to take what it considered calculated risks in order to achieve a competitive advantage. Company C had no given philosophy on risk but attempted to address each element of risk as it came along.

All three companies were roughly comparable in size, talent, and resources. Company A was the market leader, Company B was third in market share, and Company C was second. Each developed its operating plans according to its own perspective on risk and its explicit or implied strategies.

Company A (running first) decided the potential of increased margins did not outweigh the reality of increased fixed costs that vertical integration would bring. It was further concerned about vertical integration's impact on its ability to keep designs current. Company A chose to do the work of its suppliers only in the case of extreme savings opportunities or specific and chronic market shortages.

Company B (running third) decided to take the risk of vertical integration. by becoming its own supplier for much of its needs. It did so partially to improve margins and partially to offset the logistical disadvantage of being located far away from suppliers.

Company C (running second) decided to vertically integrate only when a supplier acquisition became available and appeared to be a bargain incremental purchase. Company C's primary focus was on the deal and not on its competitive or structural impact.

The results of their decisions were as follows:

- Company A remained the leader and strengthened its position by a substantial margin. The market was volatile, as the company had predicted, and its strategy of remaining as flexible as possible was upheld.
- Company B had severe upswings and downswings that coincided with the volatile market. Overall, its strategy allowed it to stay in the top five in the marketplace.
- Company C fell out of the top 10 in both sales and earnings. Its reactive and incremental strategy did not prepare it for a changing marketplace.

The bottom line of this story is that incremental or nonstrategy-based planning is often more dangerous than planning based even on a weak strategy. Business events do not occur in a vacuum. It is risky to view them in an ad hoc fashion. What looks like a good incremental purchase today may strategically sink the ship tomorrow. An implicit plan is still a plan. Your strategic decisions must precede your operating plan. Thought is required before action. Do not embark on a voyage or set your course with no destination in mind. You may not like where you end up.

There is something almost magical about putting your plans into words. The thinking process is changed and improved by the act of writing. It may be that writing about a thought only gives you another opportunity to refine your thinking. It may also be that the act of writing actually changes the chemical, electrical, or biological processes of the brain. Committing a plan to paper makes a big difference. Something about writing helps to bring a thought into better focus.

The only sure way to improve planning is to think like a CEO, bring everyone into the process, and formalize the planning procedures. Establish a planning format complete with deadlines and commitments. Review the results of your planning regularly and modify the process accordingly. Like a CEO, use correct planning to provide a road map to your success.

Chapter 4

People Management: Never Try to Teach a Pig to Think

Criticism is easy; achievement is difficult.
—Winston Churchill

Jack Fisk* was hired as a turnaround consultant to an organization that was growing in sales revenue but was losing money overall. Before he accepted the assignment, the board of directors told him that they were doing fine managing their people but that their product development was weak. They suggested that his first priority should be to upgrade the product offering.

Within 90 days, Jack discovered that their product lines were too broad, though many of their individual products were well-accepted in the marketplace. People in the organization recognized where defects existed in the products, but a high turnover in personnel inhibited their ability to remedy the problems. It seemed that each new manager who came in wanted to give his or her particular poorly performing product more time and attention. Jack hadn't yet experienced the turnover problems firsthand. From what he'd been told, the company should have had great employee relations. The company mission statement (plastered everywhere) expressed its desire to "put people first." Thousands of dollars were spent each year on employee and management seminars ranging from participative management to individual empowerment. But the company's actual performance varied greatly from the plan.

Although the product line needed to be slimmed down, Jack could see the poor bottom line performance was just a symptom of the turnover problem. When he asked about these staffing concerns, everyone kept telling him about the company's long list of human resource campaigns and programs. They spoke of psychological testing, career counseling, weekend planning retreats, and lessons in handling diversity. They pointed to the motivational posters, the employee award banquets, the employee newsletter, and even the company picnics. In addition, they pointed to their thoroughly executed annual performance reviews. All of these programs and more, they said, were proof of the company's orientation to its people.

However, when he dug deeper, Jack found that none of these programs was actually focusing on performance. Nepotism and favoritism were rampant. Pay and benefits were below industry standards. While many people left on their own, no one was ever fired for incompetence or nonperformance. Employee training seldom matched job requirements, and the company's business plans neither made sense nor were communicated to employees.

Once he identified the real source of the problems, Jack knew what to do to solve them. The company should weed out the slow-moving products from the product line, but it should also institute a whole new way of interacting with employees. There needed to be accurate and objective performance measurement systems throughout the organization. Everyone would have to concentrate on satisfying customers. A business plan that addressed key issues and encouraged continuous improvement would have to be created and made public throughout the company. Performers would have to be paid fairly and nonperformers would have to be dealt with. Stock options and incentive plans were needed to reinforce the emphasis on performance. And all of the so-called human resource campaigns that did not directly affect performance would have to be suspended. Jack was around long enough to see that his solutions produced almost immediate results for the organization.

This story does not suggest that all or even most human resource programs are without merit and should be eliminated. But actions speak louder than words (or programs) when it comes to all management disciplines—and especially the discipline of people management. If this company had been tracking employee turnover, it would have seen the high number of people leaving the company's employ as an indication of its problems in handling people—as well as the root of its overall business troubles. Instead, as the axiom goes, "They managed what they measured." In this case, they measured the number of campaigns and programs aimed at improving employee relations. As a consequence, they were tops in the industry in the number and variety of their employee relations programs but at the bottom in actual relations with employees. And their business results suffered accordingly. Had they mastered the fundamentals of *CEO Logic,* they would have immediately spotted this simple truth in the complexity of the overall situation.

A Company's Most Important Asset

Who, besides bankers, would dispute that people are a company's most important asset? Service organizations boast that they are in the people business, but when you think about it, every business is a people business. People are the only resource that can think and control other resources.

Even though most organizations profess to be people-oriented, they don't always behave that way. The way they communicate directives, delegate authority and responsibility, use performance measurement criteria, structure compensation plans, and the degree of opportunity they offer to individuals are all manifestations of their true beliefs regarding the importance of people.

7 Key Insights

CEO Logic, as it relates to people management, begins with seven key insights: First, the strength of a business resides in the minds of its people. Second, employers generally get the employees they deserve. Third, managing people does not begin with hiring, educating, or how you treat people, but with how you structure your company. Fourth, the teams with the best players have the highest winning percentages. Fifth, you build an organization from the top down, not from the bottom up. Sixth, the cost of poor selection or mishandling of people may be the greatest hidden cost that a company can incur. And seventh, shared values are the key to a positive work environment and consistent performance.

1. The strength of a business resides in the minds of its people. Let this principle become the foundation of your people-management strategy. Fill your company with clear thinkers. Spend the resources to make training and education a continuous process. Strengthen the minds of your people and you will strengthen your company. Create an environment where continuous learning is recognized, supported, and even rewarded. Stop! Check right now to see what resources are currently committed to strengthening the minds of your people. While you're at it, don't forget your own mind. Develop your capacity to listen to and learn from your own people. Human concerns are always an issue.

2. Employers generally get the employees they deserve. Look closely at your people and employee turnover to see how you are doing. The quality of your employees speaks volumes about your company's priorities.

3. Managing people does not begin with hiring, educating, or how you treat people. It begins with how you structure your company. If you want to test your people-management skills, begin by asking yourself these questions about the internal structure of your company:

- Have you created an atmosphere of opportunity that provides a level playing field for everyone and that rewards performance?
- Are people recognized for their accomplishments?
- Are there good consequences for good performance and bad consequences for bad performance?
- Is there an environment that supports and encourages personal growth?
- Does the business have a strong economic reason to exist (based on clear objectives, deeply held beliefs, a competitive edge, and a sense of mission)?
- Are quality and character major elements in the company's core values?
- Is the company willing and able to invest the necessary resources to support a steady and consistent strategy designed to keep the company competitive?
- Is leadership decisive in communicating its vision of the company's future?
- Is the company truly committed to excellence?

These questions, and the answers to them, reflect issues that go far beyond hiring techniques and creative pay plans. They are fundamental issues that are key to a company's success and provide the basis for effective people management.

4. The teams with the best players have the highest winning percentages. To win the game, you have to have the best team. To have the best team, think like a CEO and hire the best. Concentrate on behavioral characteristics, experience (skill and knowledge), and personal chemistry. Develop your goals and decide what is needed before making hiring decisions. Make sure (as a prerequisite) that employment candidates accept both the charter and the mission of their task. Hire quality individuals capable of being champions of their products, projects, or departments. Don't settle for mediocrity. No one was ever unhappy that they hired the best.

5. An organization must be built from the top down, not from the bottom up. This axiom does not imply that bottom-up programs of consensus building, individual empowerment, or the establishment of teams are invalid. They can work—but only under the sponsorship of a strong leader. Contrary to popular notions, organizations require leadership. A business is not like a house that can be best built from the ground up—that is, by hiring workers, then supervisors, then managers, then executives. The foundation of an organization comes from its vision and its values, and these concepts start at the top. Whenever possible, hire the top person first, then work down through each level.

6. The cost of poor selection or mishandling of people may be the greatest hidden cost that a company incurs. The cost of a bad hire cannot be measured by the dollar amount paid to the poorly performing individual in question. The pay will not cover the cost even when you add perks, overhead, relocation, unemployment, severance, and outplacement costs paid to the individual. The real cost is much greater. It is the cost of mistakes made, lost business, damaged reputation, and missed opportunities. The sales a weak salesperson did not make, or the cost of alienating a key customer are potentially much greater than the much more identifiable costs of recruiting, hiring, compensating, and outplacing (not to mention the financial impact of the lost productivity of the sales manager twice involved in the hiring and training process).

7. Shared values are the key to a positive work environment and consistent performance. Jeff Haines, CEO of Royce Medical Company, believes that sharing and communicating his values is fundamental to his highly successful manufacturing and distribution business (recently featured in *The Wall Street Journal*). Royce Medical employees—called associates—are empowered to satisfy customers and to participate in developing most major company policies and procedures. All of this is done while still maintaining tight cost controls and a dynamic sales orientation. Jeff fosters this positive work atmosphere not only through personal contact with his associates but also through the many physical reminders of Royce Medical Company values, such as the one that is prominently displayed in their reception area:

> *At Royce Medical, our standard is to provide excellent customer service and satisfaction. We take pride in offering our customers exceptional service and quality at every point of contact, whether it be from the manner in which our receptionists answer the phone, to the quality of workmanship that goes into our products. We care about the customers we service and the employees who service them.*

Royce associates also develop a corporate values statement every year:

Royce Medical Company Values—Fiscal 1997

The Associates of Royce Medical Company have developed a list of our company values to assist associates in the decision-making process. The combined actions chosen by each associate determine the company's success or failure. We believe that our system of values must be such that the Company, its Customers, and its Associates are all equally considered and that all three must be fairly and profitably served by them. We have created these values for the following reasons:

These Values Will Provide a predictable measurement by which we can judge our actions. When actions are within the values, we should expect support; if not, we should expect to be held accountable.

Our Values Are a Tool to assist all associates in accomplishing our mission statement which is found in our Strategic Plan.

We Wish to Ensure that our values are a constant focus and it should be clear that we each bear the responsibility to live up to all the values at all times.

We Write Our Values as a living, changing document that will be reviewed annually.

Profitability—Royce Medical must be profitable to succeed. Each associate impacts the profitability and growth of the company. We all have the responsibility to develop strategies and capitalize on opportunities that utilize resources wisely and efficiently. Through continuously improving performance and by learning from our mistakes, we create and benefit from a stronger, more profitable business.

Customer Service Excellence—Superior customer service is the result of consistently exceeding customers' expectations. The customers' perspective of the relationship they have with Royce is the key to our success. Every interaction with the customer has definite impact on the success or failure of this commitment. No customer should ever be left feeling dissatisfied with our product or service; therefore each associate has total authority and with it the obligation to make every effort to accomplish this goal.

Empowerment—Royce associates are empowered to make decisions and develop strategies that contribute to achieving the mission of the company. Management's role is to provide leadership and support to individuals who are within the values, and accountability for those who are not. Additionally, because we recognize the impact of each individual's contribution, associates will be involved in the decisions that affect them.

Sense of Urgency—We approach our work with a sense of urgency. Quick and decisive actions will help us to make the most of our opportunities.

Job Preparedness—To develop well-informed businesspeople, the company has the responsibility to provide valuable and accurate information on a timely basis. In addition, effective training and guidance programs should be developed and maintained. Each associate has the responsibility to fully utilize these programs. Additionally, a set of clear, measurable expectations should be in place and updated as necessary.

Commitment—We demonstrate commitment and dedication by doing the best job possible at all times and by going the extra mile to get the job done. All associates have the responsibility to follow up on every commitment made to customers, vendors, and fellow associates in a timely manner, and make every effort to provide the most accurate information possible.

Ethical Behavior—Ethical behavior is the standard of conduct that is exemplified by honesty and integrity and applies in all business relationships, internally and externally.

Respect—In all business relationships, always treat others as you feel they would like to be treated. Respect and consideration for the customer, vendor, and fellow associates are critically important, and should never be compromised.

Positive Environment—At Royce Medical, we are committed to creating an environment that breeds success. We believe in an atmosphere that encourages unity, initiative, and provides freedom to create. Rewards, recognition, and celebration should be utilized often to strengthen our positive environment. We should all do our best to contribute to a fun, enthusiastic, and productive environment.

Teamwork—Royce Medical Company is one team—each associate is a player. We must be willing to see the opportunity in all associates' perspectives and work in unity to achieve the company's mission. Strong internal business relationships should be continually developed through open and constructive communication and by giving equal consideration to all points of view. This will allow us to accomplish our objectives more readily, and create the potential to achieve what otherwise would not be possible.

These Royce Medical announcements and statements are important, but not as important as the daily decisions and actions that support them or the participative process that was used to create them. Jeff Haines believes in these values and has found a way to go beyond the typical corporate "public relations" approach to his customers and his associates. Almost everyone in business has learned to talk the talk, but Jeff and his associates at Royce Medical Company have learned to walk the walk.

There are whole courses offered on people management, so this chapter will not attempt to treat the subject comprehensively. It does, however, offer proven insights and practices, well-known and used among the most skilled managers, for finding, attracting, supervising, and keeping the right people. People management is really what CEOs and managers at every level do. Managing people effectively is much more than being friendly or sensitive to their needs. To manage people effectively, you must begin by learning and embracing the seven key insights. The CEO or manager who understands these insights is prepared to manage his or her organization for optimum results.

Strengthening the Foundation: Hiring

Hiring the right people for the right jobs adds significantly to the foundation created by the seven key insights. Knowledge, skill, and talent are all major factors in successful hiring. Recruiting and hiring are the first operating skills required to implement *CEO Logic* people-management strategies.

Hire for strength and be careful what you screen

Almost all strengths have the potential of negative side effects that might be looked upon as weaknesses. A person with focus may appear at times to be narrow-minded. A successful task-oriented individual in the extreme may be too tough on people. But those potential weaknesses can become strengths if the person with these traits is in the right job and in the right context. When asked about General Ulysses S. Grant's drinking problem, President Abraham Lincoln is alleged to have responded that he'd like to know what brand Grant drank so he could send all his generals a barrel. Lincoln knew that Grant was there to win wars; as long as he was winning them, the President could overlook a weakness for whiskey.

Although you have to be aware of the downside of any candidate, you also have to be careful when screening for negative qualities. Many so-called negatives may not truly be impediments to job performance. If, for example, you rejected all applicants for a sales position because they did not submit neat and organized job applications, how many potentially great salespeople might you also be rejecting? It's no secret that many great salespeople could not fill out a form (except an expense report) to save their souls.

Never try to teach a pig to think

It doesn't work and it irritates the pig. Everyone has talent; it is up to you to determine the exact nature of each individual's talents in order to hire and delegate accordingly. A high percentage of all chronic performance problems is due to assigning a person to the wrong job. It seems almost too basic to suggest that CEOs and managers alike need to assign organized people to administrative duties; high-drive, task-oriented people to production or sales responsibilities; and creative people to research and development or marketing. But when you look around your organization, you will probably see many misplaced souls struggling to survive. Do the company, yourself, and the individual a service by matching each person's behavioral patterns to the tasks for which they are best suited.

Make sure they want the job

A candidate's desire to do the work and have the job are often the most important hiring prerequisites. She also needs to have at least a minimal level of the skill and knowledge required to do the job. A history of success is another positive for any candidate. Neither skill nor past history, however, will make up for a lack of desire. On occasion, a candidate will accept a position because he has nothing better to consider at the time. Perhaps he is accepting this position reluctantly because his industry is in recession or because his last company failed. If you don't get the sense that he is planning to rush home to celebrate your job offer or if you don't think he will be calling all of his friends to boast about his new position, reconsider your offer. It is difficult for anyone to perform well in a job that he considers to be of marginal importance.

People will be as they have been

It is their nature. They will also do as they have done. Ask questions in employment interviews about past accomplishments. There is a big difference between a candidate who can answer correctly your questions about how to start up a factory and a candidate who has actually successfully started a factory. Past performance is the best predictor of future performance.

Make hiring effective, not just efficient

Many companies tend to place too much emphasis on the efficiency of the hiring process. They seem more focused on minimizing hiring expense. If you're thinking like a CEO, of course you want to hold down expenses, but you also know that the primary issue is not hiring efficiency but hiring effectiveness. You are not trying to see how many candidates you can hire on the smallest budget. You are trying to hire the right people who will perform with distinction and excellence. The key is to focus on selection, not just cost.

In any event, you will need a good hiring system that looks something like this:

1. Analyze position needs.
2. Develop a competitive analysis of position (pay, benefits, etc.).
3. Prepare position specifications and qualifications.
4. Review for internal candidates.
5. Place ads, hire a search firm, and/or begin networking.

6. Develop resume screening criteria and "knock-out" questions.
7. Prepare pre-interview questionnaire.
8. Review, analyze, and screen resumes.
9. Review, analyze, and screen answers to pre-interview questionnaire.
10. Conduct preliminary phone interview (ask "knock-out" questions).
11. Set interview appointment.
12. Prepare for interview. Arrange for a quiet office, a copy of the resume, and your list of questions.
13. Hold interview:
    a. Opening/introductions.
    b. Discussion of position specifics.
    c. Discussion of company position and history.
    d. Interactive interview to determine:
        1) Have they done this work successfully before?
        2) Can they do this work successfully now?
        3) Do they have a strong desire for the position?
        4) Is their personality a good fit with the organization?

    The answers to these last four questions will tell you *if they can do the work, if they will do the work,* and *if they will fit in* with others in your company.
14. Schedule multiple interviews with other company officials.
15. Check business and personal references.
16. Select the best candidate and make an offer.

Follow any system that generally addresses these issues. There are many good books on the subject. Think and make selections like a CEO and you will hire great people.

You will find good candidates everywhere you look

Good prospecting is a prerequisite to good hiring. Qualified candidates can be found through many sources. It is usually a mistake to direct your efforts to just one source. Competitors, customers, and suppliers may know of good candidates, but you will not find them if you do not look. Remain on the lookout at all times. Grocery stores, restaurants, and service organizations are just some of the areas to watch. Some of the more traditional employee candidate sources are:

1. Newspaper and trade journal advertisements.
2. Executive search firms.
3. Temporary or temporary-to-permanent agencies.
4. Private and public employment agencies.
5. College placement centers, high schools, and trade schools.
6. Contract employee firms.
7. Walk-in applicants.
8. Trade conventions and job fairs.
9. Human resource departments of downsizing companies.
10. Professional business organizations.
11. Referrals from your own employees.

You may even consider outsourcing the entire process. Think like a CEO and recognize that there is no shortage of places to find candidates.

To ask or not to ask, that is the question

In these days of high regulation and pervasive litigation, it is difficult to know what can and cannot legally be asked. For starters, *don't* ask questions regarding:

- Race, religion, or national origin.
- Marital status, age, age of children, or childcare arrangements.
- Charge accounts, life insurance, or home ownership.
- Credit rating or arrest records.

The Equal Employment Opportunity Policy allows for some of the above topics to be addressed as long as they are pertinent to the job and you ask every applicant the same questions.

These questions often overshadow the more important issue of *what should* be asked. The following is a brief list of topics to consider. However, I suggest you consult a true human resource authority with your final list of topics and questions.

Do ask questions regarding:

- Capabilities, past experience, previous responsibilities, and major career accomplishments.
- Previous work performance measurements.
- Education and certification.
- Previous successes outside the work environment.
- Employment gaps and resume inconsistencies.
- Excessive job hopping.
- Reasons for leaving previous employment.
- Strengths and weaknesses, likes and dislikes.
- Previous supervision.
- Self-perception and career goals.
- Problems solved or left unsolved.
- Other company interviews.
- Salary history and requirements.
- Avocations and interests.
- Knowledge of your industry, company, and products.
- Availability for travel.

Plan your interview questions and predetermine your selection criteria. But keep in mind that none of these questions or even the answers to them will take the place of sound judgment. The primary goal is not effective questioning, it is effective selecting. When interviewing, listen more than you talk. Use multiple interviewers and concentrate on issues related to past accomplishments because they will be the best indicators of future performance.

Hire up—not down

It's a common tendency in management to "hire down," that is, to hire subordinates with less skill, talent, and knowledge than you have. Whether this is a conscious effort to avoid competition or a subconscious self-protective reflex, it doesn't work. Winners beget winners and losers beget losers. When you "hire up" you are bringing in people who can help you build a winning team. As a rule of thumb, a subordinate should have greater (not lesser) specific knowledge than you, at least in his or her particular field.

Don't fish with dead worms

If you want to hire the best, you've got to have "live bait." To some degree you are not hiring a manager for a position but selling your position to a good manager. So it is a hallmark of *CEO Logic* to analyze the position in much the same way that you would analyze a product for its competitiveness. You would not offer an overpriced, undervalued, or otherwise flawed product to the marketplace—and the same goes for your open position. Pay, benefits, working conditions, responsibility, authority, title, autonomy, and opportunity for growth must all meet competitive standards. Substandard positions, conditions, compensation, and terms only attract substandard candidates.

Expect to train even the best

Because it's impossible for new employees to know everything about your business, your customers, your existing work force, your philosophy, or your circumstances, all of them require some degree of orientation and training. At a minimum, they will need a review of the history of the industry, the company, and the position. But it also pays to take the time to relay details of past successes and failures to all new employees. You may also find it worthwhile to assign short-term, well-defined projects early on, designed specifically to validate a new employee's skills and knowledge.

Hire for character, competence, and conscience

There are some aspects of a candidate that have to be fundamental, that can't be trained, encouraged, or "fixed." In order to stay with a company, employees must have:

Character: Their character was established long before you met them. Unless you are a priest, rabbi, or minister, you will not be successful at repairing character flaws.

Competence: They must be capable of understanding what constitutes right and wrong in their positions. Purchasing agents, for example, must be able to comprehend that inventory shortages are bad, inventory turns are good, competitive prices are good, and weak suppliers are bad. If they cannot understand the basics, they must be terminated.

Conscience: They have to personally care about this "right and wrong" of their position. Some are capable of understanding right from wrong but occasionally choose wrong for their own reasons. Any individual with an attitude that reflects malaise or apathy does not belong in the organization.

If you find that an employee does not have character, competence, or conscience, you'll need the advice offered in the next section.

Facing Up to Reality: Firing

No one makes 100-percent correct hiring decisions. There is not much you can do about the good candidates whom you misjudged and let get away, but you can correct the mistake of employing the ones you should not have hired. It takes courage to admit a mistake and it is difficult to inform someone that her skills do not match the company's needs, especially when compassion often leads us to stay with marginal performers for too long. But remember that individuals will never be satisfied or successful if they have been assigned to jobs they cannot handle. Effective CEOs know that the ability to face up to hiring mistakes is one of the more important steps in building a good team. Facing up to your mistake will also create an opening for a qualified candidate and will make life better for the other players on the team—and for the organization as a whole.

Even if you have the courage to face up to your mistakes and make those difficult firing decisions, that doesn't mean it's going to be pleasant or without cost to the organization. Nevertheless, there are several things you can do to ease the process.

Let them go easy and with their dignity

Amicable partings are the only ones that make sense; they are also the cheapest. When it comes time to make a personnel change in your organization, walk softly. There is no longer a need to correct the soon-to-be former employee's shortfall in performance and there is no percentage in trying. Pay a competitive severance. Allow generous notice (or pay in lieu of notice) so the terminated employee will have time to find a new job. Provide outplacement counseling whenever possible. If you're thinking like a CEO, you'll remember that the way you treat employees in these difficult transitions, will not only reduce potential legal and unemployment costs, it will also confirm your people-oriented philosophy to those who stay.

Set up a court of last resort

Send the ex-employee an exit interview form directly from the president's office with a stamped and return-addressed envelope to be sent back directly to the president's office. This process serves two functions. First, it allows direct feedback from both voluntarily and involuntarily terminated employees. The feedback can be analyzed to help reduce the high costs of turnover. Second, and equally important, these exit interviews let every supervisor know that mistreatment of an employee cannot be hidden from top management.

Face up to mediocrity

Almost every manager faces up to incompetent employee performance sooner or later. It is much more difficult to address chronically mediocre performance. Mediocre performance might be acceptable—if only you could get your customers to accept mediocre products and your competitors to limit themselves to mediocre service.

Firing is sometimes necessary for the health of the organization in spite of its unpleasant and uncomfortable nature. It, like the military tactic of "strategic retreat," is one of the more difficult disciplines to master. The key is to direct your compassion to the *way* you fire and use your business sense on the issue of *when* to fire.

Supervision and Management

Hiring and firing are undoubtedly important to building a great team in your organization, but we all know that managing and supervising are much more the stuff of everyday life. Like the other topics in this chapter, there are hundreds of books on these subjects, but my experience working as a CEO and coaching other top managers has taught me that focusing on a few key principles can produce the best results for the organization and for the people in it.

Think it through

CEO Logic dictates that you think through the true purpose of each position. Determine the key method of measurement for each key manager and each key department. Test your communication of this "true purpose" by asking each manager how her performance is measured, how her department is measured, and how they both are doing. Compare their answers to your own evaluations of the same questions. You will find more often than not that your subordinates are not 100 percent in agreement with you. This is also a good exercise for them to perform with their subordinates. Too many times, people fail because they did not clearly understand the expectations of top management. Think like a CEO and recognize that when managers cannot clearly define the measures of their performance, they are probably not performing to their potential.

Measure the right performance issues

You have probably seen a salesperson's performance review that looks like this: Organization: Good; Verbal Communication: Good; Image Presented: Good; Work Ethic: Good; and so on. Nowhere are the questions: Did she sell enough? Did she open her quota of new accounts? Was she able to hold the target margin? Did she sell the right mix of product? Did she gain or lose market share in his territory? As CEO, you have the vision, strategy, and business plan in mind when you are thinking of performance and results. So you and your top management will need to be involved in developing exactly what to measure and how to appraise performance. Don't leave performance appraisals to the human resource department.

Focus on results

Do not confuse personality, effort, long hours, style, strong credentials, attendance, or effective communication with performance. Focus on results, measure results, discuss results, strategize on results, and reward results. Top management and the company are evaluated on the results produced, so that measurement should permeate the organization.

Trust but verify

Ronald Reagan called "trust but verify" a Russian proverb, but I call it common sense. Checks and balances for important and critical issues are the keys to excellent performance, stress-free days, and restful nights. This goes for customers, employees, suppliers, shareholders, directors—everyone. Supervision and follow-up are part of the verification process. If you build in automatic or organizationally structured safeguards—such as two-signature checks, or an accounting type of separation of duties—you enhance your and other managers' ability to assure performance. Structure the work effort so that no one individual's mistakes can jeopardize a critical project. The more important the project, the more important the fail-safes.

Make performance the basis for politics

I hear many CEOs say that there are no "politics" in their company, but politics exist in every organization. Whether your company politics are explicit or implicit, political criteria are used to allocate power and compensation, and everyone knows it. I'm using the term "politics" here in a somewhat different way to indicate the methods or criteria used for determining promotions, demotions, raises, job assignments, and firings. Politics could be based on loyalty, commitment, effort, hard work, or friendship, and they are in many organizations. While these qualities are all desirable and attainable, they do not necessarily support sound business fundamentals, such as satisfying your customers and employees, or selling your product at a price you can afford. Many companies have failed with a hard-working, loyal, and committed work force filled with friends and family who were not getting the job done right or the right job done.

If you are doing business correctly, you get good performance coupled with a hard-working, loyal, and committed work force. They may eventually become your friends because you have treated them fairly. But the central question is: What will you measure and reward? The customer will not care or understand that her late delivery, incomplete shipment, or noncompetitive price happened because you hired and promoted on the basis of friendship rather than ability to perform. So promote and give raises based on merit and let positive character traits be an extra advantage. You will often find more good performers with positive character traits than marginal performers with these same attributes. Your customers will not accept marginal performance for any reason, so why should you?

Delegate routine tasks

Free yourself to address issues critical to your level. No matter how much money is involved or how important the task, anything routine can be delegated. If it has to be done over and over on a regular basis, it is routine and someone else can do it. You may have to set up strict operating parameters or a series of checks and balances, but it can be done without increasing the risk of failure.

For many years, I used to personally make night deposits. I filled out the bank deposit slips, stamped the endorsement on the checks, locked everything in the deposit bag, and took the deposit to the night drop box. It would be impossible to calculate how many hours I wasted taking care of this task. Finally, I set up a proper separation of duties and a few follow-up checks and balances, and thereafter the deposit was made just as well without my direct involvement. How many tasks like this are you doing out of habit?

Communicate positive support and confidence

People respond best when they feel good about themselves and believe that you have high expectations for them. In most companies, you cannot be with key managers all of the time. This is especially true when your responsibilities include remote operations. Project how you want your managers to think and feel about themselves after you have left. Consider how they will perform if they feel beat up, failed, or incompetent. Discuss positive steps they can take to improve their performance. Let them know you have confidence in their ability to perform and that you are counting on their contribution.

There is *no* such thing as constructive criticism

All criticism is destructive. Dale Carnegie said, "Any fool can criticize, condemn, and complain—and most fools do." There is a place for criticism but it is important to use it sparingly and wisely. Discuss the problems with the work as opposed to problems with the worker.

Design systems that allow for self-appraisal. It is easier to provide help, and is a great benefit to communication, if the worker is equipped to find his own problems. When he brings them to you, he will be more open to assistance than if you bring the problems to him. Always seek to eliminate systemic flaws or mechanical errors before addressing the potential of people problems. My father used to say, "Sign them up for the work at hand and concentrate on performance." Remember, it is nearly impossible to antagonize and influence at the same time.

Realize that personal problems are a part of business

The conventional wisdom is to keep personal problems out of business, but in many cases I find just the opposite works better. Good performers are rare; if it is possible and practical to help them when they're experiencing a personal problem, do so. That will create respect and a bond that can last for years and that can carry you through the normal ups and downs of any relationship.

There are money-makers and helpers—and that's all

In every business, there is work for which the company gets directly paid and there is work needed for support. In a service business, there are service technicians and there are helpers. In a retail business, there are salespeople and there are helpers. In a manufacturing business, there are machine operators and assemblers and there are helpers. The same is true for most departments. In purchasing, there are those who purchase and those who help. In engineering, there are those who design and those who help. If everyone knows where she stands on this basis, the operation will run more smoothly.

Give the fishing pole, not the fish

As the saying goes, give a man a fish and he will eat today, but teach a man to fish and he will eat for a lifetime. The same principle applies in business. People often take their problems to their managers, and the managers respond by finding a solution. Although that may take care of today's problem, it does not teach employees how to solve their own problems. They'll soon be back with the next one. And the manager will now have more work.

Find a battle cry

Everyone needs motivation to excel in their work and in their lives. Sometimes it is a positive motivation, such as building a dominant market share or staying number one. Sometimes it is a negative motivation, such as outdoing an unfair competitor. For thousands of years, leaders and generals have succeeded in motivating their people to pick up arms and charge the enemy in order to right an injustice or contribute to the glory of a good cause. The best CEOs galvanize their organizations with a good "battle cry" to remind their members why they are working so hard and sacrificing so much. If you make the noble purpose of each battle clear, it will generate an enthusiastic following.

Make neither promises nor threats

Do not telegraph your actions, just make your decisions and implement them when the timing is right. Like an effective CEO, take the time necessary to make your decisions, then carry them out swiftly. Do not muddy the waters by informing your targets of your considered or potential actions in the hope that the warning will change the situation. When communicating your decisions, make sure your employees know what is expected. Always act fairly and execute with authority.

Build relationships

Gary Adamson, president and CEO of Dicor Corporation, a multimillion dollar international import and distribution business, is an expert at building relationships. Gary has an honesty and sincerity about him that generates instant credibility. He truly cares about people and is a good judge of character. He is a quiet man and makes a habit of letting others speak more than he does. He is the best I know at seeking to understand before he seeks to be understood. His calm exterior belies a fierce competitiveness. He trusts people but demands, and gets, their best. He has achieved substantial business success (as owner and manager of several highly successful companies) through building long-lasting relationships with key suppliers, customers, partners, and employees. He is a true entrepreneur.

There are no gimmicks or fads to Gary's management style. He hires well and holds his people accountable to deliver on their commitments. He empowered people to perform and make decisions long before anyone coined the phrase. He provided inspiration, motivation, and a sense of purpose to his people before the management gurus started talking about vision. He made his key managers owners and created an atmosphere of growth and prosperity before these issues became popular. He is cautious with criticism and respects the dignity of others. His people find him fair, firm, knowledgeable, totally committed, and trustworthy. Gary gets great pleasure out of seeing his people grow and prosper, but he is neither ambitious nor greedy, in spite of his strong desire to succeed. He sets a nearly perfect example of how to manage people.

Gary also has built strong supplier alliances. His business thrives because of his ability to read the marketplace for his suppliers. They trust in his judgment and fairness and look to Gary for product development strategies. They know that he is looking out for their interests as much as he looks out for his own. He has a reputation for being as forthright with bad news as he is with good news.

It is impossible to capture all aspects of a good manager in these few words, but suffice it to say that Gary Adamson's quiet wisdom is second to none. He has used his relationship-building skills to grow his company. In addition, his people skills and his capacity to think like a CEO have allowed him to prosper. In the meantime, he has set a high standard for the rest of us.

Invest in others

Like many CEOs, I have spent much of my career attaining success by training and developing those around me. I have found both financial and psychological rewards in helping others achieve. Ron Minzey, however, is the best I know at this practice.

Ron gained success early in his career and has spent the last 15 or 20 years investing in others. He is a good judge of people, a fair judge of opportunity, and is willing to back up his judgments by investing both his time and his money. He is an experienced manager, a clever strategist, and a comforting mentor. His sage advice has been proven over and over by his consistent ability to make money. He is a good friend to many, loyal to his convictions, and willing to share the rewards of his investments. I have often seen him give the lion's share of a deal to the hands-on managers doing the work. Ron is proof of the axiom, "Give and you will receive." I believe that Ron might modify the axiom to say, "Give wisely and generously and you will receive more than your share."

And Finally, Staffing Matters

The ideas and concepts offered in this section will serve to round out your people-management philosophy. They include strategic thoughts on staffing matters and reflect the basic precept of this chapter: *The strength of a business resides in the minds of its people.* Use these thoughts whenever you are faced with difficult people-management decisions.

The people always win

Competent people can overcome weak systems and procedures, but good systems and procedures will fail with incompetent people. One of the reasons to embrace the concept of "letting them go easy," as we discussed earlier, is to allow compassionate managers a reasonable and fair way to address chronically poor performers. There is absolutely no way to overcome problems related to the poor performance of incompetent people, except by replacement.

Make the job fit the person

Once they've hired someone, managers often think that with training or other forms of coaching, they will be able to change her. But it never works. Every time you pick up a scorpion, expect to be stung. Likewise, expect the nature of each person to remain consistent. Job responsibilities are easily modified, but people are not. If it is not practical to modify the job, it may be time to reassign the individual or to make a change in personnel.

Count on behavioral characteristics

Effective CEOs know that you generally cannot successfully assign both sales and marketing to one manager. The sales effort requires highly driven, task-oriented individuals who can go out and bring back sales. The marketing effort requires creative individuals who can uncover the next sales trend, find a new way to package a product, or develop a better ad campaign. The two tasks—and often the sets of talents and intrinsic behavioral qualities that make successful marketers and salespeople—are seldom compatible. If you combine sales and marketing in one individual's job, you are likely to subordinate the creative manager to the high-drive seller. When you put sales and marketing together, marketing may not focus enough attention on creating new opportunities. The manager may even end up spending most of her time performing minor sales support duties, like the preparation of company and competitor sales reports.

It is better not to do a job at all

It's human nature to want to be sure all the bases are covered. But the key is to cover them well, not just barely. Top managers have enough experience to know that they can live for a time with slowness or inefficiency, but they cannot live with work done incorrectly. They understand the right answer to this fundamental question: Is it worse to do bad accounting or no accounting, bad engineering or no engineering? The discipline of *CEO Logic* requires that we resist the temptation to take what might appear to be the easy way out. If you cannot find the person to do the work right, she should not have the job.

One good manager can make the difference

Our Illinois operation of Underground Technology Inc. (UTI), a company providing damage prevention service to utility companies, was floundering. We made every possible mistake, from analyzing work content poorly to underbidding on contracts. In addition, because we had failed to determine our exact startup requirements, we overbought both vehicles and equipment. We purchased cellular phones for our field technicians because two-way radios, our normal program, were not set up in the area. At times we spent more on communication than we did on labor.

All of these embarrassing mistakes were capped off by the big error: hiring the wrong manager to lead the organization. He compounded the problem by making his own bad hires. After five months, customers, employees, and suppliers were unhappy. We might have abandoned the project except that our primary Illinois customer was a division of our largest corporate account. We had to solve these problems.

Our first step was to remove the top manager in an attempt to stop some of the bleeding. Then, after several unsuccessful attempts to recruit others, we finally hired my brother, Steve. I was reluctant for two reasons. First, although Steve and I had successfully worked together in the past, I was concerned about the problems that come with hiring family. How would other managers react? What would working together again do to our personal relationship? What would I do if he did not work out? The second reason had more to do with the nature of the task. Our company was young and lacked systems. We had grossly overestimated our capacity to manage remote operations and grossly underbid the contract. The job could have been the proverbial "widow-maker." I feared putting my own brother in a no-win situation.

Steve took over the Illinois division and began to make improvements. We gave him the same advice and instruction as we had given his failed predecessor, but this time we had a good manager. Steve saved our Illinois division from disaster. His first step was to weed out the poor performers and to begin building a team. He installed management information and daily operating systems and worked extremely long hours just to get all of the work completed on time. He knew that if he did not meet the customer's schedule, we could lose the contract. Next, he put in better scheduling to get control of the labor cost. This actually brought us to break-even. He began to work on quality and claims management, and on adding new business.

Today, this division is one of our most successful. Steve turned it around through the application of equal parts of leadership and management. He inspired, motivated, defended, trained, and disciplined his people. Like our dad, he is fiercely loyal to his people and they return that loyalty. He is intelligent, organized, and analytical. But mostly, he is good with people. He prides himself on his fairness, ability to sell, and capacity to evaluate a situation accurately. His division now makes more in one month than the whole company used to make in a year. His secret appears to lie somewhere between his people skills and his total commitment to his convictions. Steve is a living example of how one person thinking like a CEO can make the difference.

Look for diamonds in the rough

Willy Stewart was a young man of modest education and experience when the company first hired him. The organization he ran was expanding wildly, and he was clearly overwhelmed by the situation. My first impression was that Willy might not be strong enough to handle the multitude of issues at hand, but we decided to give him a chance to perform. At first, mistakes of inexperience were the order of the day. We did, however, see flashes of brilliance, particularly in his ability to analyze complex problems. With help, he worked through his mistakes. Today, Willy is a great contributor to our organization. He learned from his previous mistakes of inexperience and made them the foundation of his good judgment. His perceptive eye, excellent strategic thinking, and analytical approach to business have improved our operations immeasurably.

When we invited Freddy Galvan, a management candidate, to attend one of our monthly management training meetings, he stood out, but not always in the best ways. He disagreed somewhat arbitrarily with almost everything that was said and was almost asked to leave the meeting. There was something, however, about his energy and his confidence that impressed us. He had an enthusiasm that the company needed and a willingness to tackle any problem. Today, he is a successful regional manager managing six offices.

Both Willy and Freddy were diamonds in the rough. Today, they are vital parts of our management team. Their approach to management has been tempered by time and experience. They are continuing to improve each day as they learn to think like CEOs, and their potentials seem unlimited.

Pay too much for great performers and make them feel like partners

When you have a great performer, you never want to lose her to the competition because of money. Remember that the cost of employees is not what you pay them, or even their pay plus benefits, taxes, and overhead. The real cost is related to the sale they should have made or the production schedule they would have met, had they performed well. So, if you have great performers, never make them unhappy because of a compensation plan that understates or underrewards their value.

When your key players feel like managing partners in their respective domains, you'll find that they will take more interest and perform better when they have more than just a rooting interest in the outcome. Stock options, equity, warrants, phantom stock, or equity acting bonus plans can give them a meaningful stake in the business. In my companies, I pay key management based on bottom line or gross margin contribution, depending on their level and ability to impact these measurements.

Search for balanced partnerships

Often the tendency is to partner with individuals who possess skills and behavior similar to your own. After all, you have been successful, so why not find a clone? But the fact is that a partner who has complementary skills and behavior makes a stronger combination.

My partner, Jim Gerblick, provides terrific balance to our management team. Jim is people-oriented, with great empathy and sensitivity toward others that far surpasses mine. As president, Jim is the point man for all important relationships except banking. Employees, customers, and suppliers all look to Jim for support and information. He attends trade shows and employee functions to get a sense of the marketplace and to maintain rapport with the work force. He builds long-term relationships by using the input he gathers to shape management decisions and company policy.

Jim's "Mr. Outside" plays perfectly to my "Mr. Inside." My high-drive and analytical style may come across as tough, demanding, and impatient. I am always looking for immediate performance. Jim, in contrast, may be too understanding, too patient, and too tolerant of weak performance. Like everyone, Jim and I possess both positive and negative tendencies. We take advantage of our positives but attempt to compensate for each other's negatives. Both of us share the same values around wanting the company, its people, its customers, and its shareholders to succeed. Together, we offer a balance in our decision-making and a consistency in our execution. The key to the success of our joint effort is our mutual understanding and respect for each other's style and perspective. We believe our company prospers from our complementary differences and our ability to work together on difficult issues.

Final Thoughts on People Management

Though the majority of advice in today's business literature has to do with the discipline of people management, the real-world shortage of good people-managers suggests that few in top management have taken such advice to heart. Don't make the same mistake. Remember that every business, at its core, is a people business.

Employee participation and employee empowerment are the current management buzz words. No management program, however, has the power to affect people as much as the success (or lack of success) of the organization for which they work. *The first obligation of management is to provide an organization that makes money, provides opportunity, and treats people fairly.* Top management's ability to make sure that the company is properly structured, viable, and competitive must come first but must also be backed up by effective hiring, firing, and proper supervision.

When you're thinking like a CEO, you keep in mind that every management decision will have an impact on your people. In a sense, everything you do in business will become part of your people-management strategy. Provide a viable business, hire the best, face up to mediocrity, and manage people as you find them. Zero in on the people who make you money, and make them the kings and queens of your business. Invest heavily in your people and you will reap great returns. Think like a CEO and treat them as if you really believe that they are your most important asset. The teams with the best players have the highest winning percentages.

Chapter 5

Career Management: Control Your Own Destiny

Our future is in our hands. Our lives are what we choose to make them.
—Winston Churchill

Kirby Lakes*, CEO of Metrax Incorporated, a regional service company, was growing his company at 30 percent to 40 percent a year. In 1992, he had 58 employees. By early 1997, he had 361 employees. Kirby's priorities were to make sure all of the work was completed, to perform a quality service, to control costs, and to protect the company's assets. In addition, he managed the company's finances conservatively and spent considerable resources measuring and assuring customer and employee satisfaction. Kirby and the company were by all accounts successful. By May of 1997, however, they began to run into problems. Customers were raising their expectations, competitors were lowering their costs and improving their service, and Metrax was having trouble keeping up.

The company made most of their hires at the lowest levels and then attempted to promote predominantly from within. The company provided substantial training at the service technician level, but offered only modest training and education to middle and upper management. The management layers were thin and the ability to learn the work of senior management while on the job was limited. The primary problem driving the company's nonperformance was insufficient management development.

Kirby and Metrax were forced into a crisis management mode. After consulting with his board of directors, management team, and an outside consulting group, Kirby took these steps:

- Twice-monthly formal management training seminars for all levels of supervision.
- Regular participative meetings with groups of supervisors to document company values, philosophies, key responsibilities, and job descriptions.
- Creation of an additional management layer to be used for training management candidates.
- A change in its policy from 100 percent promoting from within to 50 percent inside and 50 percent outside.
- An internal program to identify and train potential in-house management candidates.
- A program to identify, attract, and recruit more experienced managers from outside the company.

Only time will tell if Kirby's crisis management program for Metrax will succeed. It will be a race between rising customer expectations, increased competition, and Metrax's ability to meet the challenge. Management development cannot be left to chance. It must be handled proactively on an individual basis. Kirby and Metrax are learning this tough lesson about how management development can impact a growing company's performance.

But while no business can continue to grow and prosper without nurturing its young managers, no manager can expect an organization to take charge of his career development. It's a two-part, interlocking endeavor. Building a company necessarily requires building careers. Individual management careers are the building blocks that establish a foundation for growth and continuous improvement for any organization. Yet, at the same time, savvy managers at all levels must realize that they have to be in charge of their own destinies. For both sides of the equation, career development is a key discipline of *CEO Logic*. For the organization, it means maximizing the value and potential of its most important asset: its people. For individuals, it means being aware of where they want to go and what they must do to drive their careers forward.

This chapter is targeted at managers in the throes of developing their companies, their divisions, departments, subordinates, and/or their own careers. Even professional managers need support in thinking strategically and practically about career development. Because in too many cases, careers just happen to people. That's a syndrome that I call "pinballing." Pinballing occurs when an individual bounces from one job to another based on happenstance: Dad lines up a job, a friend finds an opening at his company, a new factory opens, an old factory closes. Whatever the circumstance, you do not plan for it. It just happens to you and you react. And because you get what you manage, you and your organization probably do not get what you want and need whenever proactive management is missing and, therefore, pinballing occurs..

There is a better way, but many do not know much about it. A degree in chemistry or an MBA probably did not include a course on how to get a job, much less how to develop a career. Even individuals who have already achieved outstanding performance in their current positions may not be prepared to tackle effectively the issue of career management. Too often, they start where they first are pinballed and stay there until the next unplanned opportunity comes along or until they get kicked out.

The opposite of pinballing is strategic career management. And practicing the discipline of strategic career management, beyond developing the careers of your people and achieving the organizational outcomes you desire, will prove invaluable training for your overall mastery of *CEO Logic*. Because if you are prepared to excel in managing your career and the careers of those on your team, you are ready to excel in managing your business.

Take Inventory and Manage Your Own Career

The first step in career management is to understand your own strengths and weaknesses. Are you strong with numbers but less effective with people? Do you have creative talents but lack organization? Are you sensitive to others but lack the drive to go out and bring back scalps? Do you enjoy a lively conversation or do you prefer to avoid confrontation? Are you an idealist or are you pragmatic? There are many ways to evaluate yourself: behavioral tests, opinions of family and friends, trial and error, and supervisor appraisals. However you arrive at a profile of your strengths and weaknesses, the accuracy of the analysis is critical. *The initial career management task is to match your strengths with the needs of a potentially satisfying position.* This is akin to the idea of an organization's core competency. What do you do well? How can you leverage your special capabilities in the marketplace? You have to find a position that can use your unique strengths, but also make sure that your weaknesses will not be a deterrent to excellent performance. For example, if you are high in drive and empathy but low in organizational skills, you may want to find a job in sales with limited paperwork. Your empathy will help you understand and relate to a prospect. Your high drive will give you the strength to withstand rejection, but your weakness in administration will not hurt your performance too much. Matching your personal core competencies to the needs of the job can save a lot of heartache and frustration and can position you for greater success over time.

Align Your Actions with Your Inventory

Once you determine which position or positions might work for you, the next step is to select an industry and a company. If you want to progress quickly, look for industries in their emerging or growth phase and avoid industries that are past their prime. Look for companies within these selected industries that have solid core competencies that give them the ability to sustain a competitive edge. No other factor is more important to the success of a company.

Each industry and each company has a given set of operating characteristics. Some pay big and some pay small. Some reward performance and others reward loyalty, seniority, or hard work. Some are strict and formal while others are loose and informal. Some reward formal education while others lean towards rewarding on-the-job performance. Some require relocation, some are located only in one part of the country, and some are international. When you choose an industry and a company, you are making a strategic decision about your life that will have consequences far into the future. This seems obvious, but is often frequently ignored. If you're following *CEO Logic* in career management, you will, like the best top managers running the most successful companies, align your actions with your analysis of your personal core competencies. It is said, "Failures are divided into two classes: Those who thought and never did, and those who did and never thought."

Once you've found the industry and company where you want to be, the next step is simple: Work hard and do work that you like. It's easy to criticize and easier still to ignore this advice because it is so obvious, so simple, and so common. But we do spend a huge part of our lives working, and to do well requires long hours, tedious study, attention to detail, and hard work. This degree of sacrifice is extremely difficult unless you truly enjoy the work.

Once you have developed a strategic plan for your own career, you are ready to help others. Take the people in your organization through this same process. Facilitate their career planning by raising the questions and sharing the information presented throughout this chapter.

Secrets of Successful Career Development

The following tips distill many years of experience and observation about the ingredients of successful career development and management. All require the application of *CEO Logic* because all involve a conscious use of tactics and strategies that will enhance your performance and help you get the results you want.

Bring solutions, not problems

It is not enough to identify problems for your boss. He had plenty of them before you came along. This concept may be the greatest factor in your own career success. While others bring detailed analyses of problems to their supervisors, you need to bring answers. While others are busy explaining the difficulties of resolving their problems, you need to be busy selecting the best available alternative. It is good to define problems, analyze causes, and critically review potential solutions. But bosses want and need answers. They require practical solutions that fit the available resources and that have sufficient horsepower to get the job done. If none of the potential solutions are perfect, select the best available approach and support it with your reasoning. Offering solutions will set you apart from 99 percent of your competition and get you the recognition you need to drive your career forward.

Look at the top of the ladder

When you're looking at an organization, particularly in terms of your own chances for advancement, look at the top manager's pay, perks, life style, and responsibilities to discover the most you can expect to achieve in that organization. Certainly this analysis would not be your only (or perhaps even your primary) criterion for selecting a company. It is, however, an indication of perquisites and potential rewards. If the CEO is a member of the founding family, that tells you something about a particular company's politics. If the top person has a Wharton or Harvard MBA, that tells you how they may be looking at education and connections. If the top person earns $400,000 per year, everyone else will likely earn less. Since CEOs are generally among the most visible in their respective companies, you can learn a lot about the organization's values by looking at the individual selected to be at its helm.

Know your target and take risks

To get outstanding results in your career development and management, you have to put yourself out there. Top managers know that they have to create and seize opportunities and take the accompanying risks—both for their companies as well as in their careers. So let your goal be to get up to bat in a big inning in an important game. Get a shot at succeeding or failing on an important issue. You cannot always eliminate risk; you may not even be able to minimize it. Career planning, like running a company, is about defining the risk that you are willing to take. Develop an accurate assessment of your abilities so that you will be ready to accept the biggest possible challenge.

Find and learn from mentors and role models

Everyone can benefit from the use of mentors and role models. Role models are particularly helpful if you are willing to analyze their behavioral traits and management practices and take the time to document your findings. I have had several mentors over the years. Some have shared their business wisdom, others have talked of life. Early in my career, I looked to Dave Yoho, Marv Borr, and Mike Gilbert for this advice.

Dave Yoho is a dynamic public speaker and a successful businessman with a unique perspective on business, especially sales. I have stolen his material for so long that I can no longer remember which was his and which was mine. A convenient memory loss.

Marv Borr was a confident, high-energy, successful, and demanding retail leader. He managed by example and challenged his people to keep up. He was a genius at retail merchandising, cash flow, and finance. I learned more about these business fundamentals during my five years with Marv than I learned in any other period in my life.

Gordon E. (Mike) Gilbert is an old sage. He guided me by his style and wisdom through many corporate battles. I was young, brash, and often overconfident while he was experienced and wise. He eventually taught me to harness my passions, to temper my comments, and to manage the politics.

I had others, whom I had never met, who also served as role models and/or semiheroes. Peter Drucker, Mickey Mantle, Alfred Sloan, and others all impacted my life without ever knowing me. I probably did not picture them accurately, but my perception of them helped to guide my thinking. Using Peter Drucker as a role model taught me the importance of clear thinking and of building a philosophical foundation to use in decision-making. Many of his thoughts on strategy, people management, and decision-making became foundations for my own management thinking. His legendary capacity to identify a major change in trends caused me to develop my own system for regularly standing back to analyze the big picture. From watching Mickey Mantle, I learned how meeting the competition and striving for excellence can hone and shape a company or a career, and improve everyday performance. From reading about Alfred Sloan, I developed a healthy respect for formal strategic planning, detailed problem analysis, and action plans with accountability. His views on corporate and division charter, as well as his thoughts on organizational structure, made a lasting impression on me.

In addition, there was also my father. I did not realize until late in life how much I was affected by my dad. He was always firm in his convictions and took great pride in his work. He was nonpolitical and personally nonambitious but fiercely dedicated to achieving superior results for his company. He was demanding, trusting, loyal, and firm with his people. He had the ability to organize work and motivate his people so that a few strong leaders and a lot of average performers could consistently achieve excellence. He motivated through high expectations and rigorous individual performance measurement. He was ahead of his time on these concepts. He had the ability to recognize strengths and the capacity to believe in people. He was not a particularly sociable person but he built a lifetime of personal relationships. He was a team builder who enjoyed sharing the credit and making stars of his people. My dad was self-educated and grew up in the school of hard knocks, though you would never suspect it with his strong analytical ability. When I was young, he once told me that he was sure that I would do well. This came at a time when my rebellious nature and impetuous style had just gotten me into trouble again. I have never forgotten his prediction.

Life is not a dress rehearsal—and neither is business

What you are doing right now, today, this minute, to make the company stronger and more competitive and to better satisfy your customers is everything. In business, as in life, there is a tendency to wait and to focus on the next big event or the next perceived upcoming opportunity, i.e., the next trade show, the next performance review, the next big project. *Do not wait!* Make a difference now in every way you can—and encourage everyone in your organization to do the same. Show them that just "fitting in" and not rocking the boat are not the only behaviors you value or want. If you behave as though you think it's important to make a difference and to go for it, chances are people in the organization will take a cue from you and do the same.

Practice interviewing

Learning to handle tough interview questions and to make a positive impression on those senior to you are skills that will serve you in many endeavors. Thinking through your potential answers and determining what general approach to use will prepare you for thinking about business as a whole. *CEO Logic* is based on clear thinking about complex issues and this exercise is as good a place to start as any. Use this process to refine your basic management skills as they relate to situation analysis, problem-solving, decision-making, and anticipating responses.

Talk to human resource people, seasoned managers, and company associates. Read the many books on how to respond to tough interview questions. Practice with anyone who will listen. Look for opportunities to test your interviewing skills. Know how to answer questions such as the following:

- Tell me about your strengths and weaknesses.
- What qualified you for your former position?
- What were your major accomplishments in that position?
- Tell me how your education applied to that job.
- Tell me about your former supervisor.
- What was your reason for leaving that position?
- What are your career goals?
- Tell me about your toughest negotiation.
- Describe your planning process.
- What was your greatest success in life?

When asked for your opinion, give it

CEO Logic dictates decisiveness and candor. Top management is always looking for talented managers who know how to think and analyze and solve problems. When they ask you what you think, don't just give them confirmation of their opinion. James Garfield said, "The men who succeed best in life are those who take the risk of standing by their own convictions." To stand by your convictions you have to know what you think and you have to realize that you cannot please everyone all the time. Fence-sitters, at best, are in for an uncomfortable ride.

Over and over I see young managers who give the answers that they perceive to be expected. They probe until they find the questioner's position, then they mimic or paraphrase it. And it is true that some managers, especially senior managers, are not really looking for an original opinion, only for confirmation of their own. But forget about them. If they ask for your opinion, have the courage of a tough-minded, independent thinker—and give it to them.

Excel in oral and written communication

Throughout this book, I emphasize the importance of communication to being a top manager. The ability to articulate and communicate vision, values, and mission and to make it meaningful throughout the organization is essential—but it comes from years of practice. The way you as a manager communicate affects nearly every aspect of your business career. Subordinates need clear direction and feedback. Superiors require succinct progress updates. Customers and suppliers must understand your true position on a given subject. Bankers demand exact and positive communication. Shareholders need a clear picture of past achievement and future prognosis. So begin early to develop your knowledge of language to enable you to select the best possible words to deliver your meaning. Speak and write in plain English. Avoid big words, jargon, and convoluted references. Use analogies, examples, and metaphors to illustrate your point. Put important directives and responses in writing. Construct compelling arguments and keep your messages concise.

Watch one, do one, teach one

The capacity for effective training is central to career development and a critical step needed to implement the strategies and action plans dictated by *CEO Logic*. Watch one, do one, teach one, is an old training adage. It might better be stated: Watch one, do many, teach some. You will not learn by watching alone, you have to get active. Over the years, I have developed a phrase I use in training sessions. It is called "Hands-Off Training." This lets the instructor know that the trainee will not learn the task if the trainer keeps interfering. Trainers tend to be compassionate people and it is difficult for them to stand by and watch a trainee struggle with a particular task. So they "help" by taking over. This, of course, is not really helping because the trainee's struggles are a natural part of learning. If you want to learn, follow the adage, "watch one, do one, teach one."

Dealing with Company Politics

Politics is the art and science of the distribution of wealth and power. This is as true in business as it is in life. You are part of it; have an active impact on it or be a passive victim of it. I understand that even the mention of company politics is somewhat politically incorrect. It would be great if all companies based their political decisions (such as hiring, promoting, and job assignment) on the basis of performance alone. This, unfortunately, is not always the case. I am not suggesting that you compromise your values to get ahead. But work to understand the power system within the company and try to discern the criteria used in political decision-making. *CEO Logic* requires that you master all the methods available to implement the company's plans, and politics cannot be ignored.

Strength usually wins

It is dangerous to align yourself against the current power structure. Noble but losing campaigns will not get the job done or pay the rent. Founders, owners, CEOs, and senior management usually prevail. The pattern here is clear, but you do not have to go along with the crowd to get along. There are often high rewards for integrity and independence of thought and for standing up for your convictions, as we've already discussed. If you're thinking like a CEO, you research your facts, understand and respect the power structure, and stand your ground once you are sure of your conclusions.

Think before you fight

Think like a CEO and develop a strategy before you enter into a big fight. Pick your battles carefully. Sometimes timing affects the outcome of a confrontation. A good general does not knowingly take his troops into a losing campaign. Fight big fights only when you have the resources to win. Use strategy to get you in position to win. It does not lessen the importance or the nobility of your campaign to think before you fight or to gain and use tactical leverage in advance of the battle.

Use the rules to your advantage

CEO Logic recognizes that every organization has rules that have grown out of all kinds of experiences and issues, including predecessors who have made mistakes or errors in judgment. So while senior management becomes offended when the rules are broken, there is also usually some degree of flexibility that you can use to your advantage to get what you want. If you become an expert in the rules, their origins, and their sponsors, you'll have the room you need to get your way without violating company guidelines. For example, your company relocation policy may not allow you to pay a valued employee for certain reasonable but nonreimbursable moving costs, but you may be able to solve the problem by using the company's standard merit incentive program. This will only work out for you if your motives are clear and the final impact of your action is positive for the company. Be cautious—this is an easy place to get into trouble.

How you say it matters

Effective and persuasive communication is another issue central to implementing the strategies of *CEO Logic*. How you present an idea often affects how it will be evaluated. There once was a priest who wanted to smoke and pray at the same time, so he asked his bishop if, on occasion, he could smoke while he prayed. The bishop responded that it might not be such a good idea to interrupt prayers with smoking. Many years later, the priest asked a new bishop the same question, but this time he said, "On occasion, while I am smoking, would it be okay to interrupt my smoking with prayer?" The bishop told him that was certainly fine. The point is clear: It makes a difference whether you're perceived to be interrupting something sacred with something profane or interrupting something profane with something sacred. Although the substance of the two requests may be the same, presentation makes the difference.

Please your boss

This concept is valid whether your boss is your customer or your immediate supervisor. Find out how your superior's performance is measured before you develop your strategy. Make him look good and you will look good. Bosses have many of the same concerns that you do. They have directives from above, authority parameters, and targets to meet. Their superiors will be judging their performance much the same way that yours will be measured. Your position was likely created to help them achieve certain objectives and to solve problems or seize opportunities. Find out about the history of your position, look at the performance of your predecessors, and determine who, in addition to your boss, is expecting and measuring results. The more you know about the true purpose of your position, the easier it will be to please your boss by turning in a solid performance.

Manage up

It's going to happen to you at some point: You'll have a boss or a customer who is not as strong as you are in any number of ways. To avoid letting weak supervision hold you up, be sure to document in advance how your performance will be measured. Determine which measures indicate a fair job, an average job, a good job, and an excellent job. Once these performance indicators are set and you have documented them in an "as we discussed" letter, you have set the stage for potential success. All that is left is your excellent performance and the follow-up review meetings you will arrange.

Never wound a king

Often in business, young managers become disenchanted with the actions of someone senior to them. He may be taking unfair advantage of a position or making bad judgments. And it may be creating problems for everyone. Address these situations carefully. Generally, the best method is to approach the offender directly but nevertheless with respect for his position. You may even decide to ask for confidential guidance from your direct superior, but keep your concerns between the two of you unless the actions are bad enough to have the offender removed from office. From your point of view, the worst thing that can happen is that you tattle, the offender gets a minor reprimand, and then he is free to retaliate at leisure.

Vaccinate yourself against company politics

The best inoculation against the potential of bad politics has three components:

1. Work hard and dedicate yourself to the good of the customer and the company.
2. Generate superior performance by staying focused on critical issues to achieve results.
3. Let your word be your bond in all cases. Develop a reputation for honor, integrity, and trust.

Personal Development and Values

These thoughts on character, personal associations, sacrifice, and hard work will complete your education on career development. They may well be the most important concepts presented in this chapter.

Time wounds all heels

John D. Rockefeller said, "The most important thing for a young man is to establish credit, a reputation, and character." People who act like a "heel" sooner or later will be found out. Everyone has had associates who have opted to openly test this rule. They may appear to be successful within the organization, but their indiscretions don't take more than about six months to be noticed by an ever-widening circle of people. I have seen exceptions where a particularly clever individual has fooled his supervisors for longer periods of time, but that cannot go on indefinitely. Sooner or later he will be caught. Remember that even while he is "getting away with it," he is still suffering. Bad character is destructive to one's self-image and, therefore, bad character brings its own punishment.

If you lay down with dogs, you get fleas

Just as a CEO selects the people he will and will not do business with, pick your companies and associates well. As with partners, it never pays to do business with bad people. Bad people lack character, ethics, and a sense of fair play. Doing business with them will not only cost you money and negatively impact your performance, it will also cost you your reputation. You can find new money and get a new job but it is hard to get a new reputation.

Opportunity for money, prestige, power, or position may tempt you to consider aligning yourself with people you know to be of poor character. This is one of the few times in this book that you will hear me talk in absolutes. Laying down with dogs is *always* a mistake. It is not a good deal if bad people are involved.

Don't be average

Henry Ford said, "The question, 'Who ought to be boss?' is like asking, 'Who ought to be the tenor in the quartet?' Obviously, the man who can sing tenor." To be noticed in the most positive way, you have to perform better. If you cannot perform better, perform more—start earlier, stay later—or be especially bold in advancing new initiatives. For an ambitious manager, the first step is to stand out and get noticed. If you look, act, dress, and perform like everyone else, the *most* you can hope for is to be recognized and rewarded like everyone else. To excel, you have to do more and be more.

But advice to stand out is not a license to be odd. There must be a purpose to your individuality and this purpose must make sense to your superiors. Make it obvious to them that you are ready for more responsibility. Make your presentations more professional or more thorough than is generally expected. Spend more time validating your facts and be more prepared to accept additional assignments. Distinguish yourself in an identifiable and positive way.

Persistence is the road to genius

Attention to detail and intense commitment to excellence are hard to find. Many of the best and most successful top managers look to a candidate's intense desire to engage in the work and to perform with excellence as their number-one hiring prerequisite. They know that intensity and commitment to achieving outstanding results can overcome minor shortfalls in education or experience. Persistence provided the road to recognition for many of us who lacked the special talents or intellect to achieve in other ways. History is filled with many examples of the so-called lesser person prevailing over the more talented one because of persistent effort.

Have enough confidence to learn

No one wants to teach you things if you are always pretending that you already know them. Have enough confidence in yourself to ask for assistance or instruction in areas where you lack knowledge. Benjamin Franklin said, "They that won't be counseled, can't be helped."

When I was a young manager, I was very self-conscious about my lack of college education. I was competing with Harvard and Stanford MBAs and felt I could not afford to show my ignorance even on the most arcane subjects. Fortunately, a seasoned manager took me under his wing and explained the harm I was doing to myself. He explained that it was a sign of courage and confidence to admit my weaknesses. He said that he often noted this courage in successful CEOs. He told me that this type of honesty would not only help me to learn but would make a favorable impression on my superiors. He was right.

No shortcut goes unpunished

I first heard this comment about shortcuts from my controller. No doubt he was referring to accounting, but it is also a good lesson for career managers. Your days in school may have taught you that you could be successful while coasting for most of the semester and then cramming for the final, but that only worked in school. Real knowledge and skill only come with day-by-day, hour-by-hour diligent effort. If you coast for long periods of time on a regular basis, you will fail.

You don't have to be tough to be successful

Eric Stromsborg, president and CEO of Kett Engineering Corporation, is proof that nice guys can finish first. Eric operates a successful and growing 900-person operation that provides trained labor and management to large corporations. He is pleasant, personable, honest, easy to engage in conversation, and has excellent people skills. He has a good understanding of his personal goals and is well on the way to achieving them. A few years back, Eric's business started a period of rapid expansion. Revenues, margins, and profits were up. Sitting in his office one day, I overheard a call to the top manager in his largest division. They were discussing the tremendous upturn in business. My questions, in that circumstance, might have addressed revenues, margins, profits, credit capacities, needed resources, etc. Eric's first question was, "How is everyone handling the pressure?" Eric is living proof that nice guys often make great businessmen.

Practice self-assessment

I have made a lot of mistakes in my career, but three in particular stand out. The first had to do with ego. I was relatively young (35 years old) and president of a Fortune 500 company. The company was the largest in the county and I was getting continual compliments on my success. I finally recognized how all of this had gone to my head when I went to a division sales seminar in Nashville, Tennessee. This division was our largest and its president was one of our best. I once read a quotation from Woodrow Wilson that said, "Every man who takes office in Washington either grows or swells, and when I give a man office, I watch him carefully to see whether he is growing or swelling." I am embarrassed to say that my first few hours at the seminar were spent swelling and complaining. I am pleased only that my inexperienced and immature actions at Nashville did not become my norm. The division president, his people, and their customers were the important players at this meeting; I was just another guest. Afterwards, I knew that I had let my position go to my head and that I had to make immediate changes.

The second big mistake had to do with team-building or, perhaps more accurately, the lack of it. At another company, I was so busy meeting short-term corporate objectives that I failed to consider the team. I worked day and night knowing that if I met the goals, promotion and transfer would be my reward. Making the quarterly numbers was all that counted to me. When I finally reached the top, I discovered a trail of carnage made up of burned-out people who tried to keep up. It took years to rebuild the team and to repair the damage caused by my inexperience.

My third error was in hiring clones. I recruited and employed highly driven, task-oriented, well-organized people just like me. The company suffered, however, from a lack of creativity and sensitivity to its people.

Admitting to these past shortcomings is still difficult and painful today. I have no doubt that had I been able to make an honest self-assessment at the time, I could have overcome this poor behavior much sooner. The key to self-improvement is accurate and honest self-assessment.

Get results

If young managers remember only one piece of advice, let it be this one: ***get results***. Getting consistent results is the remedy to almost all career problems, the exception being problems relating to ethics. The first and last rule of career management is to ***get results***.

Final Thoughts on Career Management

Helping young managers grow is both one of the most gratifying and one of the most selfish deeds top managers ever perform. When a young manager finds success, it helps the company, it helps the senior manager, and it helps that young manager. It is selfish because it brings so much personal enjoyment that it can hardly be called work.

Successful career management begins with an individual's assessment of his unique strengths and weaknesses. That, then, allows for discovering the positives and negatives of potential career opportunities, matching strengths to career choices, giving the very best effort, taking charge of personal destiny, and learning to think like a CEO.

Your strengths and weaknesses are what constitute your character. There is no substitute in business as in life, for knowing and developing personal character. I will leave you with the one rule of personal conduct for your young managers that I have asked my children to live by, and also a few thoughts on character that we discuss regularly in our home.

Act like a citizen and a gentleman (I have all boys)

Being "a citizen" means following the laws of the land and the rules of the organization. Being "a gentleman" means being considerate of others. This one rule has served my family well and I hope it will be of benefit to you.

Thoughts on character:

- Every decision has consequences, some good and some bad.
- It is our job to determine our priorities and to make good decisions for ourselves.
- We are responsible—not our friends, teachers, bosses, parents, or instructors. We are the masters of our own destinies and we are responsible for our current situations, good or bad.
- We develop habits. The only question is whether they will be good habits or bad habits.
- The only way to repair a bad habit is to replace it with a good one.
- Cultivate peace of mind, physical health, family and friends, career and finances—in that order.

- Keep your promises, tell the truth, and be nice to people.
- Think now about what you want to be remembered for after you are gone.
- It is a good thing to dream.
- Success is often defined by the positive differences we make in the lives of others.
- Make a clear determination about what you should be doing now to achieve your goals.
- Whatever you choose to do in life...*do it well and get results.*

Your own "rules" and thoughts on character may be different. Whatever they may be, I suggest that you take the time to write them down. Discuss them with your own young managers, your mentors—and your family. All will be strengthened by your demonstration of clear thinking about character.

Chapter 6

Sales: Keep It Simple and Understand It Completely

I never worry about action, but only inaction.
—Winston Churchill

Anthony Reynolds*, now former vice president of sales for Marshall Manufacturing, couldn't figure out why he'd just been "counseled" out by his boss, company president and CEO, Ben Wright*. Since he had been hired four months ago to energize their 18-person sales force, Anthony had traveled with 10 of the 18, analyzed their sales presentations, evaluated market share within each of their territories, reviewed their expense accounts, listened to customer problems and objections, and introduced a new compensation plan. And he had told Ben what he thought was causing their sales shortfall: the shortage of competitive features in their products and their over-the-market pricing. He was doing everything a top-flight sales manager was supposed to do, wasn't he?

From Ben's perspective, the product deficiencies were obvious. However, he couldn't afford to wait until they brought their new product lines to market 10 months from now. He had to drive a sales turnaround now. So he hired Michael Thomason* to do it. Michael did most of the same things that Anthony had done, but he went one step further. He addressed the efficiency of the Marshall selling system. Once he was sure that the design of the selling system was logical and capable of delivering results, he looked at the number of leads, the number of appointments with prospects, the number of full-scale presentations, the number of quotes, the number of orders, and the average order size. He then set out to improve each element, beginning with an increase in the number of leads.

Michael knew—and did—something that Anthony didn't that allowed Marshall Manufacturing to achieve substantial sales increases in spite of product shortfalls. Where Anthony was confusing his sales management responsibilities with those of the president, Michael focused on the priorities of the sales manager, and took immediate action to improve this month's results by incrementally improving each element of the selling system. He understood the true purpose of his position as sales manager: to improve *both* long- and short-term sales performance.

The True Purpose of Sales

Salespeople are the dynamic life-giving element of a business. They may be, at the same time, the highest paid, least understood, and most demeaned of all businesspeople. Criticism of sales often starts with competing departments wishing to deflect criticism from themselves. This is easy to do, because sales is both integral to and dependent upon the other management disciplines. While it may be difficult to identify the exact impact that areas, such as product development, production (quantity, cost, and quality), shipping, customer service, credit administration, and pricing have on sales results, no one hesitates to lay both credit and blame for revenue performance on the sales department.

What, then, is the best, most effective way to *think* about sales? How do the savviest CEOs think about their sales function? *The answer, as with all departmental resources, lies in discovering the true purpose of sales*. Top managers know that the fundamental purpose of the sales force is to maximize revenues (or at least unit sales) without compromising margins or company principles. Individual sales representatives carry the company's sales message to prospective customers. They demonstrate product features and benefits with the ultimate goal of persuading those prospects to purchase from their company rather than another. The bottom line for salespeople and sales departments is that they must sell.

This may all seem too obvious. What manager doesn't know that the purpose of sales is to sell in order to maximize revenue? Obvious as it may seem, however, here's an example from the hotel industry that shows how easy it is to lose that concept in the midst of other pressing demands if you're not thinking about sales in the right way. In most business hotels, sales efforts are focused on selling room nights and/or food and beverage services. Salespeople (called sales managers) contact businesses, individuals, and associations in order to convince them to hold their events at the hotel. They work with travel agents and volume room-night purchasers (airlines, local businesses, etc.) and offer them special rates and services if they will contract for a large number of room nights over a given period of time.

In one hotel chain where I consulted, I asked the general manager, "Who is the best sales manager at this hotel?" The answer was, "Betty has the best training; she worked six years for Marriott and you know of their reputation for excellent sales training. John would be next because he used to work this same territory for Hilton. Mary is new to selling, and Joe is learning quickly."

I then asked, "Since Betty is Number One on your sales force, how much more does she sell than the others?" Somewhat taken aback, the general manager said she wasn't sure because her hotel didn't track room nights sold by each sales manager. They sometimes tracked the room nights sold by the whole sales department, but even then there were problems with tracking room nights "sold" versus room nights actually delivered. Still, the manager said, "Betty doesn't necessarily sell more, but she's certainly more knowledgeable."

We then discussed their selling system. This hotel's daily sales routine consisted primarily of individual sales managers fielding incoming calls, personally dropping off hotel brochures and rate cards to local businesses, and arranging hotel tours. There were no systematic efforts to identify or contact prospects, to make formal presentations of benefits, or even to see if the hotel brochures were delivered to the right persons. Sales managers were not trained in making appointments, qualifying customers, customizing presentations, or getting referrals. In short, their selling system—like that of many hotels—was weak. And it is no wonder. If you don't think about sales in the right way, don't properly design your selling system, and don't measure the right issues—in this case actual sales results—you can't manage them well.

You may be thinking that this general manager and her director of sales were particularly weak managers, but that was not the case. Business hotel management is often so focused on manpower scheduling, food and beverage activities, front desk operations, customer service, and property maintenance that they devote little time to improving the selling effort. Their poor sales efforts are not necessarily due to weak salespeople or managers but more often to a flawed system used for filling up the hotel on off-demand nights. This business hotel example tells the story. Even if the sales force perfectly executed the sales plan as it was designed, there was still no chance they would succeed. In fact, this selling system was flat out not capable of delivering the desired results. Using this system would be like trying to use a 20-pound jack to lift a 200-pound weight. It just wouldn't work. The source of the problem lay in the way they were thinking about—and measuring—results.

The Secret Is the Selling System

A design deficiency in the *selling system* reflects a fundamentally different and more serious problem from the *selling efficiency* issue faced by Marshall Manufacturing. Once a weak system is in place, it is difficult for management to see the real problem. The tendency is to keep trying to make the system more efficient rather than trying to change it. It's the proverbial case of not being able to see the forest for the trees. Management may try new training programs, more motivation, tighter discipline, better rewards, even hiring and firing individual sales reps. They may even try to increase the efficiency of each element of the selling system, as in the Marshall example. But if the basic selling system is flawed, none of these actions has a chance of working. The secret to thinking like a CEO about sales is to understand that you cannot make a poorly designed selling system work without redesigning the system. Changing the people will do nothing to improve a fundamentally flawed selling system. *The first step in managing sales is not training, hiring, pay plans, better prospect lists, or even better sales management. It is the design and validation of the selling system.*

Successful CEOs think of the selling system as a big "selling machine," where leads are put in one end and sales come out the other. To analyze the efficiency of your own "selling machine's" design, ask your team the following questions:

1. How many suspects (potential prospects) are needed to generate one prospect (someone who uses and could buy your product)?
2. How many prospect calls does it take to generate one appointment?
3. How many appointments does it take to generate one sales presentation to a decision-maker?
4. How many sales presentations to decision-makers are needed to generate one price quotation?
5. How many price quotations does it take to generate one sale?

So if it takes two suspects to generate a prospect, five prospect calls to generate an appointment, two appointments to generate a sales presentation to a decision-maker, three sales presentations to generate a price quotation, and two price quotations to generate a sale, then you now know that at current efficiency (closing rate) of your selling system, you need 120 suspects to make one sale. Your sales team can work on finding more suspects or they can work on improving their efficiency at each step of the selling process. They can also look at modifying, adding to, or deleting from the process. *The key is to design a well-tuned "selling machine" with the horsepower to generate the required revenue, margin, and market share.*

Many times, a company's selling system evolves over several years without direct input or guidance from senior management. There is often no conscious design or subsequent attempt to validate its efficacy. Peter McCutcheon*, owner and CEO of Brand Chemical Company, found his sales effort to be in just such a state.

He operated with a sales-oriented general manager, 14 outside salespeople, four inside phone sales reps, two sales coordinators, and a sales secretary. The inside phone reps, sales coordinators, and secretary were paid salary only. The outside sales force was paid a salary plus a commission for products sold and delivered within their respective geographic territories. The general manager was paid a salary plus a generous discretionary bonus loosely based on company profitability. The implied assumptions behind these compensation plans were that the inside people merely processed day-to-day orders, the general manager was primarily involved in overall operations, and the outside sales force actually generated month-to-month sales.

The selling system as it evolved at Brand Chemical had never been documented, much less analyzed or validated. For many years, the growth in overall company revenues had been quite good, so there was never any urgency to address this issue. But 1996 was different. In 1996, the company showed a year-over-year decline in revenues. This, of course, prompted new attention to the whole selling process.

Pete McCutcheon began by analyzing the existing sales process. Here's what he found:

- New business accounts could take as long as 18 months to process from first contact to first shipment. The process typically involved several face-to-face contacts by the outside salesperson, sample submission and approval, credit approval, and capacity to deliver verified. Then, once Brand Chemical became an approved supplier for specific products, Brand then performed its credit analysis of the customer. Only then did the inside sales reps begin to quote current market prices on the specific approved products. If all went well, products could then be shipped whenever they were available and the customer agreed to the price.
- Account retention was neither measured nor managed. Most accounts remained with the company, but many were lost. No regular analyses or attempts to recover the lost business were made.
- The outside sales force made mostly social (public relations) calls to existing accounts, unless customers called with specific problems.
- The company made no organized new business prospecting efforts.
- The company made no organized attempts to determine account penetration (what percentage Brand had of a customer's business) or whether other Brand products might be of interest.
- The general manager spent two-thirds of his time on sales issues.

- The sample submission process was neither tracked nor managed.
- The inside sales reps were authorized to negotiate within a price range and therefore had a large impact on margins.

What Pete McCutcheon did was to bring in outside help to design and develop a selling system. A complete system, including the necessary technology to monitor and manage the process, was developed and installed. His sales compensation plan was modified to reflect actual results expected and achieved at each step in the selling system. Leads were generated, appointments were made, presentations were given, samples were tracked, quotes were given, and sales were made. In addition, customer satisfaction was formally measured and lost business was actively chased.

Pete McCutcheon is still working on increasing the efficiency of his selling system, but now he has a good one in place and this year looks like it will be a record year.

It is up to the CEO to ensure that the company has the right people, products, pricing, quality merchandising, distribution channel, manufacturing, delivery, and sales management. It is up to the sales manager, however, to validate the incremental selling process to be sure that the system is capable of delivering needed results.

Sales Managers in the Selling System

A sales manager's job is both strategic and operational. It is to develop and discipline the selling system, measure and manage sales efficiency, build a sales team, define the sales message, solve day-to-day selling problems, and guide and motivate the sales force to meet their objectives. Further, her job is, like a CEO, to simultaneously be the chief skeptic and the chief optimist. As chief skeptic, the sales manager analyzes and anticipates problems. I have never met a successful sales manager who was not worried all the time that something, if not everything, would go wrong with each pending sale.

At the same time, sales managers must be able to generate hope, energy, and optimism in order to motivate the sales force to put enthusiastic actions behind important plans. Balancing these roles can be a delicate matter. If the skeptic role becomes too prominent, a sales force can easily be demoralized with too much gloom and doom. But being overly optimistic and unrealistic does no good either. So the sales manager, like a CEO, must be able to manage both roles skillfully to keep the troops focused on success and performance.

At the heart of the sales management process lie two key operational elements. All great sales managers have developed these skills and talents. First, they have learned how to select great salespeople. They recognize that coaching has its limits. To win consistently in sales, you need talented players who have the desire and the knowledge to sell effectively. If the potential to succeed does not already exist in the sales force, the sales manager cannot succeed.

Second, effective sales managers are great sales strategists. They must know how to think and plan for sales. They are skilled at placing the sales force in a position to succeed by addressing overall market strategies, such as new products to offer, new markets to enter, and new pricing formulas. They also have the capability to develop and implement individual sales tactics, such as customized presentations, special offers, and unique services for individual customers. They require an accurate perception of circumstances, a keen awareness of what will and will not work, and a large arsenal of programs and tactics that they rely on to attack and conquer each situation.

Timothy Pfeiffer*, vice president of sales for Gross Manufacturing, was in a tough position. His new products and pricing were being well-accepted by all except his two largest accounts. These two accounts represented 31 percent of his total business and they were not satisfied with Timothy's new offerings.

His number two account felt that it should have received preferential pricing in recognition for its volume purchases. The number one account was also unhappy with the price but was even more concerned with the lack of differentiation of product features between Timothy's offering and the others on the market. Each openly threatened to change vendors if their respective concerns were not addressed. These were neither selling system nor selling efficiency problems. They were primarily operational issues—but ones with strategic implications.

The industry was fairly small and most participants knew each other. In fact, this may have been at the core of the problem. Any significant move with one account had the potential of affecting all of the others. Tim Pfeiffer's creativity and experience served him well in his solution.

First, he developed a private brand product offering for his largest account. With this move, he was able to offer better pricing and a new package of product features specifically customized to number one's unique needs without jeopardizing his other accounts. Second, he was able to offer his number two account better pricing by introducing the existing product line to its foreign subsidiary, and aggregating both its domestic and foreign purchases for discount purposes. These moves satisfied both accounts.

I don't relate this story in order to advocate private branding, looking for foreign markets, or aggregating sales volumes of affiliated companies. The lesson to be learned here is about the need for a clear understanding of each problem and each customer, as well as the benefits of amassing a large sales manager's "tool box" of potential fixes to any given problem.

Part of thinking strategically as a sales manager means developing a sales plan for increasing sales. This analysis of the opportunities to add more customers and to sell more to existing customers considers the relative viability of making more sales calls per day, improving the selling methodology, upgrading the sales force, adding to the product line, creating new distribution channels, changing the product features, or changing the price point. It projects the cost and effect of improved merchandising and increased advertising. Developing a sales plan begins with formulating an overall strategy for growth.

Develop a formal growth strategy

Ribank Engineering was not meeting its growth objectives. The sales staff would be on target for three months, then off by 30 percent or more the next month. The fluctuations in sales levels were not only disrupting the production department but were also shaking the confidence of CEO Herb Leyman* and his management team. The dips in sales came without warning and no one knew for sure whether Ribank would fully recover to previous sales growth levels.

Herb thought the severe sales declines were due primarily to a combination of weak marketing and normal seasonal swings in business. He felt that the company's advertising was not generating adequate leads and this shortfall was exacerbating the company's typical out-of-season sales performance. His vice president of marketing, Jayne Dickenson*, had a different take. Jayne complained about factory quality and delivery problems, tough competition, and a new contract that had overwhelmed production with unexpected demands for volume. And all those problems were causing customer dissatisfaction, which was causing sales to fall. She was also concerned that 80 percent of her time was spent on solving factory problems, leaving only 20 percent for marketing.

Scott Barker*, the vice president for sales, attributed most of the sales declines to the recent loss of a large contract, the lack of leads from marketing, and the normal fluctuation in one particularly volatile segment of the business. He also noted that his outside independent representative sales force was new to the company and therefore just now getting up to speed. In addition, he felt that his company-employed sales force spent half of its time solving existing customer account problems (caused by poor quality production), leaving inadequate time to develop new business.

In reality, Herb, Jayne, and Scott were all correct in their conclusions. The business was seasonal, there were production problems, leads were not sufficient, the new contract was overwhelming, they had lost a large contract recently, some customers were unhappy, no one was watching marketing, the outside representatives were new, and the in-house sales force was not working on new business. These were all symptoms of a company growing beyond its means and thus showing signs of stress in every aspect of its business. The sales force had actually sold more than operations could currently deliver.

In spite of these stresses and strains, Ribank Engineering was still increasing its growth objectives and constantly measuring its success based on increased revenues. Everyone, including the CEO, may have been contributing to the company's problems, but the source was their inability to plan for growth. They were not thinking in a strategic way about the whole enterprise. They had not measured excess capacities, designed an effective and well-disciplined selling system, or developed a marketing system that would generate enough leads for the sales staff. Sales came when they came and operations responded as best it could on short notice. The pendulum was swinging from sales to production, over and over.

To correct its fundamental problems, Ribank's sales department needed a sales strategy and a selling system that allowed it to anticipate and forecast sales levels. That strategy needed to start with the CEO setting sales objectives that balanced new business plans with the company's operating capacities. Herb, as CEO, needed a method for measuring excess operating capacity, and Scott, as vice president of sales, needed an overall plan to manage sales and predict growth.

An outline of a typical sales growth strategy addresses at least the following issues, beginning with internal growth options:

1. How can we broaden the range of products/services sold to *existing* customers?
   - Develop a "full line" sales presentation, with collateral material, detailing the benefits of the company's complete line of products/services.
   - Analyze existing customer needs and uses.
   - Generate referrals and introductions from current departmental contacts within existing customer organizations.
   - Schedule formal "full line" sales presentations to secure new business.
2. How can we sell existing products/services to *new* customers?
   - Develop a lead generation system to convert suspects to prospects.
   - Design a system to secure appointments with prospects.
   - Develop a new business sales presentation that includes methods for qualifying prospects' needs, desires, fears, and limitations; an outline for presenting and/or demonstrating product/service features, advantages, and benefits; responses to anticipatable objections; closing questions; and a process for generating referrals.
   - Schedule new business sales presentations.

- Establish a new business task force consisting of company departmental personnel (production, customer service, accounting, etc.) to ensure attention to customer satisfaction on issues such as product quality, correct packing and shipping, timely delivery, and accurate billing. Place one individual in charge of the task force and make her personally responsible for total customer satisfaction. Give this individual both the authority to make needed decisions and direct access to the CEO.

3. How can we develop and sell *new* products to existing and new customers?

   - Assign resources, responsibilities, budgets, operating guidelines, and goals to market research and new product/service development.
   - Develop a new product/service sales presentation.
   - Establish test marketing procedures.
   - Schedule new product/service sales presentations.
   - Establish a new product/service introduction task force (similar to the new business task force above).

4. How can we develop *new* markets and/or *new* distribution channels?

   - Establish resources, responsibilities, budgets, operating guidelines, and goals for new market and new distribution channel research.
   - Establish test marketing procedures.
   - Follow the guidelines outlined in number two above.
   - Measure the selling efficiency (number of leads, appointments, presentations, and quotes needed to generate a sale) and forecast new business for each option chosen.

In looking at each of these four internal growth options, strategic thinking demands that the sales manager examine the cost, volume, potential return, risk of success or failure, time needed to achieve results, the toughness of competition, and the company's ability to execute each strategic option. Only then can allocation of resources among them be decided.

Match the machine to the task. In designing and implementing an efficient selling system, match the sales force structure to the task it faces. Some businesses separate lead generation or prospecting from other aspects of the selling system. It's up to management to determine how to apply separate resources to sales system elements, such as setting appointments, financing, unit delivery, customer follow-up, and securing referrals based on considerations, such as cost, productivity, and availability of resources. In some businesses, an item, such as lead generation, requires skills and knowledge totally different from those required for selling. In these cases, lead generation may be handled by the advertising department or even a separate lead generation department. Designing the right selling system sets the stage for successful selling.

Plan across the board for the necessary capacity. Keep in mind that continuing high growth rates demand excess capacity in all resource categories. Physical (plant and equipment), financial (cash and credit), technological (information and process), and human (company staff and consultants) resources must *all* have the capacity to meet the challenges of sales forecasts. Obviously, a manufacturing or distribution company growing at 25 percent per year will not build a factory or warehouse, establish a credit line, or develop a management information system that will only accommodate current levels of business. It is much more difficult, however, to measure excess capacity in human resources, especially those of senior management. Measuring the capacity for the sales or production work force is a matter of numbers and productivity, but doing the same for the senior management team is a totally different story. Senior management capacity must be analyzed and considered on the basis of past accomplishments and current performance. If a senior management team has no history of successful performance at planned growth levels and they are consistently falling short on current assignments, changes are needed. Management training, temporary expert help, reduced scope of assignments, additional planning, increased staff, and personnel replacements are the options. Growth can be a company's great savior or, if handled poorly, a threat to its survival. It requires careful and strategic analysis of all resources, activities, and capacities.

In line with developing a strategy for growth, it is also necessary to establish a specific charter and mission for the person in charge of sales.

Develop a charter and a mission

As much as any other key role in an organization, the top sales manager needs to have a clear sense of what she is doing to contribute to the overall business. A charter and mission statement can be useful in this effort because the speed of the boss will determine the speed of the gang. The charter details specific duties, responsibilities, and operating parameters, while the mission describes the purpose of the position, establishes specific results to achieve, and defines success. Defining the charter and mission for the senior sales position defines success of the sales organization.

A charter will specify, at the bare minimum, that the sales manager:

- Recruit, hire, and train a sales force sufficient to meet company revenue objectives.
- Develop, discipline, and measure the efficiency of a selling system with the "horsepower" to meet the company's sales goals.
- Develop a method for tracking and monitoring individual selling performance.
- Establish a system for generating, managing, maximizing, and tracking leads. It should measure the source, quantity, and quality (number and dollar amount generated) of all leads received.
- Create sales strategies that identify significant opportunities, effective selling tactics, and compelling and persuasive sales messages for each product and each type of prospect.
- Establish effective procedures for each of the elements of the selling system, including setting appointments, presenting/demonstrating, closing, and obtaining referrals.

- Develop a method for efficient and effective territory and product management.
- Design an incentive and recognition system for each element of the sales force.
- Create an atmosphere of enthusiasm and positive motivation.
- Develop a method for expediting individual sales and recovering lost business.
- Meet sales expense budgets.

The top sales management position will have many other ancillary duties and obligations, such as providing recommendations regarding product/service configuration, pricing, terms, promotions, packaging, and merchandising, as well as being the chief closer on tough deals.

The *mission* for this position will center on specific goals relating to volume, margin, market share, account penetration, and customer satisfaction.

Understand the ingredients of a great salesperson

Top sales managers understand what it takes to identify, hire, train, and develop great salespeople. They know that the best salespeople are born—*and* they are made. Drive and empathy are inborn; no sales manager can teach a salesperson to have the inner drive to make the sale or the empathy to accurately sense and perceive others' feelings. But drive and empathy alone do not make a good salesperson. Selling is a profession. It takes years of education and practice to acquire the expertise and methodology that consistently produce excellent performance. Selling is not just a matter of being an extrovert with the gift of gab. You would not expect a doctor to be able to perform surgery simply because of innate talent. Nor should a salesperson be expected to perform because of personality or some other superficial measure.

Sales training, of course, is an essential part of making a great salesperson. But it has more to do with supervision and the selling process than it does with classroom instruction. Classroom instruction and training manuals are important, but all of the classroom training can be undone if the systems actually used in the field differ from the official curriculum. Make sure that your training curriculum addresses all the key components of your well-designed selling system.

Typical salesperson training curriculum

1. Company history and credibility.
2. Specifications on products or services.
3. Prices, terms, and financing.
4. Past sales successes and failures.
5. How the product is produced (trip to factory).
6. How and why the customer uses the product (trip to customer location).
7. Why some potential customers select competitors' products.
8. Competitor analysis (strengths and weaknesses).
9. Review of the "selling machine."
10. Review of territory.
11. Sources for suspects.
12. How to convert suspects to prospects.
13. How to set appointments.
14. The sales interview:
    a) Opening and introduction.
    b) Qualifying.
    c) Presentation/demonstration.
    d) Overcoming common objections.
    e) Closing questions.
    f) Sales interview goals.
    g) Obtaining referrals.
15. Delivery of product.
16. Customer follow-up.
17. Paperwork/documentation.
18. Sales incentive plan.
19. How to call for help.
20. Books, courses, and other training aids.
21. Good luck speech.

Make the dynamics of sales work to your advantage

There is a certain dynamic to most sales situations that can be used in clever and effective ways to gain competitive advantage and produce better results. Teaching a sales force how to think about these dynamics and how to stay alert to their possibilities is one of the major mentoring roles of the sales manager.

More shelf space means more sales. Quite often, the salesperson wants to persuade the prospect that more of her product (rather than a competitor's) on the shelf will lead to better sales for the prospect. Teaching salespeople to pay attention to leverage through packaging, inventory turns, margins, availability, lead time, price point, advertising, quality, display, and image all offer the potential to increase sales. If they stock more, they will probably sell more.

Look for a sponsor or a guide. Guides are individuals in prospective customers' companies who know their way around, and, by guiding salespeople through the idiosyncrasies of a complex organization, can help direct sales efforts to where they will do the most good. They help the salesperson find the users of the product as well as the decision-makers. Encouraging salespeople to find and use guides whenever they are "stuck" in a prospect's big business bureaucracy can make an enormous difference.

Anticipate common objections. Every product or service generates a few common objections. They may be related to price, delivery, terms, quality, or features. Few, if any, products are perfect. It is the job of management to identify anticipatable or expected objections and prepare several responses for each. Prepare your sales force for these inevitable obstacles.

Do your homework first. You can maximize any sales situation through preparation. Nowhere is this more true than in trade shows. Do not go to trade shows unless you have prepared in advance by prospecting and setting firm appointments before the show. Breakfast meetings allow you to use the time before the show opens and dinner meetings maximize your time at night. Make sure your sales force plans their time carefully or they may spend your money and have nothing but sore feet to show for it.

Use the "natural" close. If the selling process goes the way it should, the close follows naturally. Salespeople spend a great deal of time learning closing questions like the "alternative close" (Do you want red or blue?), the minor point close (Will you want the leather trim?), the "order blank" or "name spelling close" (Is that spelled J-O-N-E-S?) or my personal favorite, the "erroneous conclusion close" (in which the salesperson says that he can meet the prospect's price in blue when he knows the prospect wants red, knowing full well the only available red units are more expensive. The salesperson does this in an attempt to help the prospect reevaluate the trade-offs between desired color and desired price. His hope is that the prospect will commit to the red unit and the higher price when he corrects the erroneous conclusion). There's nothing wrong per se with closing questions as long as they are not tricks or manipulations. But always focus your sales force on the natural close. A natural close follows when a sales presentation allows both the salesperson and the prospect to discover the customer's true needs, desires, fears, and limitations. Great salespeople know that if you treat prospects as if they were valued family members and help them to make the best choice, the close will happen without pressure or confrontation because the product and the price will fit the prospects' circumstances. Only then will the selection be right.

Match your resources to the opportunity. Like a CEO, use A, B, and C level resources on A, B, and C level prospects or customers. Resources in sales are mostly time and money. Both come in very limited supplies. There is never enough time or money to chase every prospect with maximum resources. Likewise, there is never enough time or money to service all existing customers with maximum resources. Even if you could, you would not achieve acceptable levels of return if you invested resources out of proportion to each potential opportunity. Ask your sales force to learn to think like CEOs and use their resources (time and money) wisely by allocating them according to the potential of each opportunity.

To move forward, add organization

Organizational skill is the primary factor that distinguishes sales managers from salespeople. Good salespeople are strong in drive and empathy and have good people skills and strong leadership ability. They already have proven abilities in prospecting, setting appointments, and closing sales. But even a great salesperson may or may not be organized and may or may not follow a system. Some seem to follow a different path for each sale. These salespeople should be celebrated and perhaps even given an opportunity to earn more, but they should not manage and direct the sales force. Effective sales management requires defined systems and organized administration. Promoting unorganized or unsystematic individuals to sales management will only lose you a great salesperson and gain you a weak sales manager.

Sales Representatives in the Selling System

The salespeople are out there to sell, to meet objectives, and to get the full potential out of their territories. Their main role is to bridge the gap between what prospects perceive they want and need and what the company has to offer. They must be experts on their products as well as those of their competitors. They must know all there is to know about financing, delivery, lead times, pricing, terms, and options. But above all, no matter what, they have to sell.

All management disciplines require balancing of competing objectives. The purchasing agent must buy at the best price while maintaining high-quality products and minimum inventories. The production manager must meet the schedule but minimize costs and rejects. A CEO must balance short-term needs against long-term objectives. Salespeople, however, must face even more of these apparent paradoxes. They must have a tough-minded commitment to selling their products but at the same time be sensitive to and compassionate about the prospect's needs and interests. They must be well-trained, coached, and prepared but must maintain the capacity to be spontaneous so that they can respond quickly to a potentially wide range of inputs. The salesperson, like a CEO, has both the best and worst of jobs in business. She can be the hero or the goat, can know both "the joy of victory and the agony of defeat."

Secrets of Successful Selling

For those who coach and manage salespeople, there are a few key ideas that, once mastered and made a part of everyday practice, can make a significant difference both in the efficiency of the selling system and in the results it achieves. This section condenses these ideas into a short list of the essentials.

Sales representatives must sell what they believe in. In sales, just as in business, selecting the right product determines much of a sales rep's future. If there is no economic reason for the product to exist, if it does not operate as advertised, or if the company does not stand behind it, salespeople will not believe in it. Tell sales candidates not to join your company if they do not believe in the products and the company, because if they do not believe in both, they will never excel at selling them.

Encourage salespeople to admit mistakes and shortcomings. Customers may doubt tales of a company's or a salesperson's past successes, but they will instantly believe stories of past failures. People find it hard to believe claims of being number one, but tales of being number two are usually accepted. This phenomenon is even more effective when telling a prospect the details of a past error. Of course, it's important to mention how the error was eventually corrected.

Remember that the company never has exactly what the customer wants. If it did, it would not need salespeople. It could get by with only a vending machine or a blind dog with a note in its mouth. The sales representative's job is to make the sale by bridging the gap between what the customer perceives as her needs and what the company can provide.

Sell it like it is. Once a product is ready for market, do not ask your sales force to introduce it by asking customers and prospects to critique it. If you ask them, they will. They will tell you everything that's wrong with the new product. To avoid this, prepare your sales message and be prepared to convince and persuade all potential buyers of the product's benefits. Too often, especially at trade shows, salespeople say, "Here is the new model, what do you think?" This is not selling, and if the company did not know what "they thought" before they finalized design specifications, it's too late now.

A feature is only a benefit if the customer says it is. Remind your sales force that a feature is a benefit only when the customer can use it and is willing to pay for it. The salesperson's job is to find which feature can provide the greatest benefit to the prospect based on his or her needs, desires, fears, or limitations.

Never forget that price is always an issue. It is not a stand-alone issue, it is a comparative issue. Many sales have been lost because the salesperson failed to address and justify the difference in price between her product and a competitor's. Knowing the strengths and weaknesses of your competitors' offerings is critical to this process. Salespeople must find and leverage the one or two features that offer the greatest advantage to a prospect. A salesperson's knowledge of her own products is only half the job.

Everyone gets a pitch, but the UPS delivery man gets five pitches a week. This was the credo of a retail sales organization I managed many years ago. Everyone says not to prejudge prospective customers. Tell your sales force to go ahead and prejudge, but give a sales pitch anyway. It is almost impossible to avoid prejudging a prospect by his appearance or his initial comments. The problem is that salespeople are not always right. Even a skilled salesperson misses on prejudgments once in a while. Think like a CEO and ask each salesperson how many good prospects she wants to let get away.

When in doubt, open with professionalism. Many suggest the best way to start a sales call is to build rapport by talking about some item in the office such as a golf trophy or picture of a boat. Getting straight to business is just as effective. Ask your salespeople to tell the prospect who they are and who they represent, why they are there, and how long the meeting will take. Many decision-makers prefer this approach. If they are bosses, they probably already have plenty of people complimenting their golf games and boats.

Facts and statistics don't sell. Individuals, not companies, make decisions. And individuals make decisions based on emotions. They "feel" a decision is right when they are comfortable with a given alternative. They later use the facts and statistics to justify their decision. So have each salesperson target her presentation to the prospect's feelings and emotions and use the facts only to support her conclusions.

Use testimonials. Suggest that your sales force use the old "feel, felt, found" approach. When a prospect raises an objection, it is answered by saying, "I know how you *feel*. Mr. Jones at XYZ Corporation (a credible company, like the prospect's) *felt* the same way but he *found* after using our widgets that his concerns were unfounded." Sometimes testimonials are the only way to overcome certain objections.

Discover the decision-making process early. Salespeople need to learn to ask who makes the decision, who is on the approval committee, who signs the contract or purchase order, when they'll decide, and what criteria they'll be using. In every company there are more people who can say "no" than people who can say "yes." Unless a contact is acting as a guide, salespeople don't need to spend their energy with someone who has no authority to purchase.

Make it easy for the prospect to relay your pitch. It will not always be possible for a salesperson to deliver her sales presentation directly to the decision maker(s). The deal may require committee approval, which occurs in a closed meeting, or the decision-maker may be at another location. Teach your salesforce to help their contacts relay their sales message by concentrating on the benefits of the product, not the features. It will be much easier for the prospect to remember that a new machine will increase production by 20 percent and reduce costs by $100,000 than it will be for him to remember the detailed explanations of 15 separate features.

Anything but a "yes" is a "no." "I will think it over" is a "No." "I will get back to you tomorrow" is a "No." "You are the best I have seen yet" is a "No." "I will take it, here is my money" is a "Yes." All those put-offs mean that the customer is not convinced yet—so keep selling.

Maximize referrals. Teach your salesforce that asking general referral questions like, "Do you know anyone who can use my product?" will be disappointing. Much more effective is a question that directs the prospect's thoughts to several specific categories of other prospects, such as: "Which of your suppliers might be a prospect for me?" and "Who do you know at XYZ Company?" or "Who do you know at your previous place of employment?"

Find a role model. Ask the members of your sales force to find a role model and analyze and document her selling characteristics. This process will give them a guide to use in their own development. Below is my own attempt to follow this advice.

My occasional business partner, Terry Ballas, is the best one-on-one salesperson I have ever met. I say this having met hundreds and hundreds of salespeople. He is a creative thinker and an honest communicator. His openness about his own human shortcomings and past mistakes is very disarming. He gives you an instant feeling of trust and honesty. His integrity is unquestioned. I have done million-dollar deals with him on a handshake. This, however, was no great leap of faith on my part. Terry's handshake is worth more than most people's signature.

Terry has a no-nonsense way of expressing himself. He has the ability to think like a CEO and to reduce the complexities of a deal down to its simple basics. He only sells that which he truly believes in, and he has a unique ability to ignore meaningless or extraneous details. He has the capacity to immediately focus on the elements of a transaction that will be critical to the deal's success. He is only interested in win/win opportunities. I have seen him walk away from potentially profitable deals because he felt the other side might not be treated fairly.

Terry brings conviction and passion to his transactions. He learns from others and uses mentors to guide him. He is a true entrepreneur in the sense that he has the creative ability to recognize opportunities that most would miss. I have watched him grow from a great salesman to an effective leader over the years. He has the capacity to imagine opportunities and to inspire others to chase his vision. Along the way, he has also developed into an exceptional manager. His natural ability to relate to others, to focus on priorities, and his sense of personal values have served him well. He is a self-made success with a clear sense of purpose. Terry is as different from a typical businessman as an accomplished artist is different from a typical house painter. Very few people can combine this level of natural talent with such a high degree of creative genius. Terry has improved his deal-making by learning to think like a CEO. If your salespeople were to meet Terry, they would truly meet a great salesman, a unique leader, and a great role model.

Final Thoughts on Sales

Selling, for CEOs, starts and ends with satisfying the customer. Everything that has the potential to impact customer satisfaction falls within the CEO's definition of selling. Decisions on product design, advertising, merchandising, manufacturing, distribution channels, customer service, credit administration, and pricing must be included when the CEO analyzes selling performance. Selling must be viewed by top management as an integral part of the marketing system. Sales departments require a viable customer base that provides a universe of prospects in adequate quantities. They also need a competitive product to sell that has a definable economic reason to exist.

The incremental sales system that identifies and locates suspects, converts suspects to prospects, sets appointments, makes presentations, and closes transactions does not operate in a vacuum. Most CEOs are aware that addressing selling as a stand-alone discipline will usually produce better short-term results, but it will be limited in scope and degree of improvement. Addressing selling as part of an entire system of satisfying the customer is a broader and more strategic way to look at the process.

CEOs and managers at all levels must possess the perception and candor to accurately assess the overall viability of their product offerings and marketing systems. At the same time, sales management must be challenged to excel with the products in hand. In my judgment, 70 percent of selling success is due to competitive products, attractive pricing, and viable marketing efforts. The remaining 30 percent has to do with selling issues, such as the number of salespeople, the quality of training, or type of commissions. This, of course, is not to say that this 30 percent is not important. But a CEO must know when and how much to focus on the narrow issue of selling versus the broader overall marketing issues of the entire company.

An example of the need for this type of decision-making can be seen in the encyclopedia business. In the past, competition in this industry was based on putting together a good reference book, producing it efficiently, and selling it through proven channels. The industry recognized that a good reference book at a good price alone would not sell. Sales and marketing expertise became the defining issues between good and bad performance for companies within the industry. The industry developed and implemented some of the best one-on-one, single-call, retail sales systems ever. Their direct mail, door-to-door selling, infomercial, and telemarketing programs were phenomenally successful.

The initial rationale for this selling approach was based on the impulse nature of this particular buying decision. Today, however, the industry is now facing a much greater obstacle than sticker-shock and the tendency for qualified prospects to procrastinate. Computerization and online sources of information are threatening their ability to sell their product. The CEOs of these encyclopedia companies can no longer solve their problems by simply improving their incremental selling systems. They need a new product, one that takes full advantage of modern computer hardware and software. They need to understand CD-ROMs, online services, and hyperlinks. In short, the new product will not be a transcript of the old product on a computer disk. It will need to add new dimensions. As you may know, this transition process is underway and will continue well into the future.

The point is not about the advantages of computer disks over paper books. It is about top management's need, at times, to address the entire marketing philosophy of a company—rather than take a sales manager's perspective, which is necessarily focused on the validity and the efficiency of the incremental selling process.

Chapter 7

Numbers: Don't Be Fooled by the "Accounting"

The farther backward you can look, the farther forward you can see.
—Winston Churchill

It seems almost too obvious to say that good numbers focus management on the right issues and bad numbers generate bad consequences. But here is a story about how the obvious can be overlooked—with disastrous results. I once worked with a sales-oriented manufacturing company with highly educated and very bright top management, including the chief financial officer. They generally ran a fiscally conservative operation: They followed up on receivables aggressively, gave detailed audits to accounts payable (and took discounts when appropriate), built safeguards into the payroll system, managed cash flow closely, and kept long-term debt low and short-term debt moderate. Their monthly and annual financial statements were prepared in-house by well-trained division controllers and audited by an outside CPA firm. Each of the division's controllers reported to a general manager whose main orientation and preoccupation was to deliver sales to drive revenues. Everything seemed in order, so what could be the problem?

Following the lead of the largest division's general manager, each division's sales force held a contest each month to reward its members for high productivity. Each month-end was complete with celebrations and disappointments—steak for the winners and beans for the losers. As with many successful sales-oriented companies, everyone in this organizational culture bought into the "selling is everything" mentality. That's where their performance was measured, that's what they were rewarded for, and that's where they focused.

They were, however, so focused on meeting sales goals and achieving high numbers that many in the organization lost perspective. Their selling zeal led, over time, to bypassing one of accounting's control mechanisms. And that led to distortions in the numbers.

The sales staff, in its effort to meet monthly goals, found a way to book sales before product was shipped. Sales agents would identify a unit in finished goods, or occasionally still in the production line, that had been designated for a specific customer. They would arrange for advance credit approval on that unit and would fill out a document that notified accounting of the need to invoice the customer. The sales agents hoped, of course, that the units would be shipped before the accounting department did their shipping audits or before the customers got upset about being invoiced before they received their products. This "billing process" continued for several months—until finally someone got caught.

The tip-off came when it was discovered that a particular past-due receivables balance involved a unit that had not only not been shipped, it had not even been produced, despite the fact that it was 30 days after invoicing. The customer complained of being wrongly accused of slow payment, the sales agent was in trouble, and the company was embarrassed. Further investigation showed that this was not an isolated incident. Just under $1,000,000 in sales had been booked but not shipped.

It was relatively easy to fix the accounting problem in this case; it was harder to address customer concerns and complaints, but they also were eventually handled and resolved. That, however, wasn't the worst of the problem—and it wasn't the end of it. For the several months of erroneous billing, sales, accounts receivable, and production volume had been overstated while finished goods and raw materials were understated. No one in management could use the financial statements or the daily operating control reports to diagnose the company's real performance until the "billing problem" was corrected. The statements they'd been using to track performance made the operation appear to be doing fine (except for the past due receivables), even though there was nearly a $1,000,000 sales shortfall. There were significant additional consequences to these particular bad numbers. The bank nearly pulled the company's line of credit, the securities and exchange commission demanded further investigation, public shareholders became upset, the company was paying taxes on profits it did not actually earn, bonuses and commissions were overpaid, and, of course, the sales force was eating steak when it should have been eating beans. Good numbers do not always ensure success, but bad numbers are always a problem.

Run the Numbers—Don't Let Them Run You

Why spend so much time and effort understanding, refining, and validating the "numbers" relating to business? What do the "numbers" have to do with thinking like a CEO? My own concentration on numbers is particularly confusing to those who are aware of my love/hate relationship with the accounting profession. They know I feel that accounting department presentations are at best some slight distortion of reality and at worst a huge misrepresentation of the facts. Further, the numbers (as traditionally presented by accounting) do not usually provide insight into the most critical issues for a business, such as customer or employee satisfaction, potential threats from the competition, opportunities for growth, or a company's competitive edge. In short, traditional accounting-generated numbers do not always help managers make better management decisions. And the one to change that is top management, including a CEO who knows how to think about and manage the way numbers are produced, reported, and interpreted.

The main reason for producing timely, accurate, and meaningful numbers is that managers need them to control their operations and make decisions. They are, of course, also required for various governmental or stockholder reports, but the primary task of accounting is to make sure managers have the appropriate means to run their business. Poor operating controls are universal features of weak management and troubled companies. It is almost impossible to attain successful results if you are using bad or poorly presented accounting information.

When presented properly, numbers can and must act as an early warning system—a beacon to warn you away from treacherous waters. They are not the business itself, but they can and should provide an accurate *picture* of the business and its performance. That's why it's so crucial to educate your accounting department not only to produce accurate and timely numbers but also to understand the way top management will use them in making decisions. The people in accounting must learn that timeliness and accuracy are not the only measures of good numbers. They must—with top management's guidance—choose measures that have the potential to impact the bottom line by influencing the behavior of key operating managers on crucial issues.

David Cilano* had a contract labor business that was struggling along, making a little money most of the time. He asked me to help him figure out how he could improve his results. We looked at all the traditional measures of performance, but something was missing from the picture projected by his financial statements. Although the reports and systems used were not perfect, they met general standards of completeness, timeliness, and accuracy. What we discovered, however, was that the most important problems and opportunities of his business were buried in the detail. As a contract labor business selling trained labor, a major key to success was manpower utilization, that is, direct labor hours paid to workers versus direct labor hours billed to customers. But from the numbers that David was getting, it was difficult to see how they were doing on this critical measure. Labor and labor-related costs were spread throughout the profit and loss statement, so it was difficult to get a complete snapshot of manpower utilization. Top management could not easily compare revenues with costs. And if it is hard to see a problem, it is harder still to solve it. The key to correcting this deficiency was to concentrate all direct labor costs into the Cost of Sales accounts. In this new presentation, David and his managers got the same basic information but in a way that allowed them to easily compare revenues generated from labor sales with the relevant labor costs. Once they could focus on the amount of labor paid to workers but not billed to a customer (the inverse of manpower utilization), they could take corrective action. As a result, the company began making substantial margins.

You might argue that this management team would eventually have focused on the key issue of manpower utilization without benefit of consolidated numbers, but the question then becomes: When? And "when" is an important issue. As it was, the improved measurement of labor utilization resulted in better management of the labor paid to workers but not billed to customers. This improvement reduced the company's labor nonutilization factor from 15 percent to 2 percent, and earned them millions of dollars in the process.

Having a clear and accurate picture of performance and results is essential for managers at all levels. The right financial data should form the foundation of operating controls, allowing management to measure past efficiency and productivity in a timely fashion, to establish individual and collective accountability, and to create reliable information to be used by management in such areas as decision-making and forecasting.

Thinking About Numbers Like a CEO

As CEO and holder of the entire picture of your organization, your role is to make sure that accounting provides meaningful performance indicators to help you and your management team control your business. You can't assume that your accounting department and managers will necessarily do that without your clear and firm involvement. You must insure that accounting personnel understand that it is their top priority to help all operating managers make better decisions. This role is not inconsistent with their obligations to meet GAAP or CPA guidelines, public reporting requirements, or tax responsibilities. It is not a matter of either/or; it is an issue of priority and balance.

Management needs and uses accounting information as the basis for key decisions about issues such as pricing, costing, expense and cash control, resource allocation, theft control, asset utilization, return on investment, and credit needs. Effective accounting allows for better defined targets, more accurate progress and status reports, a clear understanding of past performance, and a basis and method for future planning. That is why the "numbers" play such a major role in management. In my experience, there are a few very critical principles that top managers can use as a framework for thinking like a CEO about the "numbers." Within these concepts, the theoretical is paired with the very practical in an effort to give you the best and most useable insights into the numbers as they apply to everyday management.

Ensuring financial reports answer management's questions

What information do operating managers need to do their jobs? Where does it come from? What form will make it most useful? And how often do the operating managers need it? For example, a typical accounting income statement will show labor, material, and overhead expenses as they relate to a production department. The production manager and his people, however, may not find this information adequate in its "normal" aggregate form. Such information as cost of quality, manpower utilization, raw material shortages, machine utilization, and individual process cost might better meet production's information requirements. Close the gap between the information provided by accounting and the information that operating managers need to perform.

Remember that accounting only reports the past

Top management's issues—such as sales, costs, expenses, cash, and credit—are all in the future, but accounting only reports what you've already done. Thoughtful CEOs use accounting primarily for verifying and analyzing past performance: Did we do what we thought we did? How well did we do it? CEOs and all managers need to understand both the strengths and the limitations of accounting data. Not using accounting information at all would be like driving at night without headlights. But using accounting data as your only decision-making tool would be like using the rearview mirror as your only navigating device. Effective CEOs know that accounting alone is an insufficient indicator of total company performance. Statements of accounting are good financial indicators, but they will not measure customer or employee satisfaction, the threats from competitors, or even a changing financial climate. Successful CEOs understand that they need to analyze the past, but only as an effort to stay focused on the present and the future. Accounting is a management tool with great strengths—and clear limitations.

Forecast the past

Try this procedure as a training mechanism for key operating managers. At the end of each month, but before the company's monthly financial statement comes out, ask all operating managers to forecast each line item on the financial statement covering their operation for the month that has just passed. If, for example, it is March 31st, a manager in control of his operation who understands the accounting process should be fairly accurate in predicting what the

March financial statement will say. After all, this manager was responsible for those revenues and expenditures during the past month, so he should know what was sold and what was spent. If the "predictions" are wrong, then either the manager was not fully on top of the operation or the accounting is wrong. When operating managers know and understand the accounting process, they are able to track and manage their daily revenues and expenditures. When they understand basic bookkeeping, they will know when the financial statements are right or wrong. Making sure that operating managers are savvy about financial matters provides an important check and balance to the accounting process. It also encourages both groups to be involved in each other's work and keeps them both on their toes. One tip: It's a good idea to go very easy on this program for the first several months. The idea is to train operating managers, not to beat them up or criticize them.

Make forecasting a management activity

Forecasting profit and loss, balance sheet issues, and cash flow are the primary basis for plan versus actual analysis in many companies. Accounting data do not include forecasts for customer and employee satisfaction (i.e., market share, customer survey indexes, employee turnover, and employee survey indexes). These common omissions are a symptom of relegating the planning responsibility exclusively to accounting. Accounting personnel should be involved in plan preparation and presentation, but management must be the driving force in any planning project.

Remember that a ratio is just a ratio

Ratios, often used to measure profitability, liquidity, solvency, or asset utilization, are not facts; they are only indicators of information relating to the facts. In spite of this shortcoming, operating ratios can be helpful in managing a department or a company, as long as those using them remember that because they are general, they are often imprecise measurements. Liquidity ratios, such as the current ratio (current assets compared to current liabilities), for example, attempt to represent a company's ability to meet its short-term financial obligations. So if current assets equal $1,000,000 and current liabilities equal $500,000, then a current ratio of 2 to 1 would indicate that the

$1,000,000 of assets that will liquidate (turn into cash) in the next 12 months will be sufficient to cover the $500,000 of liabilities that will become due in the next 12 months. In other words, a company with a 2 to 1 current ratio should be able to generate more than enough cash to pay its bills.

This, however, is not always the case. Pending acquisitions requiring additional cash may not be reflected in the financials. An unanticipated increase in revenue may require an unanticipated investment in inventories and receivables to support that revenue growth. In addition, balance sheet timing (representing an end-of-the-month snapshot) may distort perceptions due to the actual daily swing in the numbers. Short-term revolving debt may technically reflect a short-term obligation, when in fact its principal will be renewed year after year. The timing of current assets or current liabilities may be front- or back-loaded within the 12-month time period.

Any of these elements may affect how accurately this liquidity ratio measures and reflects a company's ability to meet its financial obligations. Use ratios, but use them only as general indicators. To validate ratios, look through the numbers with the eyes of a savvy CEO to ascertain the fundamental realities.

Customize reports for their different audiences

It's often up to top management to remind accounting personnel that different audiences need different presentations and information. The IRS requires information in a format that is different from what the SEC requires. Shareholders are interested in share prices, return on investment, current operating performance, and future prospects. Lenders want reports on collateral and cash flow issues. Suppliers want to know if they will be paid in full and on time.

The same financial package cannot be made to serve all internal constituencies either. The board of directors may want an overview while middle managers require down-to-the-dollar detail. Most accountants, unless otherwise directed, will present financial information their way—the CPA way. That may satisfy their friends and associates at the next CPA meeting, but it may miss the target for important audiences. It's up to top management to have in-depth discussions with accounting managers and staff about the many different purposes and uses of information. Face-to-face meetings between them and the various users can be especially useful. The accountants I know seem to enjoy and appreciate the opportunity to get input directly from users, in spite of the fact that they rarely seek this input on their own.

Make financial reports readable

Small print, Rhode Island-sized paper, weird fonts, gray ink, and unclear categories are just some of the things many accountants think are acceptable! They also like to put things alphabetically because it makes their work easier, even if "vacations" may have nothing to do with "vehicle expense." Top management needs to make sure that statements and reports are organized so that the categories are meaningful to those who will be using them. For example, arrange revenue and expense groupings so they are relevant to operating managers, reflect performance, and measure accountability. And if you really want your managers to work with the financials, spend the money to make the reports easy to handle, easy to understand, and easy to read.

Tie the numbers down

There is no worse feeling than finding a huge shortfall or discrepancy between the month-end management reports and the official month-end financial statements. No top manager can make good decisions based on bad information. You should not have to wait for the official financial reports (sometimes as much as two to four weeks after the end of the month) to know how well you are doing. Dependable daily and weekly operating reports increase the timeliness of your feedback and therefore allow you to move sooner on any given issue.

To avoid month-end surprises, tie daily operating reports and management information directly to the company's official financial report information. Sales volume information should be taken directly from invoices to customers. Labor cost data should come directly from payroll processing. The key is to take daily operating numbers directly from source documents, not from documents such as call sheets, production estimates, or procurement manager surveys.

Discipline source documents

Source documents, such as customer billings, supplier invoices, and checks written and received, are the foundation of accounting information. If you as a manager want accurate accounting, you must make sure that those source documents are processed and controlled properly all along the way. Firm procedures that minimize handling and protect the documents are requisite for accurate account coding, proper authorizations, and correct journal entries. They are also the first place to go for answers regarding financial data. Properly processed source documents provide either the answers or the names of the people to talk to for answers.

Integrate the accounting system

A fully integrated accounting system may seem too technical or too trivial for top management's attention, but successful CEOs know that nothing good happens when you cannot trust the numbers. A sales or revenue entry should be input directly from the source document (probably an invoice) and the computer should automatically generate the corresponding receivable. The receivable should only be able to be cleared by a cash receipt (another source document), and the computer should automatically credit cash when there is a receivables-clearing entry. Such a well-integrated system keeps things running smoothly, minimizes the opportunity for mistakes, and makes cheating more difficult. For example, the more automatic and the fewer ways to clear a receivable, the more difficult it is for anyone to pervert the system. Operating or accounting procedures will not take the place of honest people, but having the checks and balances does not hurt in helping people with their honesty.

Make sure numbers reflect reality

Make financial reports reflect reality with respect to timing, division, department, and account. If the financial statement reports that $1,000 in sales travel was incurred by the Colorado Sales Department in December, then that is the exact way it should have happened in real life. If the numbers do not relate to reality, they will not be trusted. When the numbers are not trusted, they can become the source for excuses and false rationalizations. Accounting will reflect reality only when accounting policies are sound, when the accounting system is validated, and when documents, coding, and input are disciplined.

Analyze investments 6 ways

In his book *Drucker on Asia,* Peter Drucker advises all managers to control the numbers by looking at their investments with six key factors in mind:

1. The expected rate of return.
2. The payout period and the investment's expected productive life.
3. The discounted present value of all returns through the productive lifetime of the investment.
4. The risk of not making or deferring the investment.
5. The cost and risk in case of failure.
6. The opportunity cost.

Recently, I advised a CEO of a $42-million-per-year service company who wanted to develop expansion guidelines for his senior management team. We integrated much of Peter Drucker's wisdom into his expansion strategy communication. Following is a synopsis of the CEO's instructions to the team:

- Business expansion is to be based on existing and clearly identified opportunities. No speculative investments.
- Each expansion investment must exceed the cost of capital, generating at least a 20 percent return on investment.
- Each investment involving a new capacity (e.g., new facilities in new territories) must pay back 100 percent of the fixed investment within the term of the contract.
- Less profitable investments will be considered whenever those investments would further strategic defenses. In particular, investments will be made to offset potential threats from competition.
- The cost of failure must not exceed the cost of the initial investment.

- Expansion will be pursued aggressively where it either utilizes existing (fixed) capacity or serves to reduce the overall concentration of business with any one customer. The current goal is to reduce concentration with the largest customer by half within three years.

With the advent of computers, there is no reason to settle for just one or two of the six investment feasibility calculations. Thinking like a CEO means turning the analysis of the numbers into a business decision based on the probability of success and relative contribution of strategic alternatives.

Make the numbers more meaningful—talk with accounting

As a top manager, you can serve your company well by making sure your accounting department is focused on measuring the right issues, not just on measuring issues right. That means working with operating managers to select the measures that are central to driving your business. It is not enough for accounting to measure the costs of jobs; they must also learn to measure the value of the underlying work. Accounting information must be able to influence behavior and help operating managers make the right choices about issues such as outsourcing, the selection of sales distribution channels, products and customers to emphasize, projects to undertake or abandon, managers to promote, or resources to apply.

Use these questions to open a dialogue with your accounting personnel as a first step in making the numbers more meaningful:

- Can all accounting personnel discuss the company's vision of the future and how its specific operating strategy affects their work?
- Can all accounting personnel describe the company's core competencies and the resulting benefits they generate for customers?
- Do accounting personnel understand the information needed by each division or department head to run his or her areas of responsibility?
- Can accounting personnel describe key decisions regularly made by each division or department head?

- What is the primary purpose of accounting's numbers?
- Do our accounting systems and reports show which customers and products are most profitable?
- Does our accounting accurately define our company's cost position within our industry?
- Which operations generate the most cash? Use the most?
- Where are our biggest investments? Are we controlling them effectively?
- How are we using source documents to produce management information reports?
- What specific recommendations has accounting offered to improve the bottom line this year? Do you have others? How can we encourage you to uncover more?
- How could we take advantage of upgraded information technology?
- How is the accounting department's performance measured and how is it doing?

Final Thoughts on the Numbers

Effective CEOs know that good numbers are essential because they:

- Guide management decisions.
- Measure performance.
- Draw attention to both successes and mistakes.
- Reflect reality by offering a window into the operation and its value.
- Provide early warning signals.
- Inspire confidence and trust, just as they can serve as a barrier to theft and expose misuse of funds.
- Present a historical point of reference that is useful for moving ahead and taking risks.
- Meet IRS, CPA, GAAP, and SEC requirements.

When presented correctly, good numbers produced through sound accounting can help managers at every level cope with the complexities of almost any operation. Numbers can, however, also easily distort reality. Revenues can be booked before shipments are made. Operating expenses can be improperly capitalized and contingent liabilities can be ignored. Sales and/or expenses can be shifted to incorrect time periods, deposits can be erroneously booked as revenues, and inappropriate reserves can be created to hide existing or pending problems. CEOs who are savvy about numbers and understand their value and their limits use formal measures such as internal cash controls, physical inventories, fixed asset reconciliations, and external audits together with proper decisions about hiring, separation of duties, checks and balances, verifications, integrated financial statements, and accounting policy safeguards to help defend against distortions.

They also know where to look for signs of trouble. Indicators of potential problems can include a sudden request to change auditors, a major change in accounting policy, fired bookkeepers, out-of-balance cash or operating ratios, shortfalls in inventories, changes in amortization rates, miscoded expenses, catch-all accounts, new account categories, or unexplained changes in amounts capitalized. Diligent CEOs are personally involved in accounting policy, bad debt or inventory write-offs, major adjustments to sales, and monthly financial analysis. They compare current profit and loss, balance sheet, and cash flow numbers with similar statements for last year, with current year-to-date, with last month, and with sales. They know that good numbers do not turn up by accident. Managers at all levels play a role by staying on top of the numbers.

Top management in particular should be able to use accounting numbers as a mechanic would use the readings from a diagnostic machine. Each reading, when accounted for correctly, should have a specific and valid meaning that reflects a fundamental reality. Think like a CEO about the actual fundamental transaction reflected by each number and you will seldom be fooled by "bad numbers." Then you can depend on the numbers to reflect the simple fundamental realities that underlie even the most complex business issues.

Part 3

Cash, Crisis, and Opportunity

Why learn banking, cash management, turnarounds, and acquisitions? Chapters 8 through 11 are about these disciplines of management that absolutely must be learned before taking the post of chief executive. A crisis in any one of these areas will be met with an urgency that will not allow time for on-the-job training. Each of these areas is ruled by the logic of one critical element: *cash*.

These cash-dominated disciplines also affect day-to-day operations of managers at every level. Lessons about the need to make budgets and conserve assets, to accurately assess risks and focus resources, and to negotiate like a pro are important to success in more normal times as well. But when times of crisis and opportunity turn your focus to matters of cash, you will not want to rely entirely on your gut instinct. Mistakes in any of these four disciplines can prove fatal to a company. It pays for every manager to understand them strategically—inside and out. Here, more than anywhere else, *CEO Logic* is critical to survival.

Chapter 8

Banking: Master Their Rules

In finance, everything that is agreeable is unsound and everything that is sound is disagreeable.
—Winston Churchill

Albert Raines*, CEO at Firstline Plastics, Inc., was preparing to visit his fifth bank in five months, attempting to secure a $750,000 receivables line of credit. His business was profitable and growing, so he couldn't understand the four turndowns he had been given. He thought he'd done everything right, but the process seemed confusing. All four of the banks had accepted his multipage application complete with references, and all four took approximately 30 days to reject his request. They didn't seem to pay any attention to his company's profitability or its excellent loan repayment history. He needed the line of credit and was puzzled by the banks' attitudes.

When asked about the reasons he had been given for the four turndowns, Albert said that the first bank told him it did not offer receivables-backed lines of credit; the second bank was concerned about his high (perhaps out of control) growth rate; the third bank said his personal financial statement was weak; and the fourth bank was frightened away by the three previous rejections. I asked Albert to tell me about the form of his previous applications and the content of his interviews with each loan officer. He said that he went to each bank, filled out their forms, and answered their questions about his business and the loan request honestly. Obviously, this approach was not working. But why?

As it turned out, some of the bankers' concerns were actually justified. In particular, much improvement was needed in managing the company's growth. What each bank was looking for was to be assured that the business was sound, that management was in control, and that the loan would be paid as agreed. To accomplish this, we added to his application a new business plan that dealt with the growth issues and we changed the way the loan application was handled. That made a difference with the fifth bank and Albert got the loan for his company..

The first thing a CEO learns about bankers is that they are different from the rest of us in the business world. Their background, their training, their hours, their culture, and their view of business are different from ours. Who but a banker would ask their customers to stand in line, follow strict protocols, and fill out a document perfectly, just so their customers can give them money? If you or I were in that business, we would find a way for our customers to drive by and throw their money at us if they wanted to. We would be the ones following strict protocols and filling out special documents, but that is not the way it is in banking. There's nothing very strategic about dealing with banks, but it does require an understanding of the rules and a knowledge of how banking decisions are made. The rest of this chapter is devoted to an inside look at the logic of how to deal more effectively and efficiently with bankers to get what you want—and give them what they need.

The Brave New World of Banking

This is a new era in banking. Take whatever you thought you knew about the banking "relationship" and throw it out. Follow instead these three "new" rules of banking to understand how your bankers think.

Rule #1: Bankers lend only when they perceive zero risk

To get money from a bank, you must fully answer all potential negatives. When loan officers look at your application, they are looking to screen out all risks. Most loan officers do not have the authority to say yes, but they can say no. A loan officer is encouraged to screen conservatively—and is rewarded for doing so. Look what happens when she makes a loan. If she makes a good loan (one that is paid back on time and in full), she is sometimes given a pat on the back. If she makes a bad loan, she runs the risk of being fired and disgraced. Wouldn't that affect the way you looked at a loan application? Making this decision is not hard, even for a banker!

In the old world of banking, bankers evaluated risk using the "five Cs":

1. **Character**—Can you be trusted? Do you have a history of making payments?
2. **Capacity**—Do you have a way to pay back the loan?
3. **Conditions**—Do you have answers for the "what ifs" about your operation, such as what if there is a downturn in business or what if key members of management leave?
4. **Collateral**—Is there back-up security that could be liquidated if necessary?
5. **Capital**—How much money does the business owner have at risk?

In times past, a loan applicant did not have to satisfy all five criteria to get a loan, but probably needed two or three. Those days are gone. Now, bankers will accept no greater than zero risk. To achieve this end, they ask (and often get) triple assets. They require specific collateral, business tangible net worth, and personal guarantees. If you have $1,000,000 in receivables, a $1,000,000 business tangible net worth, and a $1,000,000 (liquid) personal net worth, they might lend you $800,000. This is their way of achieving what they perceive as "zero" risk. If your receivables go bad, they have the net worth of your business. If the business fails, they have your personal worth. If it were legal for them to take your first born child, they would. Remember that a banker will consider your investments to be assets only to the degree that they can be liquidated. That is the way it is, and that is the system with which you must contend.

As a loan applicant, you must be able to answer the main questions that help them evaluate the risk and how they can avoid it:

- How much money do you want? And what are you going to do with it?
- Why is this loan good for your business?

- Why do you need the bank's money to do it?
- When—and how—will you pay it back?
- What happens if your plans do not work out?

You may, by the way, have heard about "relationship banking," whereby you can build a long-term relationship with your bank and bankers that will make the whole lending process more personal—and easier. Forget it. It is gone. Just as you start to understand the bank, you will probably get a new loan officer, new bank owners, and/or new policies. Rather than depending on one bank for all your cash needs, it's better to build "relationships" with more than one bank in order to defend against this turnover phenomenon. And keep in mind that the bank's concern is to get the loan paid back, not to support your business. To put it bluntly, banks do not make good partners. So if you are looking for a partner, look for someone who shares your concerns.

One twist to building "relationships" with a number of banks is to look for special borrowing opportunities. New loan officers, new bank presidents, and newly reorganized lending institutions often offer unique and favorable lending. Many times these individuals and organizations are anxious to put business on the books. They may not be a source for bad loan risks, but they can provide discounts or approvals for loans that may otherwise be considered marginal risks.

Rule #2: Match funding to the business's operating needs

Many companies have run into trouble because their capitalization did not match their operating needs. A franchise company I know, for example, made several mistakes in its initial and subsequent capitalization. As a startup, they had to grow, but their capital structure did not allow for the investment required to support that growth. As a result, the company was both underfunded and incorrectly funded. It was underfunded because it forced management to sell future franchises in order to pay current expenses. As soon as the business hit a 90-day lull, it was out of money. The business was incorrectly funded because all initial and subsequent funding required short-term servicing. Interest, and sometimes principal, amortization was scheduled monthly and quarterly from the beginning. All of the invested funds demanded immediate servicing. The fact that there was no patient money invested in the company exacerbated the under-funding problem. It is usually difficult to support growth *and* pay significant interest, principal, and dividends. In this case, the better the franchise company did operationally, the worse their cash position became. This was a classic case of a profitable company plagued by constantly running itself out of cash.

Rule #3: Find a lender who offers your kind of money

It's just as important to match the kind of loan you need to an institution that offers financial products that meet your funding parameters. We often hear the term "creative financing," conjuring up financing structure involving senior and subordinated loans, junk bonds, mezzanine lending, or preferred stock with warrants. These things do, of course, exist but they do not constitute creative financing. The match and the fit are where the creativity comes in. You would not go to a Chevy dealership to purchase a Ford and you should not go to an asset-based lender for a cash-flow loan.

When you're looking for that match between your funding needs and a lending institution, consider what specific loan products they offer. Each loan product comes complete with particular rules and guidelines. You may not, for instance, find a residential real estate loan at a business bank or even at a commercial real estate lender. So you can save yourself time and lots of energy by avoiding the obvious "no." Do not waste time applying to lenders who would not say "yes" even if you had perfect credit. Always check in advance of your application to determine the type of lending products offered.

That's the first step, but you can save yourself even more time by going one step further. Give a verbal outline of your business, lending needs, credit history, and collateral to the loan officer before completing a credit application. Check the loan approval process and the lending (loan approval) authority of your loan officer. Ask the question: "If everything I have told you is true, would you make this loan?" If the loan officer cannot answer, see a supervisor. Take this extra step to shorten the loan approval time dramatically and avoid having needless loan rejections appear on your credit report.

And one last word of advice. Become familiar with a banking rating service, such as Veribanc, Inc., P.O. Box 461, Wakefield, MA 01880, (781) 245-8370.

Proposing the Loan

Use a loan proposal to paint a picture of your company for the bank. If you need bank financing, you will need a loan proposal. The loan proposal is the window through which your bank first sees your business. It becomes the foundation of your loan officer's presentation to the bank's loan committee. Use it as a vehicle to demonstrate how your business is fundamentally sound and why the bank should lend you its money. The following outline is offered as a guideline and as a menu of suggestions to consider. Your loan proposal, of course, will need to be customized to your specific lending needs. You may require a shorter version for small loans, more or less emphasis on a particular section, or added or deleted sections. Answering these questions will also help you think through whatever changes in your business you are proposing to fund. The more professional your loan proposal, the better first impression your bank will have of you and your business.

Loan Proposal Outline

1. **The deal—in a nutshell:** Provide a brief description of the amount needed. Describe what you intend to do with the money, why this will be good for the company, how and when you will pay it back, and the collateral available. Include a quick snapshot of your company: annual sales, profits, number of employees, and who owns the company. Describe the business in simple terms and language, i.e., products/services, customers, method of distribution, locations, age of company, and recent trends.
2. **Management—character and capacity:** Detail your organizational structure. List key personnel, their functions, and major areas of contribution. Identify who can run the business in your absence. Include key-man life insurance policies and describe any buy-sell agreement. Provide resumes of all key players. Attach your signed and dated current (within 30 days) personal financial statement. Enclose your personal business income tax returns for three years.

Note: Review your TRW and Dun & Bradstreet credit reports in advance of your loan application. Follow up to correct any inaccuracies.

3. **Description of business and conditions:** Describe your business and industry conditions. Explain why this loan is good for your business at this time.

Describe your product or service:

- How long have you been in business?
- How is the product made and/or purchased?
- What is your market niche?
- What benefits do you sell? Describe all unique product or service features, i.e., patents or trade secrets.
- Which product produces the most sales?
- What have been the most significant changes in your industry and business in the last three years? What changes will take place in your industry during the next several years? How will your company have to change to meet these challenges?
- What distinguishes high-profit companies from low-profit companies in your industry?

Describe your customers:

- Who is a typical customer?
- How do you acquire customers and how many do you have?
- Who are your largest customers?
- Who are your most profitable customers?
- Why do your customers buy from you instead of your competitors?
- Do you give discounts?
- How do you distribute your products to your customers?

Describe your suppliers:

- Who are they?
- Who are your back-ups on essential items?
- What are your suppliers' terms?
- Have you experienced supply shortages? Why?

Describe your competitors:

- Who are your competitors, i.e., name, location(s), size, specialties, strengths, weaknesses, age, profitability, market share, and overall market strategy?
- What is happening to your market share? Why?
- How are you different from your competitors?

Describe your labor/work force:

- How many employees to you have?
- What is your employee turnover rate?
- What major skills are required of your employees?
- Is your work force unionized?

Describe your equipment and facilities:

- What major items of equipment do you use?
- Where are they located?
- Do you own or lease them? On what terms?
- What insurance coverage do you carry?
- What is your current order backlog? What has it been in the past?

Miscellaneous:

- Describe automated accounting procedures.
- Provide details of computer hardware and software.
- Give legal details of company formation (S Corp., C Corp., etc.).

4. **Financials:** Describe why you need the bank's money and how much of *your* money will be at risk.

   - Include a minimum of three years of balance sheets, profit and loss, and cash flow statements in summary format. Provide audited financials if available.
   - Supply interim internal financials (since fiscal year-end).
   - Explain all existing debt in detail, i.e., copies of notes, terms, original amount, name of lending institution, and payment history.
   - Explain any extraordinary items or changes from last year.
   - Highlight owners' investment in the company.
   - Pre-answer all obvious questions in footnotes or addenda.
   - Explain the nature of the financials, i.e., reviewed, compiled, or audited.

   Provide details regarding collateral:

   - Receivable aging and payment history.
   - Background on customers.
   - Receivable write-offs.
   - Credit approval process.
   - Credit safeguards, i.e., letter of credit or deposits.
   - Percent of receivables concentrated on any large customers.
   - Invoicing and collection policies and procedures.
   - Inventory valuation method.
   - Inventory description.
   - Inventory liquidation procedures and timing needed (pre-arrangements are best!).
   - Physical inventory count, frequency and type of audits.

5. **Purpose and amount:** How will the bank's money be used? How much do you want, when do you want it, and what will you do with it?
   - Report and expand on the summary offered in "the deal."
   - Explain the exact purpose for the loan.
   - Show how the loan will increase sales, improve cash flow, or create higher profit.
   - State the loan amount requested and explain how this amount was determined.

6. **Financial projections and repayments:** Tell them how you will pay the loan back, when you will pay it back, and how you will pay if something goes wrong.
   - Indicate which of four ways you will repay the loan:

     a. Another loan.
     b. Liquidating or selling off assets.
     c. Additional equity investment in the company.
     d. Excess cash flow from profitable operations.
   - Back up your loan request with well-reasoned sales forecasts.
   - Provide contingency projections (e.g., 20 percent more sales, 20 percent fewer sales).
   - Projections need to include pro forma balance sheets, profit and loss statements, and cash flow projections for the period of the loan request.
   - Projections should be monthly for the first year and quarterly thereafter. Yearly may be sufficient in the out-years.
   - Be sure to reflect the new interest on the profit and loss projections. Also reflect new asset acquisitions and the corresponding depreciation on the projected balance sheet and profit and loss.
   - Define the bank's risks and offer solutions to them.

- Provide a break-even analysis.
- Document the company's ability to match revenue declines with cuts in expenses.
- Explain any large line item by describing its nature and historical and projected size.
- Explain all changes in ratios.
- Explain how the bank's loan will be impacted by your three projections: most likely, best case, worst case.
- If the worst-case scenario can handle the loan repayment easily, then state this plainly in the narrative.

7. **Loan proposal summary:**
   - One-page loan proposal summary, including the most important points from each section.

Tips for a Successful Loan

Nowhere else in business can your simple intentions become more mired in a complexity of detail than in the world of banking. Let me offer you some experience-tempered suggestions to smooth your way to a successful loan.

Avoid the 7 most common mistakes

1. Failure to communicate clearly your understanding of the key success factors in your business.
2. Projections and financial schedules that do not foot or that contain math errors.
3. Projections that lack common business sense, e.g., that require 80 percent market share or 400 percent increase in sales, require more production capacity than is available, or do not match industry projections.
4. No description of internal financial controls or checks and balances.
5. No identified milestones or targets to serve as checkpoints on your progress towards projections.

6. Inadequate current or historical financials.
7. Misspellings, bad sentence structure, or poor grammar.

The devil is in the details

1. Closely review and personally negotiate all critical issues, such as those relating to default, cross-default, cross-collateralization, time to cure, penalties, personal or corporate guarantees, special fees, interest rate calculations, prepayment issues, compensating balance requirements, and special loan covenants (such as minimum working capital, minimum net worth, percent of receivables/inventories, and reporting requirements). You will also need to negotiate prohibited events such as asset sales, salary restrictions, dividends, and certificates of compliance.
2. As part of paying attention to details, consider all of the possible fees. Interest rates are not the only costs of a loan. Administrative fees, origination charges, appraisal costs, compensating balances, processing tariffs, and early payment penalties are just some potential additional costs. Construct a cost matrix consisting of all monies to be spent acquiring and servicing the loan, then include in this matrix all loan covenants, requirements, and restrictions. Comparative shopping is the only sure way to obtain the best deal for you and your company.
3. Before closing, review draft copies of all loan documents with a lawyer specializing in banking law. Banking law is different, and so are the liabilities and potential hazards that your corporate lawyer may not know well. It's a good idea to use a competing bank's lawyer for this process.

Keep it simple and easy

1. Do not overly complicate the loan proposal by offering or describing complex issues that are not material to your financial position and are not required to get the loan. For example, if you own 100 shares in each of 125 small companies and include this information as part of your financial package, the banker will probably ask you to verify

ownership and explain these investments even if they are not material to your financial position or loan application. Such inessentials can clutter a loan proposal, take excessive administrative time, and slow up the processing of the loan.

2. If your business does not fall into a known category (retail sales, hotel, residential builder, etc.), help your banker out by finding a commonly known business that looks and operates like yours. Fill in the blanks to the statement: "My business is just like...." You can also make your loan officer's job easier—and help speed the approval process—by providing two or three copies of your loan request and walking her through the proposal.

Cash is always king

Have a separate cash flow page explaining the sources and timing of your personal cash flow. This is particularly important when you have multiple sources of cash flow, including salary, dividends, sale of assets, or outside equity investment.

Get off and stay off

Take these 14 tips to stay off personal guarantees:

1. Calculate in advance of negotiations how much it would be worth (to you) to be off of a loan guarantee.
2. Consider a compensating balance.
3. Always ask to get off or stay off of personal guarantees.
4. Ask your banker if everyone signs a personal guarantee.
5. Ask about the circumstances of those who do not sign personal guarantees.
6. Ask what those companies have that you do not in terms of ability to pay back the loan.
7. Work on your answer to the banker's question, "Why don't you want to sign personally—aren't you going to pay back the loan?" (Answers might include, for example, "It will cost me flexibility," "I have a board resolution against signing personally," or best of all, "My other bank does not require one.")

8. Ask that the guarantee be released on a portion of the loan, at a future date after making payments as agreed, when the company net worth exceeds a certain amount, or when the debt coverage ratio, cash flow, or collateral reaches a certain amount.
9. Remember that most personal guarantees are released fully only when changing banks and the release is made a condition of the change to the new bank.
10. Do not give up. Keep asking and keep bargaining to get off the guarantee.
11. Get an indemnification guarantee rather than a joint and several guarantee.
12. Offer collateral instead.
13. Attempt to protect certain assets, such as home or minimum net worth.
14. Replace the debt with equity.

Begin the loan renewal process immediately

1. Set the stage for lower rates, better terms, or a lesser personal guarantee if you achieve certain targets and repay as agreed.
2. Keep the loan officer aware of any material changes in the company or the industry.
3. Keep all promises and meet all covenants.
4. Get to know the senior people at the bank. Get an organization chart from your bank. Update this chart every six months.
5. Get on the bank's mailing list for annual reports and internal newsletters.
6. Refer other good businesses to the bank.
7. Avoid overdrafts.
8. Give the loan officer advance notice of all significant problems.
9. Know your bank and loan officer's lending authority.

Maintaining the Banking "Relationship"

Although long-term bank relationships are dead, short-term relationships are essential. One of the best ways to start a relationship with a bank is through a referral from a good customer. Once you have gotten to know or have received a loan from your bank, the key to maintaining a productive relationship, in addition to making the payments as agreed, is information and communication. The more they know, the more that reduces their sense of risk—and that can be crucial if you need to renew an existing loan or apply for a new or different type of loan. Give your loan officer information on your company, your industry, your banking history, and yourself. Show your banker not just your office, but your products, your factory, your customers' use of your products, and so forth. It is impossible to give bankers too much information for their files. Don't forget to look at your company the way the bank does. Ask the bank for their "analysis of your account" and the "spreadsheet for your account." These are the forms the bank uses to analyze their profit or loss on your account(s).

In communicating with your bank, document your discussions. Letters are better than phone calls when communicating with banks. Keep the bank informed of good news and bad. Bankers hate surprises.

Go to bank receptions, meetings, and the like. Invite your banker to your company Christmas party and/or annual sales or management meetings. Know the names and backgrounds of loan committee members.

It also doesn't hurt to know your bankers personally. The more you know about their outside interests, the better chance you have for building a strong personal relationship with them. Familiarity and common ground are the keys to good relationships. It also pays to go out socially with your banker and her spouse—but make sure all social occasions (dinners, etc.) spent with your banker are purely social. No business questions.

Do your bank favors

The best thing you can do for your bank is to repay the loan as agreed. The second best thing is to refer a good depositor (not a borrower). Loan officers get promoted by the deposits they bring, not the loans they make. Talk and write about deposits when possible.

The best time to raise capital

The best time to raise capital is when rates are low and you do not currently need the money. If you wait until you need money, it is likely that others will be borrowing as well, causing rates to be high.

Final Thoughts on Banking

The best story on "creative financing" I know began when my partner and I decided to build a private jet center on land that we had leased for 30 years. The total cost of the project was approximately $7.7 million. We raised $1.5 million in equity through a private placement. Nothing creative there! The loan, however, proved to be another story.

The basic problem was that we could not locate a lending institution who would loan us $6.2 million for a project on leased land. Finally, my partner located a professional loan broker who, for a fee, taught us about "creative financing." His trick was simple. First, he checked our numbers and projections with his own computer software program. Next, he walked the project site with us and reviewed the specific actions identified in our business plan. Then, he did the "creative" part. He put together a straightforward loan request and proceeded to contact 65 lending institutions (mostly banks and savings and loans).

The results were as follows: 63 unequivocal turndowns, one "maybe," and one interested in doing the deal. We chose the latter. When we asked our loan broker what he would have done if we had received 65 turndowns, he said he would have gotten more "creative," which meant he would have contacted 65 more!

P.S. The loan has been paid as agreed.

Chapter 9

Cash Management: Keep the Lifeblood Flowing

In critical and baffling situations, it is always best to return to first principle and simple action.
—Winston Churchill

David Greenbaum* had been hired by Old West Savings Bank to take charge of a fairly small ($10 million annual revenue) company that was having cash flow problems. Originally founded by the current CEO's grandparents, the company had a strong history of financial performance and, in fact, was still generating profits. But David could see that the company had made some mistakes in managing its cash flow, mistakes that are all too common in small businesses.

As he got into the operation and saw what was going on, David first discovered that the current CEO had used a large amount of cash to buy out another shareholder. This left the company with very little cash reserves. Then top management made an inventory error and overstocked certain items, which further depleted its cash reserves. But management stubbornly would not admit the mistake; they refused to take a loss in order to liquidate the overstocked items. David found that the company could have survived the inventory overstocking error if it had not used so much of its cash in the stock buyback.

Always remember that cash is king. When it comes to cash management, *CEO Logic* means realizing that profits do not matter if you cannot make payroll or pay your bills. Many businesses fail because of poor management. Others fail because of improper capitalization, weak markets, poor expense controls, poor product development, lack of marketing, or even misuse of funds. But it is far more common, even for companies that do everything else right, to fail because they have incorrectly anticipated their cash needs or have improperly managed their incoming and outgoing cash flow.

The Lifeblood of Business

Many senior corporate managers have a very distant relationship with and sketchy understanding of cash and cash flow. They may never have seen a payables check or a night deposit. In a large organization, cash management for a division (even for very large divisions with revenues of $50 million to $250 million) may be handled completely from the corporate headquarters. I have known division general managers and controllers who have never had to worry about money in the bank to cover payroll or the accounts payables run. Money was "automatically" transferred from corporate to a so-called "zero balance account" to cover checks just as they cleared the bank. An increase in inventories or receivables only meant a higher loan balance with corporate, and the worst consequence of a misjudgment in cash needs was a stern letter from the chief financial officer.

Those outside the corporate womb know all too well that their reality is quite different. In the real world, checks can actually bounce, creditors can get upset, and employees can start searching for more stable employment. This chapter's lessons in cash flow were not learned in my years as a corporate warrior; they were pounded into me in the strongest way imaginable during my time as a struggling entrepreneur in an undercapitalized operation. The subject of cash management may not be as interesting as management strategy or as exciting as sales, but it can make the difference in whether your organization lives or dies.

Be careful when and how you grow. Growth in business is more dangerous to cash flow than is a decline in business. Growth in sales is immediately followed by a growth in receivables. Certain types of growth are more costly than others. New products and new markets (territories) often require additional investment in fixed as well as operating assets. Unmanaged growth is a serious threat to a company of any size. Plan your needs and continually measure cash utilization.

Cash flow lessons usually come hard. Miss funding a payroll and good people may leave the company; fail to cover payables and key suppliers may hold critical shipments; fail to pay the bank and you may face foreclosure. When serious negative cash flow hits your company, you will have very little time to react, and no room for error in your reaction. *CEO Logic* dictates that you understand how each operating decision affects cash flow and that you manage cash flow issues proactively. You can increase sales, decrease expenses, and increase profits and still go out of business if cash flow is not managed well. Increases in inventories or receivables have to be funded. Trade payables have to be paid down, and accrued liabilities eventually have to be paid out. Provisions need to be made for new capital expenditures and replacements of plant and equipment. You cannot manage by profit and loss alone. Mastering the balance sheet and cash flow statement is the first step to effective cash flow management. As Benjamin Franklin said, "There are three faithful friends: an old wife, an old dog, and ready money."

Maintain cash flow vigilance. There should be just one person (either a top manager or someone who reports often and directly to a top manager) in charge of measuring, monitoring, and controlling all cash flow issues. Arrange to get frequent—even daily—cash position reports and monthly cash flow projections. Do contingency cash flow plans to determine the potential impact of "what if" projects. When top management is involved personally and paying attention, everyone can see the importance of cash flow. In my organization, when there is a big collection day, we take the receivables people out to lunch. When someone finds a way to improve cash flow, there is always a celebration. This is another one of those times when actions speak louder than words.

Cash Reporting

In monitoring cash flow, there are two critical reports: management cash flow reports and daily cash position reports. With these two tools, you will be well on your way to controlling your cash flow needs.

Management cash flow reports

In monitoring cash flow, there are two critical reports. Management cash flow reports measure the changes in cash. They also distinguish between cash from operating sources and cash from debt and equity sources. They differentiate between operating uses, capital acquisition, and financing (payback) uses. Some accounting cash flow reports list all sources and uses together. The management cash flow report separates these items and matches operating sources and uses before going on to capital items.

A good management cash flow report clearly indicates three issues:

1. How much cash was generated and used by operations?
2. What actions generated this level of cash (where did the cash come from)?
3. Where did this cash go (what was it used for)?

For example, you want a cash flow report to tell you that you started with $10,000 and that you generated cash from operations by earning profits (plus depreciation) of $120,000. This was done while concurrently increasing inventories and receivables by $20,000. This $20,000 increase in inventories and receivables reduced your operating cash to $100,000. Then you used $20,000 of the operating cash to purchase equipment and $75,000 to pay down the revolving loan. Finally, it would show that you ended with $15,000. The explanation in this example is oversimplified in that it does not address all of the sources and uses, but it makes the concept clear.

Management cash flow

10,000	Beginning Cash Balance
120,000	Earnings and depreciation
(20,000)	Build-up of inventories and receivables
100,000	**Cash from operations**
(20,000)	Equipment purchase
(75,000)	Pay back loan
15,000	Ending Cash Balance

How much cash was there to start the period? ***$10,000.*** How much cash was generated? ***$100,000.*** Where did it come from? *Earnings and depreciation minus the inventory and receivable build-up.* What did you do with it? ***$20,000** for equipment and **$75,000** to pay back a loan.* How much cash was there at the end of the period? ***$15,000.*** If your cash flow reports do not provide this information or are confusing to read, change them.

Daily cash position reports

Cash management is the one discipline to manage daily. Arrange to have a cash position report in your hands every working day. This report, at a minimum, will need to indicate:

- Cash received.
- Loan balances.
- Receivables, payables, and inventory (if material to cash flow) levels.
- Payroll.
- Capital expenditures.
- Large checks issued.
- Cash on hand.
- Credit line available.

The example that appears on the next page is one way to present this information.

Forecasting Cash and Credit Needs

A top manager who has a picture of the entire organization and its financial health in mind understands the importance of forecasting cash and credit needs, not just issues of profit and loss. Many companies forecast only revenues, costs, and expenses as a part of their regular planning effort because they follow the logic that the balance sheet is for ownership and the profit and loss statement is for management.

Cash position report

September 5, 1997

Bank Balance Per Bank	100,000
Add: Today's Deposit	23,813
Less: Tonight's Clearings (est. from below)	60,000
Long Term Loan Pay Down	0
Automatic Loan Payments	0
Sub-Total (balance before A/R line activity)	63,813
Add: A/R Loan Draw (if needed)	
Deduct: A/R Loan Pay Down (if available)	50,000
Total Cash Position Tonight	13,813

Working Capital	
A/R Line Balance (this morning)	250,000
Add: Today's Loan Draw	0
Deduct: Today's Loan Pay Down	50,000
Working Capital A/R Line Balance (tonight)	200,000

Working Capital A/R Line Availability	
Accounts Receivable Balance Tonight	3,181,382
A/R Line Limit 80% or 3.0M	2,545,106
Less: A/R Line Tonight	200,000
Unused A/R Line Available	2,345,106
Net Line (if all checks cleared)	2,180,745

Accounts Receivable Balance	3,123,593
Add: Today's Sales	81,602
Deduct: Today's Collection	23,813
Total Accounts Receivable Tonight	3,181,382

Average Weekly Payroll

	Total	# of Checks	Amount Per Check
Jun-97 Avg	$221,543	394	$562
Jul-97 Avg	$222,470	390	$570
08/01/97	$229,308	390	$588
08/08/97	$228,331	399	$572
08/15/97	$235,021	411	$572
08/22/97	$236,708	413	$573
08/29/97	$244,053	412	$592
09/05/97	$235,497	411	$573

Accounts Payable

Checks over $5,000:		Expense	Cap Ex.
08/15/97	SW Fleet Co.	10,000	
	Western Tel.	9,738	
	NW Gas Co.	13,364	
08/22/97	Western Tel.	9,330	
	Martin & Co.	14,317	
	S&R Furniture		51,481
08/29/97	Sunset Fleet	5,947	
	Amtel-Co.	8,758	
09/05/97	Horizon Cellular	15,697	
	NW Gas Co.	13,109	

Outstanding Checks/Clearings Statement:	
Jan-July	12,542
W/E Aug 8	13,889
W/E Aug 15	1,261
W/E Aug 22	24,574
W/E Aug 29	64,401
W/E Sept 5	121,507
Total Outstanding Checks	238,174
Expected Clearings Tonight	60,000
Tomorrow's Cash Balance if all checks clear	(164,361)
A/P due within next 7 days	208,000

To some degree, this is true. The balance sheet does indicate the book value or net worth for owners and the profit and loss statement generally reflects management performance for a given period of time. Management does, however, control several balance sheet accounts. Cash, inventories, receivables, payables, and short-term debt lie primarily in the hands of management and require as much planning and control as do sales, costs, and expenses. Introduce management to the balance sheet and when you become an owner, you will keep more of the money you make.

Use short-term resources for short-term issues

Whenever possible, use short-term money, such as revolving debt or receivable lines of credit, for short-term (operating) needs, and long-term money, such as equity or mortgages, for long-term (capital) needs. Use your short-term debt to fund operations. Growth in sales will no doubt result in a corresponding growth in receivables. The bank will cry foul if you use your operating loans to make capital acquisitions. They expect that you will stay within the spirit as well as the letter of the agreement. This guideline also applies to human and physical resources. Hire temporary help, rent temporary vehicles, and rent temporary space for short-term projects. Avoid the long-term risk of not fully amortizing the assets. Do this even if the high cost of short-term resources lowers your short-term margins.

The ins and outs of credit and collection

Credit extension, billing procedures, and receivables collections are obvious places to begin cash flow management. The operational side of an effective cash management system begins in these areas. Procedures need to be established and disciplined, people need to be trained, and results need to be measured and monitored. Each individual involved in these functions will contribute more by having complete knowledge of the entire process as well as by knowing what part he plays in ensuring proper cash management. The performance of these individuals will also be greatly improved by their understanding the overall importance and potential consequences of managing cash. The items below will start you down the path toward professional cash management.

Credit collection starts with credit extension. Sometimes managers in highly sales-oriented companies tend to cut corners when establishing terms and payment guidelines with new customers. They may also be tempted to shortcut or slight the credit analysis step. They are using credit extension—as most companies do—as a sales tool. (In fact, companies would demand cash up front if it would not hurt sales.) Credit, however, can easily get out of hand if the sales department is managing or influencing it too vigorously.

Top management, being in charge of the big picture, including cash flow, must set firm credit guidelines independently of sales. Payment terms must be confirmed by the time of the first billing, or better yet, before the first sale is made. Then accounting can gently but persistently enforce the terms, according to the overall guidelines.

Slow billing means slow collection. How you send out invoices makes a big difference in how you get back payments. What happens to your billing operation during vacation? What happens on sick days? What happens during personnel transitions? If nothing happens, remember this maxim: A company cannot collect the money if it doesn't mail out the invoices. Too many times, an accounting team will put together a great billing strategy and then fall down on execution, mainly because they are not as good at managing as they are at crunching numbers. By creating independent checks and balances, top management can verify that billing is accurate and timely and that the system is running well. Bookkeepers must be advised that the billing job is not done until accurate invoices with the right backup are in the hands of the customer.

Learn your customer's payables rules. Most customers, like your company, have detailed procedures for processing payables checks. Sometimes they require special proof of delivery. Sometimes they require prior field office approval. Some need purchase order numbers and some must receive the invoice by a certain cut-off date. If those procedures and prerequisites aren't followed, their payments to your company may be slowed or delayed. We once discovered a major customer that did not age invoices with amounts under $2,000. Our response to this news was just what you might expect—many $1,900 invoices.

Measure receivables to control cash flow. There are four basic ways to measure receivables:

1. Largest to smallest.
2. Current, 30-, 60-, 90-day aging.
3. Number of days' sales in receivables.
4. Degree of credit risk.

The reason for analyzing receivables is to uncover potential late-pay problems, expose administrative difficulties (such as lost invoices or incorrect backup), and measure the quality (meaning the likelihood of payment) of a receivable as well as the quantity of money due. Each measurement category implies a different set of management responses. Largest to smallest tells you where to start first. The aging raises the flag that a problem may exist with a particular account or invoice. The number of days' sales in receivables measurement tells you if your overall collection efficiency is improving or declining, and the degree of risk evaluation will indicate accounts that require special attention.

Understand the driving force behind no/slow payment patterns. All your receivables problems can be placed in one of three categories:

1. *Should not pay* because the product or billing was not right.
2. *Cannot pay* because the customers do not have the money.
3. *Will not pay* because the customers are attempting to be "shrewd" or perhaps even unethical.

It is clear what to do about the "should not pays." Fix the problem and apologize for the inconvenience. For the "cannot pays," attempt to improve your collateral and try to extract a partial payment and a payment plan. The "will not pays" require accelerating personal contact. Anticipate their antics and move proactively to block them. Do not allow them to use standard excuses. For lost invoices, fax new ones. For improper backup, verify requirements before invoicing. Document all of your actions and let them know in a nice way that you have played this game before and you are ready.

Buy and Sell Only What You Need

One of the surest ways to get into cash flow problems is to buy more than you need. Inventories need to be large enough to avoid production problems, to get the best purchasing discounts, and to insure shipping efficiencies. But they also need to be small enough to maximize inventory turns so that your company can minimize cash investment and carrying costs (such as interest on the money; material handling expenses; cost of storage facilities, theft, damage, or obsolescence). As a rule, it makes sense to tend toward tighter or smaller inventories. There always seem to be more hidden carrying costs with large inventories than can readily be identified, while the consequences of a too small inventory will be all too obvious.

Sell off what you don't need

Do not wait, turn it into cash now. It is generally a good idea to dispose of excess assets. Sell off these items on an "as soon as practical" basis. Unless you are being paid to be in the storage business or there is no current market for this stuff, move out excess assets. There are hidden costs to keeping these items around and they will usually never be worth more than they are today. The 15 percent restocking charge to send back excess raw materials or supplies, for example, may be the cheapest way out.

Watch the Details

CEO Logic dictates that managers be responsible for many details, as well as the strategic or general issues of business. Cash flow management details are among the more important of these. Keep your eye on the following operational details—each with the capacity to affect cash flow.

Print checks when they are needed

Printing checks before they're needed understates payables and increases the risk of early mailing, which can have a severe effect on cash. Sometimes bookkeepers and accountants will want to print checks before they need to be mailed because cash is tight and they want to be ready to respond immediately to pressure from creditors or merely as a matter of convenience. Before computerized accounting, printing checks early did not matter as much, but with today's systems, open payables are relieved at the instant the check is cut. This is a poor practice and should be avoided.

Have the CEO sign the checks

There's nothing like signing the checks to give a CEO a clear sense of where the cash is going, even in a very large organization. In cases where that is not practical, limit the number of check signers and personally communicate (verbally and in writing) the check-signing criteria. Do occasional random spot checks.

Signatures all mean something

Many individuals in a company are required to sign various documents verifying certain information. Many of these signatures are prerequisites to spending money. As such, they can have a significant impact on cash. Receivers or packing slips are signed by the person accepting the goods. His signature means that the count is correct, there is no apparent damage, and the item is the one that was ordered. The main issue, of course, is proof of delivery.

Those authorized to make purchases sign to reflect their assurance that the purchase is within their authority, the price is fair, the quantity is accurate, and the quality is what is expected.

Payables people and sometimes managers sign invoices to verify proof of delivery and authorization. They are also certifying that the math is correct, the discounts are taken, and the money to cover the check is available. Signatures on invoices are actually requests for checks to be cut.

Checks signed by the CEO or his designate indicate that all backup documents (receiver, purchase order, and invoice) are in order. It also signifies that the purchase is a normal, ordinary, and valid business expenditure. This signature means it is all right to send out the check.

Inform each person involved of the purpose and meaning of his signature as it relates to cash management and the overall success of the company. In addition to issuing this information in writing, many people like to use ink stamps, which give brief indications of the same data on each document, and act as a reminder of and prompt to important responsibilities.

Deposit money every night

Even when deposits are small, the deposit runner is out sick, or there aren't deposit slips, make sure the money gets in the bank every night. Money is always important, even small amounts of money—and everyone needs to understand and act on that principle. It's up to top management to create an organization where cash is treated with care and discipline and never taken for granted. The CEO doesn't have to make the deposit, but he must make sure that those who are responsible for the deposits take their roles seriously.

Make the payables public

On a random basis, invite the payables person, the controller, the purchasing agent, the production manager, and even the sales manager to review and approve the signing of payables checks. In a roundtable format, start by selecting a portion of the current payables run. Make sure that each check has all of the backup documentation attached. Then discuss with everyone present the issues of quantity, quality, cost, and necessity represented by each invoice. It is amazing how often the people running a company are "introduced" to new information at these roundtable payables meetings!

Final Thoughts on Cash Management

The most effective CEOs know that cash flow requires management and see it as a separate discipline of business that requires its own strategy and action plans. Many organizations, especially small ones, generate detailed plans for future revenues, expenses, and profits but leave future cash flow to chance. Often the cash flow report (if any) is relegated to the annual banking package and remains subject only to the whims of the accountants. That can lead to trouble, because many accountants know everything there is to know about debits and credits in the general ledger but can lack even the basics on cash management.

I once hired a controller who seemed to have all the right experience and credentials. He had attained both a CPA and an MBA. He had worked in similar businesses and for a CPA firm. He passed our accounting test with flying colors. However, it was only a matter of weeks until he ran us out of money and nearly put us out of business. He had never worked in an organization that was tight on cash and he had no concept of cash flow. He printed and mailed the checks regardless of cash availability. If it was not for emergency loans, the business would have failed. The lesson learned was that cash requires top management oversight—it's not something to be left to chance.

Too often, businesses fail to determine their operating and capital costs of expansion. They do this in spite of the fact that both internal and external growth uses cash. External expansion costs are usually addressed because of the obvious need for acquisition financing to fund it. Internal expansion costs may be less well-managed despite the need to fund the growth in inventories, receivables, and fixed assets.

Within the discipline of cash management, there are several sub-disciplines:

- Crodit colloction.
- Credit extension.
- Trade payables management.
- Payroll administration.
- Tax management.
- Capital budgeting for equipment and real estate.
- Inventory management for raw materials, in-process materials, and/or finished goods.
- Banking.
- Excess cash investment.
- Operations budgeting.
- Theft protection.
- Currency management.
- Acquisition financing.
- Cash flow forecasting.

Each area of cash flow offers separate opportunities and threats. Whether the issue is inflow or outflow, debt or equity, short-term or long-range, each demands responsible and professional management. Top management must analyze the company's capacity to manage each of these concerns, because mismanagement of any one of them can take an organization down.

Chapter 10

Tough Times and Turnarounds: Match the Cure to the Illness

Nothing in life is so exhilarating as to be shot at without result.
—Winston Churchill

Stratford Real Estate (SRE) was in trouble—and Bert Wheeler*, the CEO, knew it. His sometimes flamboyant, personable, and tough-minded deal-maker approach to business seemed to have misfired as times had changed in the real estate development market. He had always been a fierce competitor, at times inflexible, totally focused on his own self-interests, and highly litigious whenever a dispute arose. Those traits had carried him successfully through many tough battles during his career in the commercial real estate development business. But times and the marketplace had changed, and Bert's tough and tenacious (some might say ruthless) negotiating skills no longer applied. His ability to outmaneuver, out-threaten, out-accuse, and outlast his opponents helped with his past-due loans but didn't do a thing to increase his cash flow. Bert called on an outside consultant, Walter Kellerman*, to advise him on a turnaround.

When he looked into SRE's financial position, Walter saw that the company had been living off development (construction management) fees provided by the individual project lenders that each development partnership later capitalized into the total cost of their respective projects. The cash flow problem came to the forefront when the development market slowed down. Timing gaps in projects under development soon became timing gaps in development fees normally paid as the projects progressed, which, of course, negatively and severely impacted SRE's cash flow.

Walter's further analysis revealed a reasonably qualified development staff, but both his shopping center and office building leasing staffs and the property management company hired to run his hotels were all barely adequate. In addition, SRE's bookkeeping was neither accurate nor timely.

With Walter's guidance, SRE developed a turnaround plan that began by getting control of the cash and credit and ended with structural reorganization and other measures to help the company weather the crisis and return to financial health. Specifically, the plan included:

- Negotiation of an orderly (and nonlitigious) restructuring of the loans for the troubled shopping centers and office buildings. This included a negotiated "give-back" of some properties under terms highly favorable to SRE.
- Formation of a hotel management company to operate the hotels and generate substantial monthly cash flow to SRE.
- Reorganization of the shopping center and office building operations to concentrate on generating, evaluating, and closing potential tenant leases for each property.
- Investment in dramatically upgraded accounting hardware, software, and personnel.
- Restructuring of the hotel management contracts to compensate SRE for its accounting and management information system upgrades.
- Hiring of a hotel management professional skilled in managing SRE's type and volume of hotel properties.
- Upgrading of hotel general managers.
- Set-up of management information systems that allowed each property/investment to be monitored and measured individually.

These steps allowed Bert and SRE to get out from under the substantial personal and corporate threats of foreclosures. Further, dependable monthly cash flow (money received irrespective of the number of projects under development) was generated to SRE through its new hotel property management division. The new property management teams were able to improve substantially the net operating income of each property.

10 Steps to Turning Trouble Around

Tales of tough times and turnarounds abound in today's business news. The press makes heroes out of people like Jack Welch at GE, Al Dunlap at Scott Paper, and Lou Gerstner at IBM who have waded into large companies in serious trouble and turned them around. We consider them heroes because they overcame what seemed like overwhelming and insurmountable problems. But as the Stratford Real Estate story illustrates, turnaround, even from a dire situation, is possible in any case if those involved are able to recognize the problem, accurately analyze the source causes, develop effective strategies, and are willing to take the strong medicine that will effect the cure. Tough times often call for extraordinary measures; how extraordinary is determined by the degree of organizational difficulty.

Every turnaround has its own set of distinctive problems and opportunities. Therefore, each will need strategies and action plans customized to its own unique circumstances. There are, however, certain essentials common to most, if not all, turnarounds. Following are 10 critical steps you will want to consider if and when you find yourself and your company in extraordinarily tough times.

Step 1: Recognize the seriousness of the problem. Many turnarounds fail because the depth of the trouble was underestimated or the seriousness of the problem was determined too late.

Bert Wheeler could see that he was in serious trouble—and that his tried and true ways of operating weren't going to work this time.

Step 2: Take a realistic look at your ability to survive. Every company must have an economic reason for the business to exist. And it must have access to cash and/or credit to make it through the crisis. Those ingredients must be in place to support a turnaround. No valid purpose, no financing—no turnaround.

SRE's markets were sound. The elimination of bad loans, the reduction in expenses, and the creation of management fees addressed the cash and credit issues.

Step 3: Stem the losses. Maximize current revenues, minimize current expenses, and focus everyone on the core opportunities.

SRE found ways through restructuring to get more revenue out of its property and hotel management businesses and reduce its debt. And Bert brought in Walter Kellerman as a professional resource to help analyze the situation and find ways to compensate for operational shortfalls.

Step 4: Get control of all resources, especially cash. Put cash and credit immediately under tight management. Develop a separate and individual strategy for each major resource (physical, financial, human, and intangible). Prioritize.

SRE immediately worked on upgrading its accounting operations and personnel. The company also increased cash flow by establishing a hotel property management division and restructuring the management contracts.

Step 5: Stabilize the organization. Make major changes and cutbacks as soon as is practical, then calm everyone down.

SRE made quick and decisive changes in accounting personnel, office and shopping center leasing staff, and hotel management.

Step 6: Determine the source of the decline. Analyze and identify the root causes of your problems.

SRE jettisoned investments and properties that could not be turned around in an orderly and nonlitigious fashion, so that it could concentrate on its core profitable businesses.

Step 7: Design a fix. Determine a broad course of action and communicate it to everyone.

Besides the structural and organizational changes it adopted, SRE also upgraded by investing in hotel professionals and accounting that reflected and supported its core opportunities.

Step 8: Recapitalize. Restructure debt and equity to meet the future needs of the organization.

By working with its lenders, SRE was able to arrange "give-backs" that served both parties. Eventually, SRE was put in position to recapitalize the company.

Step 9: Make profit. At this point of the turnaround, it is time to add profits to cash flow. Short-term financial health may be based on cash flow, but long-term viability requires profits.

SRE, with its new managers, new accounting, divested losers, and recapitalized balance sheet was now in a position to generate both profits and cash flow.

Step 10: Reposition the company for success. Reshape the business to ensure a sustainable competitive edge.

SRE's restructuring took it out of troubled times and got it ready for a much more prosperous future.

These 10 steps reflect a disciplined, structured way of thinking about tough times that can address any combination of threats to an organization's viability: impending property foreclosures, unpaid and unsatisfied creditors, inability to make payroll, loss of major customers, inability to obtain credit, major warranty or contract liability, new government regulations, or especially damaging new competition. The 10 steps to turnaround are practical and logical ways of seeing the big picture and analyzing what must be done—steps that can take an organization out of panic and chaos into recovery. When everyone else is clucking that the sky is falling, it's up to top management, armed with the lessons learned from *CEO Logic*, to take charge and figure out what the true problem is and what medicine is needed to cure the illness.

At such times, survival may supersede other more traditional goals. Cash flow will often become more important than profits, and pricing for margin may be necessary in spite of its impact on market share. Management in a troubled company may need to be more decisive, more dictatorial, and less tolerant of weak performance than in more normal times. Management must take greater care and pay more attention to planning in the company's relationships with bankers and trade creditors. Everything must be measured and managed on shorter time intervals. Risk must be minimized; growth and earnings must be de-emphasized; and proven winners must be chosen while proven losers must be abandoned. And in these times of great trouble, if a change in management approach cannot be accomplished, then a change in leadership and/or management may be necessary.

The thoughts and perspectives that follow might be viewed as a menu of philosophies, strategies, and tactics that enhance the 10 steps to turnaround and that leaders can choose from however and whenever they might be needed.

Control All Cash, Absolutely and Immediately

Control of cash—both incoming and outgoing cash as well as leases and other credit instruments—is the first rule of management in tough times. If possible, the CEO should sign all checks personally and place tight controls on all cash commitments, e.g., leases, service contracts, long-term purchase obligations, and the like. As the lifeblood of the organization, it's possible that you may have been hemorrhaging cash; if that keeps up, the company will literally bleed to death.

You can live without increased sales, you can survive without profits, but you cannot make it without cash. No turnaround will be managed without adequate cash and credit to finance the operation. Protecting cash means doing whatever it takes: selling off excess assets, reducing inventories, collecting past-due receivables, divesting losing or marginal divisions, reducing compensation, downsizing the work force, borrowing more money, or getting additional equity investors. If you do not find the cash you need, there will be no time or opportunity to go on to other turnaround strategies.

Tighten up review schedules

Part of controlling cash is close monitoring of both sources and uses. You may need to hold daily sales and cash flow meetings and have weekly reviews of strategy and biweekly meetings with suppliers and bankers. Because of the nature of the risk, it may also be advisable to shorten the time frame for project reviews. In tough times, top managers cannot afford to look at cash flow once or twice a month; they may need to look at cash flow once or twice a day. The time frame depends on the level of risk the organization is facing. Setting daily goals and holding everyone to them is needed to generate a sense of urgency at every level of the business. Everyone needs to think of the company as if it were a patient in a hospital. Different sets of monitoring and supervision are needed for intensive care patients than for patients who are only in for evaluation.

Bring in your own controller

As a top manager, you must have absolute control over the money and absolute confidence in the numbers. Bringing in a new controller whom you know well and have worked with before can give you that control and confidence. Whether you are new to an organization or have been at the helm for a long time, you will not make good decisions with bad information. When problems are severe, there's no room to take a chance on faulty accounting or weak cash controls. If it seems that such a change would be too disruptive or that your present financial help is performing well, an outside auditor can render a helpful opinion. You and your staff may be too close to the details to make a fair and independent evaluation. It's also possible that existing top management is part of the problem.

Make the banks and creditors owners

In very troubled companies, the banks and creditors are already "owners" but they may not know it. Convince them that the company's interests and theirs are the same. Show why your turnaround plan is better than any other option they may be considering. If top managers are proactive rather than reactive, they can prevent banks or creditors from taking matters into their own hands. When bankers or creditors are uninformed or they lose confidence in management, either can be easily frightened into making bad decisions. Keep them all overinformed and remember to keep their interests in mind when developing your plan. Once banks and creditors are persuaded that your plan to improve your operations also provides their best opportunity to receive their funds, they will act like partners instead of adversaries. And that will give the organization access to resources that might not otherwise be available.

Strategic Leadership in Tough Times

Leadership must provide the energy as well as the analysis and action plans. Stabilizing a chaotic situation has as much to do with confidence, decisiveness, and powers of persuasion as it does strategy and access to key resources. Effective turnarounds require equal parts of management and leadership. At certain times, management thought and action drive results. At other times, strong and enthusiastic leadership is the only effective medicine. The following thoughts can help you determine when and how to present a leadership image that will inspire loyalty, willingness to engage difficult issues, and trust.

Take charge with authority and confidence

Tough times make it essential to manage and lead with strength and savvy. Top managers are responsible for assessing the risks, evaluating the threats and opportunities, making decisions, and then going forward with conviction. Bankers, employees, suppliers, and customers all look to the CEO for leadership. Weak or indecisive actions can be severely damaging (if not fatal) at any stage of the turnaround.

Decisive actions at the top must be mirrored throughout the organization. One way to make that happen is to issue immediate orders that show everyone that a new day has come, that will grab their attention and focus them on the new targets. You might institute a hiring freeze, require CEO approval of all capital expenditures or CEO signature on all checks, cut back on travel, eliminate temporary help, reduce supplies, or eliminate departmental spending authorities. Many of these actions are more symbolic than substantive, but the idea is to communicate an immediate change in direction. One caution, however: Be careful about using the much publicized "sacrificial lamb" approach. In troubled companies, it is usually not necessary to look for scapegoats. Balance the need to shock the system with the need to maintain a motivated work force. Terminate someone only if it is absolutely necessary, i.e., because they have stepped out of line, they have refused to support the plan, or the company just cannot afford them.

Take only one big hit

Write-offs, reserves, and staff cutbacks are often necessary, but avoid the death of a thousand cuts. Initial moves must be bold enough to carry the organization through the turnaround. Bankers, creditors, employees, and shareholders can understand and deal with one big cut much better than they can contend with many small cuts. Employees, for example, will operate more effectively if they feel they survived the one big cutback and are assured that those who survived the cut are safe.

Keep the focus on strategic thinking

During a turnaround, your sustained focus on strategic thinking as well as specific remedies will make all the difference in the company's recovery. Keep in mind these few principles:

Emphasize your core business if it offers the core opportunity. Some call this keeping your eye on the ball or getting back to basics. In most companies, there are one or two elements of business that are central to the success of the enterprise. Focus as many resources as possible on the problem or the opportunity that will have the greatest impact on the turnaround. If you're thinking like a CEO and concentrating on the big picture, you can come back to other smaller issues when day-to-day survival is not at stake.

Pick your poison and run with it. Most turnaround strategies are based on asset liquidation, cost reduction, and/or increased revenues. Whether you plan to sell the business, merge with a larger organization, divest a division, make current operations more productive, make an acquisition, enter new markets, offer new products, sell off assets, or liquidate the company, make sure everyone is aware of the plan and singing from the same hymnal. The CEO has the primary responsibility to establish and communicate the direction and to keep everyone focused on the target.

Plug the hole first. The first step in resolving a big backlog of problems is to stabilize the backlog. Forget "first in" and "first out" strategies. Those customers currently in the backlog are already upset or disappointed. Take care of the next customer who comes through the door. Do not let the backlog grow. This way, each time you solve a problem, the backlog gets smaller.

Find the small victories. In really tough times, top management must help give the organization a reason to continue on. Looking for interim victories is a useful strategy. For example, focus salespeople's incentives on the activities that will lead to closing sales, not just on the final act of closing. Pay small amounts for leads, appointments, presentations, quotations, and offers. Let the sales force feel good about successfully completing each of these interim steps. Positive attitudes are the foundation needed to survive a downturn and to rebuild a business.

Becoming a turnaround hero

The idea of accepting a CEO turnaround position with its high compensation, increased power, and elevated visibility may seem inviting, but in order to succeed, the elements must be in place to keep it from becoming a "widow-maker" assignment. To achieve an ethical, legal, and economic turnaround, three elements must be present:

1. There must be a willingness to let the CEO control the business.
2. There must be enough cash and credit available to support the turnaround effort.
3. There must be an economic reason for the business to exist.

Turnaround leaders come in many forms

We often picture turnaround leaders the way many picture great salespeople, as bold, brassy, dynamic speakers made in the image of Lee Iacocca. But strong leaders and great salespeople come in many packages. The key to their success lies in the use of their special talents and skills, not in their ability to imitate an Iacocca. Jake Thomas*, successful CEO of a $300 million commodities distribution business, is a good example of an extremely effective leader cut from a different mold.

No one would describe Jake as bold or brassy. His description would include words like intelligent, meticulous, tenacious, perceptive, fair-minded, honest, and successful. He is always a gentleman and rarely raises his voice. I know of no person in the world with greater integrity than Jake. His education includes a Wharton MBA, and as you might suspect, he is a great thinker.

Jake has a conservative operating philosophy and is extremely thoughtful and cautious with key business relationships. I have no doubt that suppliers, customers, bankers, and key managers all value his professional approach to business. He is a quietly compassionate man who cares a great deal about society and his community. He has an abiding desire to do the right thing. His style is to take calculated risks but to avoid mistakes. He is a prudent buyer but a bold investor in projects he believes to be viable.

One of his greatest attributes is his ability to recognize and handle a crisis. He is alert and aware of potential problems and has the ability to focus immediately on the critical issue at hand. Proper resources are applied to the situation, and mistakes (if any) are quickly corrected. Jake has the capacity to remain calm and think clearly when others may be losing control. Throughout any ordeal, you can expect Jake to act decisively but with a proper degree of caution. Agreements will be thoroughly documented and both sides will fully understand the terms of the negotiation. He operates with humility and extreme respect for others. He manages his worldwide business in a fashion that keeps him out of turnaround situations. His business is successful, so Jake will probably never wear the turnaround label. He may not look like the so-called "classic" turnaround leader, but he is the kind of leader that I would want in a crisis.

Final Thoughts on Tough Times and Turnarounds

Tough times and turnarounds demand new strategies. Using *CEO Logic* to manage these difficult circumstances often means focusing on short-term emergency measures and forestalling long-term strategic objectives. The following story tells the first half of a turnaround. The jury is still out on the second half.

Dynamic Technology* was getting pressure from its bank to liquidate (pay off) its loans. It had not missed any loan payments but was in violation of several loan covenants, including minimum net worth, minimum current ratio, and minimum debt coverage ratio. When the new CEO, Andrew Worth*, came on board, he saw that Dynamic's problems stemmed from a customer's bankruptcy. Too much of Dynamic's business had been concentrated in that single account, which took Chapter 11 when its top management stole substantial sums of money from the company about 18 months earlier. At this point Dynamic had still not fully replaced the lost business and was now facing an additional threat from another large customer that was starting to look shaky.

The previous CEO, who was owner and operator of the business, had made some additional mistakes, such as changing the salesforce compensation from straight commission to salary only, which resulted in lower sales. Apart from this and a few other missteps, the business was operated efficiently. Andrew at first thought that he could satisfy the bank by taking on a partner with new capital. On further reflection, however, he saw that it was unlikely that he would find a partner to invest in a Sub-Chapter S business with negative net worth that was losing money (and customers). The same problem existed in trying to find a buyer for the whole business.

Andrew's eventual solution was radical but necessary. Because Dynamic's sales were comprised of two major product line offerings, split about 60/40, he decided to look for a strategic buyer for the 60 percent product line. By finding a buyer in a related business who would not have to add fixed overhead to take on this product, Dynamic could price the product line according to the positive effect its margins would have on the acquiring company. By focusing on the marginal contribution to a strategic buyer, he could avoid the issues of overall business losses and negative net worth.

Andrew's radical strategy worked. Dynamic sold the product line to a strategic buyer for enough money to pay off the bank and fund a turnaround. The other half of the turnaround will occur when Dynamic builds up the former 40 percent product line and replaces the 60 percent product line that was sold.

The lessons learned from this story are twofold. First, it's always a risk to concentrate too much business in one account. Second, sometimes the pieces are worth more than the whole. It took CEO logic for Andrew to recognize the seriousness of the situation and CEO creativity for him to find and implement a strategy to solve the crisis. Andrew's solution saved Dynamic from a seemingly intractable circumstance and put the company in a position to rebuild its future.

Chapter 11

Acquisitions: Don't Buy It If You Can't Improve It

The process of the creation of new wealth is beneficial to the whole community.
—Winston Churchill

Tomeco Enterprises*, a $35 million company that sells consumer items to pharmacies and discount stores, was losing sales, money, and market share. Revenues and profits had been decreasing for nearly two years, and the owners had just fired all of top management except the chief financial officer. The company's revenues peaked just three years earlier at about $70 million with pretax profits of $10 million. So what happened to this formerly successful company?

Tomeco's attempt to buy another company caused management to completely take their eyes off the ball. The CEO and his management team developed an acquisition strategy, researched potential target companies, met with each target's executives, determined prices, arranged financing, and made offers. The more they chased the acquisition, the less they managed their own business. Eventually, Tomeco did make a small ($4 million per year) acquisition, but by this time, its core business was failing. Tomeco learned that all potential opportunities bring risk, and acquisition opportunities bring more than their share.

Acquisitions bring opportunity and risk together in a way that generates great excitement. No other factor in business produces more energy and enthusiasm than the potential of buying a company. And no other event has the potential to be so distracting to management. Distraction from everyday management issues, however, is certainly not the only, or even the primary, risk related to the acquisition process. Even when separate nonoperating resources are used for acquisitions, it is still possible to handle an acquisition poorly. Managing acquisitions is clearly a separate discipline from all other operating responsibilities, requiring its own special knowledge, skill, and talents. Following are thoughts offered to guide you through the exciting and often treacherous world of acquisitions.

To Acquire or Not to Acquire?

The average acquisition manual contains about 150,000 words, or 500 pages, of detailed information regarding all aspects of the buying process. If you hire the right help, you will not need most of this information. But *CEO Logic* dictates that you, as a top manager, do have to think strategically about how acquisitions in general (as a strategic move) and in their specifics (as a particular target is identified) fit into your overall business. Thinking this way involves a number of crucial decisions that only you and a critical few in your organization can make:

- How important is it for us to expand?
- Would it be reasonable to attain the same benefit through internal development?
- What are our acquisition objectives?
- How defendable (hard-to-copy) are the core competencies of the firm targeted for acquisition? How does it leverage its core competencies into unique or distinctive customer benefits?
- What is the threat of outside competition?
- How will our existing competition respond?
- What are we really buying—key people, product lines, access to special processes or resources, customer base, etc.?
- Is the price right? How will the final price affect return?
- Can our planned improvements really be made? Will we have human, physical, financial, and technological resources to achieve our postacquisition goals?

- Can our current management team work with the new people in the target organization?
- Will there be adequate overall management with proper incentives to perform?
- Have we clearly defined our postacquisition expectations?

These questions are vital to your acquisition's strategies and decisions. The following sections provide insight and criteria to help you think clearly about these matters.

Grow from Within or Acquire from Outside?

The first decision that has to be made is highly strategic. Time, cost, risk, availability of target companies, financing alternatives, capacity to manage, and strategic fit will drive the decision about whether to expand through internal development or through external acquisition. Does your company possess the financial capacity and the know-how to build a new company from scratch? If so, how much would it cost to start and operate a new business compared to the cost of acquiring a similar operation? Are there willing and affordable acquisition candidates available? How much longer would it take to develop internally than to acquire externally?

Bob* and Jason Hendricks* owned and operated Medihelp Incorporated, a 524-person temporary help company that provided manpower and other services to hospitals and doctors. Bob was the recruiter and Jason handled outside sales. The company started as a six-person organization and grew steadily for nine and a half years. Both Bob and Jason sensed the need for dramatic growth in order to compete with their much larger competition. At the company's then current size, it could not afford to make the investments in technology or senior management required to keep competitive.

There were three main factors driving their decision to acquire rather than to develop internally. The first was their need to grow by at least a factor of 10 to be competitive. This was not possible to accomplish internally within a practical time frame. Second, several other companies Medihelp's size or slightly larger were facing the same pressures, which might make them available for merger or acquisition. Third, each potential acquisition candidate had a strong foothold with customers inside its respective geographic regions.

It became clear to Bob and Jason, as well as to many of their similarly-sized competitors, that they needed to combine their resources to enable them to compete with the four large national industry leaders. Medihelp correctly analyzed its internal versus external growth alternatives and completed its industry roll-up by acquiring several of its competitors.

Thinking About the Acquisition Process

Define your goals and develop a plan before you get started. *Planning without action may just be dreaming, but action without planning can do real damage.* After making the decision to acquire, there are several steps to take.

1. Develop a formal acquisition plan with specific objectives:
   - Company size.
   - Geographic location of targets.
   - Type of business (industry).
   - Type of products/services.
   - Incumbent management requirement (are you requiring that existing management be both strong and willing to stay on?).
   - Required minimum earnings and cash flow.
   - Turnarounds (troubled companies) considered or not.
2. Develop a buyer's package (information which establishes your credibility as a buyer). Give specifics on your company personnel, past transactions, amount and source of funds, and major affiliations.
3. Identify specific potential target companies by name, size, year founded, locations, products, and markets served.
4. Verify (screen) target list.
5. Deal only with dedicated sellers.
6. Contact targets.

7. Conduct a preliminary evaluation of acquisition feasibility.
8. Request minimum information from target (i.e., historical financials, resumes of key managers, and information regarding transactions with large customers).
9. Attempt to get exclusive negotiating rights.
10. Look for one-time salable items, such as property or equipment not used in daily operations.
11. Determine maximum price and terms.
12. Negotiate price, terms, and deal structure.
13. Draw up a Letter of Intent.
14. Perform due diligence.
15. Draw up contracts.
16. Close.

Do we know what we are buying?

There are many ways to define and think about an acquisition opportunity, but the real focus of any deal has to be on the target company's core competency. Are you purchasing a special operating capability? Relationships or contracts with customers and/or suppliers? Key managers? A new distribution channel? Warehouse or manufacturing capacity? Access to new markets? A new sales force—or what? In evaluating a company for acquisition, keep in mind that its resources come in more forms than just financial assets. Non-balance sheet items, such as reputation, undervalued property, franchise distribution agreements, special access to raw materials or to transportation or energy, intellectual properties (patents, trade secrets, etc.), established market share, terminable expenses, synergistic opportunities, or government permits can be important to a transaction. In particular, one-time liquid or salable items can have a big impact on both acquisition price and return on investment. Knowing what you're buying may seem like an obvious point, but consider this story.

Some years ago, a large diversified company purchased a sizable distribution company, selling aftermarket parts and supplies to the automotive industry, to add to their own distribution division. Soon after the deal was done, several key managers and sales representatives of the newly acquired company left to form their own company. They took most of the customer and supplier relationships with them. The buyer ended up with several warehouses full of parts but very little new business. The moral of the story is that buyers must know exactly what they are buying and structure the deal so that after they pay their money...they get it.

What will we do with it after we catch it?

Beware of untempered enthusiasm. Most acquisitions fail! Top managers need to avoid the "dog chasing a car" syndrome. What will you do with it if you catch it? Are you buying assets for liquidation or are you buying a going concern? Assuming the purchase is not for asset liquidation or breakup purposes, and you did not overpay, a primary key to successful acquisition is your *alternative operating strategy*. After you own it, how will you improve it? What core competencies did you purchase? How well are they being handled now? How will you strengthen or better leverage them in the future? How sustainable is their competitive advantage? What enhancements do you bring to the table? How much and what kinds of competition do you face? In the long run, the strength of defendable core competencies (in addition to the purchase price paid) will be major factors in the future success of your acquisition.

Because you will probably pay a market price that reflects full value for what the target company has already accomplished, any substantial return will be provided only by future operational improvements that you can make. No improvement usually means marginal (if any) returns. When thinking about ideas for improving the acquisition, these possibilities (and others) are worth noting:

- New products for existing markets.
- New markets for existing products.
- New distribution channels.
- Improved economies of scale.
- New operating (management or sales) strategy.
- New suppliers.
- New manufacturing systems.

- Additional capital investment.
- Elimination of duplicate expenses.

Hal Abrames*, CEO of Deacon-Marston Importers, built his $92 million specialty products business primarily through acquisition. He and his partner made 14 acquisitions over a 12-year period. Prior to founding Deacon-Marston, Hal was a senior vice-president responsible for North American investments in a large, $2 billion private equity fund. There he developed his acquisition skills. Hal, in this position, was paid a salary and substantial bonus, plus a small equity piece of each deal. Over the years, these equity holdings became quite valuable. Hal then teamed with Ira Marston* whose prior experience included operating an $850 million international medical supply company. When the medical supply company was purchased by a large conglomerate, all of Ira's stock options vested, making him a wealthy man.

Hal and Ira each put some money up to form Deacon-Marston. Each of their subsequent acquisitions added to their strategic strength. Their first purchase formed a strong U.S. foundation. The next eight gave them a substantial presence in Europe, Asia, Canada, Mexico, and South America. They followed that with two acquisitions that brought in new technology and stronger senior management. The final three filled in the geographic gaps to further strengthen their existing market position.

Each acquisition brought new products, sourcing opportunities, distribution channels, technology, or management skills. Hal and Ira formed a "best practices" team facilitated by outside consultants to ensure potential synergies came to fruition. These founders used their combined acquisition and operating skills to build their company by making strategic acquisitions. Each purchased company stood on its own, but each also benefited from the new association and improved overall Deacon-Marston operations.

Bottom-fishers are the exception

"Bottom-fishers" occasionally are able to scavenge a particular asset of value, such as a distribution channel, product line, name brand, patent, or sales force at a bargain price from an otherwise dying or troubled company. Their alternative operating strategy is usually to install the bargain asset into their successful company. Their general plan is to increase revenues and margins without increasing fixed overhead. This excellent opportunity is well worth taking advantage of whenever the target asset is a good fit within your operation.

Are we buying a trophy—or a cash machine?

The primary valuation issue in an acquisition often comes down to future projected cash flow. This is true whether you're paying with cash, stock, notes, or earn-outs. Your future economic and operating assumptions (such as future growth, investment, margin, or overall market forecasts) will significantly affect the return calculations. They have the potential to make or break the deal irrespective of the valuation formula used.

No matter what valuation method is used to determine a price (i.e., cash flow multiple, fair market value, last transaction value, liquidation value, capitalization of revenues, capitalization of historical earnings or cash flow, price/earnings ratio, market value added, economic value added, discounted cash flow, or market comparisons), the final price has to allow for an acceptable return. In determining a value for the company, buyers often pay too much attention to pricing techniques and not enough to core competencies and operating assumptions. The intrinsic value of a company generally resides in its capacity to offer customers a unique or distinctive benefit by virtue of a hard-to-copy core competency. Technical valuation methods are as much or more sales tools to convince lenders, etc., as they are effective measures of values.

How are we paying for it?

Match the funding structure to the operating strategy. Use "patient" money for acquisitions requiring time to develop. More than one acquisition has failed because a long-term deal was funded with short-term funds requiring short-term (monthly, quarterly, or annual) servicing. Do not let your funding structure prevent your success. When developing your funding strategy, take your future (post-acquisition) operating plans into account, not just your initial purchase needs.

How will the deal affect the target company's management?

Every business is a people business. Management is critical to every venture. And every acquisition has an effect on the managers in the company being considered for acquisition. If the deal will make the ongoing managers richer, it will probably affect their motivation to perform. If the deal makes someone other than the ongoing managers rich, there may be jealousy or resentment. The ongoing management team must perceive enough personal investment or future incentive in the deal structure to maintain their motivation.

Who do we need to help us do the deal?

Because most operating managers are not experienced or skilled in acquisitions, it's well worth the expense to obtain investment banking or some form of mergers and acquisitions help early in the process. Investment bankers and M&A consultants can offer many services:

- Deal flow.
- Information on recent similar transactions.
- Financial analysis of acquisition targets.
- Deal structure advice.
- Access to lawyers, tax specialists, and accountants.
- Access to public markets.
- Access to private debt and equity acquisition financing.
- Help with negotiations.

You may, however, want to note that investment bankers generally get their money through fees. As the buyer, you may feel that because you have hired them, their primary allegiance is to you. But because they will probably do only one deal with you but may do many deals with those who provide the acquisition funds, their allegiances will at best be split. In addition to their primary concern for maximizing their own fees, they will want you to succeed—but they will also have an interest in the well-being of the banks and investors they work with all the time. Caution is also recommended when "your" investment banker offers to show his "support for your deal" by offering to invest with the buyer.

It is to your advantage to have your attorney prepare the sales document because then it is drawn from your—not the other side's—description of the deal points. You will be in a better position to tie down loose ends and clarify vague issues. Many deals are lost during the preparation of the final documents. It is a good time to be proactive and in control.

Negotiating the Deal

Finding the right deal with a defendable competitive edge that you can strengthen and improve is the most important element in the acquisition process. Negotiating price, however, may well be a close second. Your negotiations, to be consistently successful, must begin with character...*your* character. Integrity, sincerity, and a sense of fairness are prerequisites for long-term performance in this arena. These traits need to become the foundation of your negotiating skills. The following thoughts will guide you through key negotiating issues, but it's important to remember that substance is always more important than form.

Identify potential deal-breakers early

Issues such as product liability, unfunded pension plans, environmental liabilities, product warranty obligations, golden parachutes (costly severance obligations to key employees), goodwill that will need to be written off, and poison pills (expensive events triggered by a change in ownership) can each prevent a deal from closing. As a buyer, identify and search out these types of issues early in the acquisition process. As a seller, get these issues on the table from the outset.

Tips to negotiating like a pro

People make selling decisions when they understand the deal and it makes sense to them. The first priority in a negotiation is to *make sure the other side comprehends the advantages of your offer*. They will not get to the second step of comparing your offer to others if the proposed transaction is too complex to understand. Keep the terms as simple as possible and verify that the other side understands all of the potential benefits.

During a typical negotiation, the other side will present many ideas, arguments, and positions. You will, no doubt, find many points of disagreement. Weigh each issue separately and gauge your potential for success in each before proceeding. Your case may be strong on a particular issue, but your opponent may be intransigent on that point. On another issue you may feel confident of success, but your analysis might indicate that winning this small battle will not help win the war. *Focus on issues where your case is strong and the point is worth winning.* Look for opportunities where the other side is susceptible to your arguments and the issue is significant to the outcome of the negotiation.

It is often wise to *avoid the issue of price in early negotiations.* If the other side asks about price, tell them that you like the business, but you want to know more about the operation before making an offer. If they suggest a price (which will, of course, be too high), tell them that it seems to be in the ballpark but you need more information. Build a relationship with the sellers and learn the details of the business before taking on the issue of price.

One of the best techniques for handling negotiations is to let the target company's negotiators know early on that you have an advisory board or an investor group that will be reviewing all proposed transactions. Put together and use this advisory board, even if its only charter involves this acquisition, and relay this fact to the other side's negotiators early in the negotiations. The board may not be important now, but it will become essential later on. Then begin the process of building rapport with the principals and increasing your understanding of the company's operation.

When you get to the stage of negotiating price or other critical components of the deal, *remind the target company of your advisory board.* You can then ask for the other side's help in convincing your board of the validity and reasonableness of their price. Use of the board in this way will allow you to maintain your rapport with the other side while still asking tough questions:

- What should I tell the board is the basis of your price?
- Can you help me with my board's questions about this internal rate of return calculation?

- How do I explain to the board the difference in your price and these recent comparative market prices?

Set your board up with financing, operating, negotiating, legal, and accounting expertise, and listen to the advice given. This approach will help you make better negotiating decisions as well as improve your negotiating leverage.

Pinpoint the motivation of your seller. What is the desire, the need, the fear, or the limitation he is attempting to address? When the other side says the price is $4 million, this represents their perception of the best way to meet their own requirements. Learn why they selected this price. Learn their personal and business tax situations and what they plan to do with the money. Armed with this information, you may find an alternative option that is more acceptable to both sides.

When you offer a price, stop. State your price confidently and support its credibility. Avoid apologies or negative modifiers. Do not say, "I am sorry, we can only offer, $1 million." Say, "Because of the positive trends in this operation, I am able to offer $1 million." Then be silent. My old friend Dave Yoho used to say, "The world record for silence after stating a price is 30 seconds." Test the record. Avoid changing your offer during the same negotiating session. Let them know several times that you feel the offer is fair. Discuss changes only at the next session.

Gather all the information possible

It may not always be true that the side with the most information wins, but it is always true that the side with the most information has a great advantage. If you "play it by ear" and wait until the negotiation is underway to begin to research the facts or develop your negotiation game plan, you may find yourself at the mercy of the other side. Be prepared to modify your negotiating position as you collect and verify new information. Pay close attention to the other side's apparent logic. It takes reliable (verified) information and a proactive game plan to control the agenda. Controlling the agenda is a primary factor in the outcome of any negotiation.

Evaluate financial aspects of the deal

Your goal in the negotiation is to move the other side to a price that is based on current cash flow. Because you want to achieve your return through operating improvements, you should be both willing to pay and able to finance any price that is reasonably based on current cash flow. A way of achieving this end is to persuade the other side of the need to provide a logic to their price. This "logic," of course, will need to be based on current cash flow.

Do not overpay and *do not pay for your own planned improvements*. Give the seller full value (if you must) for that which he has achieved, but do not increase your offer because you believe you can make future improvements. A patient buyer is a prudent buyer, and a prudent buyer will not overpay.

Every deal, at a minimum, needs to provide a return that exceeds your cost of capital (which is the combination of cost of debt and cost of equity). The eventual goal of every deal is economic performance. Your cost of capital sets a floor on that measurement.

Focus on next best alternatives

Knowing your next best option gives you the power to walk away from a deal when the other side is too tough. When the terms of your current best option fall below your next best option, take the latter. It may also serve you well in the negotiation to inform the other side of your next best option when the deal gets close.

By the same token, the other side will be motivated to accept your deal as long as it exceeds their perception of their next best alternative. Discover their alternatives. Analysis of the other side's options is generally best accomplished in the early stage of negotiation. Gather as much information from the outset as you can, from contacts at every level. Make sure that all members of your team are aware of this need to secure information so that they will be alert to comments made by the other side.

Leave yourself room to work

Resist the temptation to start with your best offer even when the other side has demanded it. The other side will sometimes announce that they will only consider one offer from your side. This, of course, is a negotiating ploy designed to put your side at a disadvantage. If they are truly interested in selling, then there is some motivation driving them. Discover that motivation and you will find the key to persuading them to join the negotiating process on a more reasonable basis.

The conventional wisdom about negotiating is to start low and give up small increments. The hope is that this stalling tactic will help you outlast the other side. This works when the other side has extreme pressure to sell, there are few interested buyers, or your side can afford to be patient. My own experience, however, has been that the circumstances of most potential transactions do not provide this advantage. Unreasonably low offers and meaningless concessions can negatively affect your credibility as a buyer. And credibility once lost is hard to regain. Without the perception of credibility, the other side will quickly lose interest.

Avoid bidding against yourself or splitting the difference

Often the other side in an acquisition negotiation will decline to counter in an attempt to force you to bid against yourself. You offer $6 million and they respond by saying that your offer is not enough. When you counter at $6.3 million, you are bidding against yourself. Press the other side to take a position. The negotiation has started, so make it a two-party game. Be resolute in your efforts to persuade them to engage. Like so many things in life, one can play, but two is more satisfying.

As a negotiation gets close, one side frequently will offer to split the difference. The tendency is to be a good sport and accept the offer. But keep in mind that the side that offers this option will usually pay the whole difference. This is a good time in the negotiating process for a pause. After the break, suggest that your really need to stay with your last offer. More times than not, the other side will agree to your terms.

Use emotion and patience to your advantage

Usually emotion is not a positive ingredient in a successful negotiation, but the strategic use of planned emotion can be very useful. Spontaneous emotion, which can easily get out of control and kill a deal, needs to be hedged by breaks that allow both sides to get themselves under control. Planned emotion, at the right time, however, can signal to the other side that you are at your limit. This is not to suggest that you pretend or fake emotions, for this ploy is easily seen through. But there is often an appropriate time (usually near the end) in a negotiation to let your true emotions show.

You can avoid anxiety or panic by being patient and preparing for the long haul. Most deadlines can be modified or ignored. Set your own time limits to allow for protracted negotiations, and control your stress level. You will think more clearly and make better decisions if you minimize distressing situations.

Due diligence is not just a formality

Buyers want the business intact; customer, supplier, and employee relationships in good order; liabilities well-defined, and no surprises. They are looking for a clean deal with substantial future opportunity. Sellers want the deal to close; the price and terms to be as agreed; minimum taxes; no leftover liabilities; employees treated well; no hassles; and no surprises. They want a clean deal completed as originally agreed and often a clean break from the past.

The purpose of due diligence is generally presented as a way to ensure no surprises. It is a process to gain and verify needed information pertaining to the transaction and the operation. It is also used, however, to enhance a negotiating position, to adjust price or terms, or to provide an out. Buyers and sellers need to manage this process closely. It will be a time that each side will learn much about the other.

Each due diligence effort will be customized to the needs of the particular deal. The focus of these analyses will be to increase understanding, to ensure that the business operates as projected, and to look for hidden problems. Generally, issues relating to financial statements, personnel, processes and procedures, product and services, customers, suppliers, government compliance, legal, competition, and the industry will be covered.

Details common to the due diligence process include:

- Verification of a specific business operating model.
- Identification of undervalued, overvalued, and unrecorded assets and liabilities.
- Balance sheet, profit and loss, and cash flow verification.
- Tax and accounting impact on the business, shareholders, and surviving entities.

- Transfer of assets (third-party consents, credit agreements, contracts with customers, union agreements, pension plans, etc.).
- Agreements with dissident shareholders.
- Indemnities, holdbacks, contingent payments, warranties, and representations.
- Problems and incentives relating to key people.
- Key management personal and business references.
- Customer, supplier, and work force interviews.
- Royalty agreements.
- Pending or potential litigation.
- Determination of postacquisition capital requirements.
- Payoff or transfer of seller's debt.
- Broker's or finder's fees, and banking agreements.
- Successor liabilities, insurance coverage, and contingent liabilities.
- Legal and regulatory review.
- Competitor, market, and industry analysis.
- New business plans and opportunities.

Professional legal representation experienced in buy/sell transactions will help you to fill in your own due diligence agenda.

Acquire like a professional

From time to time, I have suggested that you find a role model and critique and document his characteristics. This process helps you focus on the traits you may need to develop in order to emulate your role model's success. Howard Koff, CEO of Westbury Financial, sells big-ticket products to sophisticated and knowledgeable buyers. His clients are not only skilled in negotiations but also usually have world-class experts to assist them in making decisions. Howie's clients often own sizable businesses, and in this sense, his sales efforts often parallel the acquisition process. Howie's secrets are simple to articulate but hard to execute. First, he is a world-class expert himself. Dealing with the best for 25 years has advanced his knowledge and sharpened his skills. Second, his primary interest is to discover his clients' needs, clarify their objectives, crystallize their thinking, and then develop the best plan possible to help them. Third, he has researched, developed, and maintained relationships with the most knowledgeable people in his industry. He can and does call on these expert resources often. Fourth, he is very perceptive, listens well, and maintains perfect records. His acute attention to detail is legend in his business. Fifth, he is fully prepared to walk away from a deal (even a quite profitable deal) if he cannot meet the client's expectations or if the client asks him to compromise his ethics. Sixth, Howie is a perfect gentleman and is totally under control even in extraordinarily tense situations. He always presents an image of strength, confidence, and class.

When he plans his negotiations, he breaks them into four parts:

1. Precontact research.
2. Meeting to determine needs, interests, and concerns.
3. Meeting to discuss various potential alternatives (floating trial balloons).
4. Meeting to present or offer his solution to their special circumstances.

The trial balloon step is one that many negotiators miss or pass over lightly. But by testing the currents, Howie is able to confirm his perceptions and validate potential feature advantages or approaches prior to his final presentation. Most negotiators go right to the offer. Howie's approach to selling presents a model outline for successful acquisitions. Develop a similar approach and you can achieve success.

Final Thoughts on Acquisitions

Consider the following two stories. In both, target companies were acquired by the same company, for the same reason—bargain asset availability. In neither case did the acquiring company have a particular strategy for expansion. It considered itself to be an opportunistic "bottom-fisher" looking for "bargain" purchases. It held to this "bargain purchaser" philosophy in spite of the fact that it was not in the asset liquidation business. Its intention was to operate these acquired businesses as independent ongoing concerns.

In the first case, the company purchased the assets only of a dying business at 25 cents on the dollar. The product involved had good name recognition, but the target's parent company limited the use of that name to three years because it wanted to protect its core business, which used the same brand name in an unrelated industry. This venture enjoyed short-term success because the acquiring company was able to produce the product without adding production capacity.

After three years, however, the acquiring company could not compensate for the loss of the brand name. General market improvements eliminated the excess capacity, forcing it to add production facilities. This combination forced the division to be liquidated, probably at less than 25 cents on the dollar!

In the second acquisition, the company purchased assets "cheap," the brand name represented quality, and the business was operated as an independent ongoing concern. The acquiring company figured its own management and sales expertise would provide the fuel for success. Problems occurred when the parent company's human resources became spread too thin to provide any real help to the newly acquired division and additional division management and a new sales force had to be hired—a need previously discounted by management's overconfidence. The acquiring company believed the experience gained from its successes in its core business in a related industry and the lessons learned from previous failures would carry them through.

They could not have been more wrong. The old-line brand name did stand for quality, but it also stood for old-fashioned. The so-called bargain facilities were outdated and in ill-repair and, in fact, were eventually liquidated for less than originally paid. The acquiring company had no sense of the competition in this new industry, and the results of this "bargain" purchase were disastrous.

The acquiring company was not stupid. It had built its very successful core business primarily through "bargain" acquisitions in the past. The difference was that the market had changed. In the company's early growth years, the industry was in its emerging phase.

This made production capacity a major factor in a company's ability to grow and prosper. In the industry's later years, the market matured, lowering the relative importance of production capacity. In this currently saturated market, successful companies focused primarily on product design, price, and marketing, not on production capacity. The absence of a valid expansion strategy proved fatal to both of these acquisitions.

Had this ill-fated acquiring organization been using *CEO Logic*, they would have remembered the first rule of successful acquisitions: *Don't buy it if you can't improve it.* Determine in advance what you will do with it after you own it. Even companies with defendable core competencies are often fully priced for that which they have already accomplished. Substantial returns will generally result only from the improvements the buyer can add.

If you are contemplating your first acquisition, you may want to consider sharing both the risks and rewards. A high number of acquisitions fail. Overleverage, seller's fraud, loss of key management, overpayment, inability to improve the operation, new government regulations, inadequate management, and unforeseen pressures from competition are some reasons for failure. Consider sharing and spreading the risks and rewards of acquisition through the use of partners and investors or, in effect, by using other people's money. Bringing others into the deal may dilute your return but it may also prevent your downfall. Unless you are an acquisitions expert, walk slowly down the acquisition path and be fully aware of the risks at hand.

Part 4

Character, Ethics, Communication, and Wisdom

These final chapters offer insight into the human side of the business equation. Together, they address the enduring issues of character, ethics, communication, and wisdom.

These human elements of *CEO Logic* provide the energy, direction, and courage to make the organization perform. Chapter 12 offers guidance on how to select the right goals and motivate others to want to achieve them. Chapter 13 reduces complex issues to their simple cores, through brief bits of wit and wisdom from the trenches of business. Chapter 14 reunites the theoretical foundations with the practical disciplines of management, guiding you on your path to mastery of the *CEO Logic* that will open the door to your own extraordinary success.

Part 4

Character, Ethics, Communication, and Wisdom

Chapter 12

Leadership: Nothing Mystical, Nothing Magical

There is a precipice on either side of you—a precipice of caution and a precipice of overdaring.
—Winston Churchill

Leadership is one of those perennial topics about which hundreds of magazine articles and books are written. Often we know more about what it isn't than what it is. We read stories in the business news of Apple Computer and the differences between Gil Amelio and Steve Jobs and we wonder why Jobs seemed such a strong leader and why Amelio seemed to flounder. Besides historical factors at Apple, what about Jobs appeared to soothe the stock market and rejuvenate the spirits of a beleaguered company? The answers are not simple or easy, but they are remarkably straightforward. The ability to persuade people to follow—through a combination of motivation and vision—is the essence of leadership.

Leadership begins in the minds of the leaders. Learning to lead is not a matter of following rules or getting an MBA. True leadership, like so many other aspects of being a top manager, is intimately tied to thinking in a way that capitalizes on an intelligent combination of education, experience, and self-knowledge. Too often, discussions of leadership stress only the mechanics. Courses that teach public speaking, written communication, employee motivation, case-study analysis, and ways to disseminate information are indeed helpful. But leadership can only begin to be developed in the classroom. True leadership emerges from within the individual through experience. The ability to perceive a situation accurately, the capacity to recognize a significant opportunity or threat, and the judgment to select the right course of action come as much from trial and error and instinct as they do from formal study.

Role models who embody effective and inspirational leadership are essential because they demonstrate not only to what to *do*, but how to *think*. J. Terrence (Terry) Lanni, chairman and CEO of MGM Grand, Inc., is one of those role models for me. I have never worked directly with Terry, but I have come to know him well through personal contact, his reputation, our time together in the Young Presidents' Organization (YPO), and my knowledge of the consistent results he has achieved with major corporations. He is an excellent judge of people. I am embarrassed to admit it, but twice I should have given more weight to his evaluation of people and have suffered the consequences. This will never happen again.

Terry has the unique capacity to get the right take on a situation immediately, no matter how complex. His ability to perceive and evaluate high levels of detailed information is matched only by his ability to stay focused on the central issues at hand. He is both analytical and creative. No doubt his early background as a chief financial officer, his MBA from the University of Southern California, and his years as a corporate president have contributed to his distinctive style of leadership. Terry is an independent and original thinker, and always appears to know exactly where he wants to go.

His pattern of results and his impressive list of accomplishments speak to his ability as a strategic thinker. But he is also a man of unequaled character who is truly committed to his beliefs and values. He is charitable with both his time and money and always makes his family a priority. He has learned to manage himself as well as others. He is decisive in his actions and has assessed his own strengths and weaknesses well. He appears to know when to act, when to pass, and when to seek help.

Terry's leadership skills are enhanced by his professionalism, style, and unwavering honesty. Terry is one of those few extraordinary leaders with force and vision who has learned to think like a CEO and who always seems to make the right moves.

Business leaders have the primary responsibility to make the organization perform. Employees, suppliers, shareholders, and customers all depend on the leader to fulfill this obligation. She does this by achieving the twin objectives of leadership: vision and motivation—

the vision to know the right course to follow and the ability to motivate others in the organization to help realize that vision. And neither a valid vision nor effective motivation can be achieved without the primary elements of leadership: passion, ethics, courage, communication, judgment, and insight. Passion supplies the energy, ethics generate trust from constituencies, courage provides the backbone needed to make tough decisions, communication delivers the message needed to motivate and define vision, judgment supports good decision-making, and insight provides the capacity to select the right people, the right role for yourself, the right goal, and the right strategy. Top managers know that the passion and judgment to select and follow the right course and the ability to effectively communicate a strong message are the forces that allow an individual to achieve.

Thomas Shin*, founder of Resort Lodging Partners, met both leadership objectives. Two years ago, Tommy and his family moved to a resort town in the Sierra Nevada Mountains. Although their move was primarily a personal life-style decision, Tommy's extensive real estate development background caused him to analyze local situations for development opportunities. He continued this land development exercise until he came across a piece of lake property.

This particular piece of land had previously drawn the interest of many developers. In the past, difficult zoning issues, Forest Service concerns, distance from the main resort town, lack of direct ski access, and earlier development failures drove off other developers. Tommy, however, could "see" through these issues and was able to develop a valid vision for the property.

He recognized that this property was located at the "gateway" to the city. Further, he saw the city's need to generate more resort traffic and more city revenue. He used these issues to convince the city managers that it was in both the city's and Tommy's best interest to develop this "gateway."

It took courage to go up against city hall, the Green lobby, and the Forest Service. It took insight and vision to see through the many problems in order to find the core opportunities. It took effective communication and strong powers of persuasion to help each interest group discover its own advantages in the proposed development. It took ethics and judgment to find the right balance among competing interests. But most of all it took great passion to generate the energy to take on this formidable task.

Tommy Shin's ability to develop a valid vision, along with his power to motivate others, turned a problem parcel of land into a profitable real estate venture that helped the city and enhanced the environment. Tommy met the twin objectives of leadership, developed a great property, and earned the respect of the city residents and managers.

Valid Goals and Effective Motivation

While current discussions of leadership often turn to skills, technique, and style, they neglect substantial issues such as character, accuracy of perception, capacity to attract followers, and validity of concept. A *good* leader persuades others to join the cause, but a *great* leader combines motivational skills and the raw power of great communication with a cause that is valid, just, and right.

A leader's motivational skills can be measured by the degree of commitment that her followers show. The purpose of motivational leadership is to ignite energy and enthusiasm in others so that they will want to join the cause and become believers in it. From that energy and enthusiasm, followers must be spurred to take action and to do so in a way that gets the most out of available resources. People like responding to these leaders' calls for action. When it is successful, motivational leadership promotes consensus, loyalty, personal dedication, a sense of common goals and an active willingness to engage the work. In short, motivational leadership promotes enthusiastic followers.

The tools of the motivational leader range from communicating compelling argument to reinforcing desired behavior. The styles of individual leaders can be equally diverse. Contrary to common belief, successful leaders have been democrats, autocrats, and dictators. Some have been teachers, some facilitators, and some expediters. Many have been active participants; others, hands-off delegators. Some have flown the flag of quality. Some have marched under the banner of innovation. Others have been dedicated to low price or customer service. All have promised allocation of needed resources, reward for achievements, and the glory of success. Most have inspired a high level of commitment and belief.

Motivational leaders often rely heavily on managers to sort out complexities. Sometimes leaders serve the dual roles of leader and manager, but more often they do not. Managers staff, plan, and organize in support of their leaders and provide the infrastructure that makes it possible to meet the leaders' goals. The leader determines where the business stands competitively and where it ought to stand; the managers, then, can determine the right strategies, staffing, organization, and action plans to get there.

In spite of the power of this ingredient of leadership, all motivational leaders are not necessarily great leaders. Motivating employees to engage in the work is important, but leaders must also be addressing the right issues. That is where *CEO Logic* comes in, because *great leaders must be able to think about and identify valid goals*. The selected destination must be both achievable and worthwhile. In other words, the effective business leader of today must be able to select the right war to fight. The "right war" might be defined as one that is both winnable and worth winning.

The Vietnam War may or may not have been worth winning, but because of the way it was managed politically, there was no way to win it. In addition to being unpopular, the war became terribly costly in both human lives and money. It's a mistake in business as in war to think that taking on causes without proper management will be rewarded. It bears repeating: The right war must be both winnable and worth winning.

Today, it is politically correct to speak of participative leadership. It is likewise "incorrect" to weigh the contributions of a single leader too heavily. The two, however, are not mutually exclusive; rather, they are complementary. Other managers' or employees' abilities do not diminish the contributions of the leader and vice versa. Great leaders at all levels of business have learned that widespread work force involvement is the secret to creating widespread commitment to a course of action. If you want people to be committed to a project, you need to think about how they can participate from the beginning. And you must think strategically about how you will take up the leadership role in a way that complements what they are doing. Often, the people in an organization are the specialists responsible for particular tasks and assignments and the leaders are the generalists who must keep the big picture. While both are equally valid and necessary, the best view for navigating the right course will come from the leader's overview and perspective.

There is no such thing as a magician or wizard in business. These are the fantasies of business magazines and books. There are only experience, hard work, and fundamentals. The closest that business comes to magic is when it conjures up inspiration, insight, and talent. Even these elements, however, are often more a product of perspiration and persistence than of "genius." In the rest of the chapter, we will further develop several of the most potent aspects of leadership, aspects that are central to top managers' ability to expand their thinking, their understanding of the leadership role, and their growth as leaders.

Leadership vs. Management

Leadership and management are not the same thing. While there is some overlap, management generally makes decisions on issues, strategies, and action plans, while leadership supplies the vision, enthusiasm, communication, confidence, passion, and values that will drive those decisions. Managers are on the ground organizing the people and figuring out which tool to use for which job, whether to work one shift or two, and who should be on point and who should bring up the rear. The leader, in contrast, determines what the work should be, communicates the noble purpose behind it, defines the goal, and reassures the troops that they can accomplish the task.

Every important project requires a high degree of management, but the level of leadership becomes more critical when the number of people involved increases and the length or scope of the project is extended. It takes a good manager to organize and assign the work so that a difficult task *can* be handled efficiently. It takes a leader to motivate the work force so that a difficult task *will* be handled efficiently. A manager's goals arise out of necessities, while a leader's goals arise out of opportunities. Leadership must set the course, the destination, and the deadlines for management to meet. Management defines the methodology, but leadership defines the success. Leaders set expectations, managers try to meet them.

Managing as a leader

When you think like a CEO, you understand that there are three "macro issues" to manage: *meeting the needs of today's operations, improving today's methods,* and *preparing for tomorrow's business.* Everyone has to manage the business that comes in today, and most try to improve the methodology and efficiency of the way they are doing that business. But few apply adequate resources to developing tomorrow's business.

I recently looked at an investment opportunity involving a telecommunications technology company. Its current offerings are state-of-the-art and its management team strong. They have a firm grasp of their three-fold management task: First, they have the resources and systems to manage their day-to-day operations. Revenues have been growing at 5 to 15 percent per year and the company makes excellent returns. Second, they have separate human, physical, financial, and technological resources dedicated to making refinements and increasing efficiency by learning to do better what they already do well. Third, they have recognized the need to raise substantial sums of money to develop the next generation of products and managers. By managing all three issue, they are competing well today and preparing to lead the way tomorrow. As it turned out, another group beat me to this investment. I have every confidence they will achieve great rewards.

The practice of great CEO leadership

Think big to grow. A small business cannot be operated with small business systems and then suddenly make the change to big business systems. Unlike switching on a light, there is no instantaneous way to make this transition. Effective CEOs know that they have to take the time early on to develop the right operating systems. If you want your small business to become a big business, operate it like a big business today. Put in the systems, the people, and the structure now to make your business grow and prosper. If you run it like a small business, it will stay a small business.

Understand that time is always a factor. Time is more a factor today than ever before. It has become a strategic weapon and, as the saying goes, time really is money. Successful companies know they must focus on reducing the time cycle for nearly every function. For example, competition has begun in many industries to reduce the time it takes to develop new products. In some cases the time taken from concept to production has been reduced fivefold. What used to take five years, now takes one. Always look to improve your results by reducing the time cycle for each major element of your business.

Learn to ask the right questions. The first step to getting the right answers is to ask the right questions. Good leaders and managers develop clear insights into the true purpose of the work in order to ask the right questions. The right questions help bring order and consistency to complex issues and serve to direct attention to the right subjects.

Mark Schwartz, CEO of Specialty Merchandise Corporation (SMC) leads and manages a multimillion dollar operation. His company sources gift items internationally and packages them with more than 20 different marketing methods in order to create great business opportunities for everyday individuals. Some of his members (customers) make extra cash and some make millions.

SMC's turnkey business gives its members everything they need to become successful independent businesspeople. Step-by-step selling instructions, business operations manuals, an enormous warehouse offering nearly 4,000 different high-margin products, and more are all provided to its members for a very low startup cost. Mark and his team support their members with state-of-the-art distribution systems and free, unlimited advisory service. SMC communicates this offer primarily through infomercials.

Watching Mark produce these infomercials is where I first saw his strength of leadership. As the cost of television time kept rising, SMC's cost per inquiry rose with it. Mark began to address the issue by first defining the problem in detail and then by conducting a thorough situation analysis. These first two steps were designed to help Mark determine the right questions. Questions such as these were developed:

- What are the factors with the potential to significantly affect the cost per inquiry?
- What is the exact deviation between desired results and current results? What, if anything, went wrong? When did the problem start?
- Does it occur in all regions at all times of the year?

- What facts and what history do we have on this issue?
- What alternatives are available?
- How can we test our assumptions?

These questions and more like them reflect Mark's leadership style. He is bright and analytical. His Stanford MBA gives him a good base for strategic thinking and his operating experience drives him to make practical choices. By asking the right questions, Mark draws his people and his outside associates into the process.

SMC's answer to improving the productivity of its infomercials turned out to be threefold. First, SMC improved its expertise at buying TV time. Second, it improved the message in the infomercial. Third, it improved the fundamentals of the offer presented in the infomercial. Asking the right questions was the key to getting the right answers.

Fight apathy. Because apathy and complacency are the twin foes of enthusiasm and performance, top management cannot allow them in their organization. Let everyone know that enthusiasm for the plans and missions of the company are the stuff that strong companies are made of. Participation by all in the process plus the abilities to motivate and to energize others are your best defenses against apathy and complacency.

Use influence to motivate and control. According to Ichak Adizes, in his book *Mastering Change,* there are three ways to motivate and control:

1. *Authority*—The legal right to give directions and make decisions.
2. *Power*—The ability to extend or withhold an incentive or a punishment.
3. *Influence*—The ability to persuade someone that the desired direction is in their own best self-interest.

In my opinion, influence is the only method that makes sense as a primary motivational strategy. Even though you will need to use power and authority on occasion, they must still be supported by influence. Top leaders remember that power and authority may achieve initial success, but long-term effectiveness comes from convincing others that the direction in which you want to go is the right one for them and the company.

When you hear yourself saying, "Do this because I am the boss," you are attempting to use *authority*. When you say, "Do this and I will reward or punish you," you are trying to use *power*. But when you say, "Do this because it is right for you and the company," you are calling on the most powerful force...*influence*.

Might does not make right

Abraham Lincoln said, "Nearly all men can stand adversity, but if you want to test a man's character, give him power." The primary safeguards against abuses of power in an organization are character, humility, and judgment. It is easy for the power that top leaders are given to spawn arrogance. Arrogant leaders fail to apologize for their mistakes and may not even see their errors. On occasion, leadership arrogance can deteriorate into condescension and self-permissiveness, as when managers talk down to people or refuse to follow their own rules. This assumed superiority can undermine the whole company's culture and reverse previous leadership gains. Leadership and the power that comes with it carry clear and certain responsibilities and obligations. A wise leader uses power sparingly and with great discretion. She recognizes that neither wealth nor power equals wisdom.

Tell everyone the secrets

Share the plans, problems, analyses, alternatives, solutions, and major portions of the financial reports with every manager in your company. People respond and perform better when they feel trusted and consider themselves an integral part of the team. The old argument that people take wrongful advantage when they know too much about the company's business does not hold water. It is absurd to think that they will be able take your complete method of doing business and give it to a competitor. Think how hard it is to get the people in your own organization to do it your way even when you pay them, train them, measure them, counsel them, and command them. And if you are effectively managing for the future, even if they could copy your current systems perfectly and had all of your resources available, they would only be able to copy your way of doing business the way you *used* to do it.

It is impossible to make good decisions without good information. When you tell the secrets, you take away the "I didn't know" excuse. Share information openly and encourage participation and questions on any subject and you'll reap the rewards.

Incentives are the clearest communication

There is no better way to inform a manager of the importance of an issue than to pay her for it. The sales force is often the best directed department in the company because they get commissions. Every salesperson can tell you immediately what results define a good day. Ask an engineer, administrator, or accountant if she had a good day. Then ask why. You will see the difference.

Celebrate the victories

It is easy to show your feelings when things go wrong. Everyone takes the time to address mistakes. But it takes conscious effort and discipline to remember to recognize and celebrate the victories as well. All of us respond well to being recognized and appreciated, just as everyone responds poorly to having achievements ignored. We all know that reward systems are important, but sometimes we do not follow through with appropriate resources.

Recognition and celebration do not have to be expensive. You can use or encourage others to use a book such as Bob Nelson's ***1,001 Ways to Reward Employees***. From it, a menu of ideas and programs can be created that make sense for you and your managers to use whenever good things happen. Take the time and make the effort to follow through. Assign several people in your company the task of reading Bob Nelson's book. Ask them to make recognition recommendations. Then spend the time (and money if necessary) to make these new forms of recognition an integral part of your company.

Build on core competencies

A core competency is a specific capability of your company that provides special values in the form of unique or distinctive benefits to your customers. To be meaningful, this core competency must be hard for competitors to imitate. Every long-term successful business is built on core competencies, irrespective of whether that business has formally identified them. Without them, competitors can—and will—successfully attack. Define your core competencies in explicit detail to strengthen both your offense and defense.

Use adversity to grow

Every stroke pleases somebody—that is true in business as it is in golf. Out of adversity comes opportunity for someone. Tough times provide the arena for great managers, leaders, and companies to show their strength. Good times, and the resulting high volumes, can hide a lot of weaknesses. Nearly everyone looks good in an up market. Use down markets to expose big weaknesses and to make big gains.

Final Thoughts on Leadership

Winston Churchill said, "When the eagles are silent, the parrots will jabber." As a leader in your organization, you are the eagle. You are the glue that holds the organization together and keeps it on course. One leader at the department, division, or overall company level can and often does make the difference between success and failure. The secret of leaders at all these levels lies in their particular abilities to think like a CEO.

Successful CEOs who have mastered great leadership bring at least these 10 essential qualities to their positions:

1. *Insight:* The capacity to accurately perceive opportunities, problems, and solutions.
2. *Judgment:* The ability to learn from the results of past decisions and actions and the incorporation of specific knowledge and basic education into thinking and behavior.
3. *Passion:* The force that generates energy.
4. *Energy:* The fuel for the action required to carry out plans and strategy.
5. *Motivation:* The ability to attract and inspire followers.
6. *Communication:* The skill to deliver the message.
7. *Courage:* The quality that enables tough decisions, engagement in difficult situations, and staying the course under fire.

8. *Compassion:* The trait that allows for empathy, understanding, and overall sensitivity to people.
9. *Ethics:* The principles required to make sure you can and will be comfortable with your results.
10. *Honest self-appraisal*: The capacity to identify what you do and do not know in order to define the right role for yourself.

I was once told a story of an entrepreneur who built and managed a fairly large company. He was generally successful, with a few exceptions. A good public communicator, especially through speeches and letters, he was known as a decisive leader, both inside and outside of the company. His personal qualities and character were widely esteemed throughout the industry. His reputation on Wall Street was good, and he was believed to have developed a superior management team, conservative financial controls, and an open style of communication. Everybody seemed to think highly of his leadership style.

In reality, however, everyone is a composite of both good and bad qualities, strengths and weaknesses. This entrepreneur's most significant flaw was that he did not know his own weaknesses. He did not know what he did not know. In the early years of his career, his vision of the industry was on target, because of continuous contact with his customers and employees. In his later years, however, his vision began to become flawed, as his contacts with customers and employees became more and more limited to public speaking engagements. As his informal contact with them diminished, his vision of the industry became less viable. Both his customers and his competitors were evolving with changes in the marketplace, while his own perspective remained static.

This entrepreneur's problems were not limited to his outdated vision. He also got into trouble when he departed from his role as leader and tried to assume certain management responsibilities. He understood the value of participative management, but those personal qualities that gave him strength as a leader became overbearing when applied to management. His reputation for fair and equitable leadership became tarnished when his management style led him to rationalize poor performance on the part of friends and family. As a leader, his drive, confidence, and commitment served him well. As a manager, his pride and prejudices limited his effectiveness.

This leader's great strength was bolstered by his commitment to his vision for the company. When that vision became blurred, the company's operating performance suffered. As the operating results deteriorated, this man of commitment felt more and more obligated to intervene in management. The power and charisma that served him so well as a leader created a barrier to communication in his role as a manager. His employees and customers were actually afraid to approach him with bad news; no one wanted to challenge his views. When challenges were brought, he often responded with personal criticism followed by personnel changes.

The only remedy for confidence that turns to arrogance was spoken hundreds of years ago by the Oracle of Delphi: "Know thyself." Know your strengths and flaws, stay close to your customers and employees, and delegate in areas where you have weaknesses. Stay in touch with these issues in order to avoid the problems that this once-great entrepreneur faced. He had the opportunity to create a market leader; instead, the organization never achieved its full potential.

Motivational and visionary leadership, whether in the person of a CEO or a departmental manager, always finds a way to define valid objectives and to energize the work force. Leaders come in various packages. Some are great public speakers, some are people of few words, but all find a way to communicate effectively. Some present an image of urban class and sophistication, some reflect a more rural wisdom. As with CEOs, there is no common size, race, gender, or religion that characterizes leaders. Some are great judges of people, while many have developed a talent for quickly correcting their misjudgments. Some have the capacity to be predominately right on the first attempt and others have built a compensating persistence. But all successful leaders have learned the central discipline of *CEO Logic*: to stay focused on the simple truths—their visions at the heart of their complex organizations.

Chapter 13

Secrets: Wit and Wisdom from the Trenches

I am always ready to learn, although I do not always like being taught.
—Winston Churchill

This chapter is an eclectic collection of ideas and reflections. Many have been in my arsenal of wit and wisdom so long that I have forgotten their origins. Undoubtedly, I have borrowed many of them, although I then modified them through experience. A few may even be original. Peter Drucker talked of the "mixed ancestry" of his ideas; Mark Twain spoke of being "a retailer of ideas" as opposed to "a manufacturer." I have expressed nothing so profound or eloquent, but am pleased to "borrow" their thoughts on originality.

I believe that reducing complex ideas to thematic axioms helps with communication and understanding. Nothing more clearly indicates ignorance of a subject than an inability to explain it succinctly. Einstein explained his Theory of Relativity in a simple formula. We in business, then, can certainly try to capture a simple management concept in a few words. I am sure you have experienced the pain of listening to a speaker (executives and politicians are particularly good examples) who did not follow Einstein's example.

Each miniconcept is designed to remind us in a small way of our values, obligations, and responsibilities. The more concentrated and vivid I can make them, the better they work. A purchasing agent (or perhaps we now call them procurement executives), for example, may have difficulty understanding the importance of minimizing investment and expense by increasing raw material inventory turns. But use the following phrase and the concept becomes crystal clear: "You can only eat like a buffalo and poop like a butterfly for so long!"

The thoughts in this section are, by design, general in nature. It wouldn't be hard, if you wanted to, to find exceptions to these axioms. Many philosophies (and all strategies) must be customized to specific situations in order to be valid. However, I find that most of these thoughts are applicable most of the time. I offer them as another way to help you begin to think like a CEO about the simple truths at the heart of most management decisions.

Management

- *When two otherwise capable and intelligent managers call each other fools,* they are usually both right.
- *You need two advertising managers,* one for the great idea, and another to keep you from changing it.
- *Back people up*. Either fire them or vindicate them.
- *Effective leaders achieve balance*. They have the need and ability to achieve and to lead, balanced by a degree of humility and emotional maturity.
- *Force movement*. Drive yourself and your management team toward decisions, not discussions.
- *Think*. Don't let the urgent drive out the important.
- *Demand departmental strategy*. Require a design, a theme, and a purpose for all major activities.
- *Let each person know he is building a temple,* not just carrying rocks to the top of the mountain. A serious part of leadership is "meaningful" communication of your vision for the company.
- *Policies, procedures, and sophistication* are needed at lower and middle management levels. At top management levels, you need only simple fundamentals. For example, warranty managers need settlement guidelines, authority levels, sophisticated legal advice, and sophisticated technical procedures. When it comes to warranty, CEOs need only this simple fundamental guideline: "Do what is fair and right."

- *Prioritizing is the answer* to time management problems—not computers, efficiency experts, or matrix scheduling. You do not need to do your work faster or to eliminate gaps in productivity to make better use of your time. You need to spend more time on the right things. Create uninterrupted "chunks" of time and minimize or eliminate from your schedule those items that do not relate to priority issues.

Strategy and Decision-Making

- *Decide how you're going to decide.* Weigh the moral, intuitive, and intellectual content of your decisions and consider them in this order: First, give the most weight to the moral aspects of your decision; second, consider the intuitive "feel" of each alternative choice; third, analyze the intellectual elements.
- *Watch incremental decisions.* Never cease to think of the business as a whole.
- *Regularly summarize your status.* Every three to six months, write a summary of the company's current position, recent mistakes and accomplishments, recent changes inside and outside of the company, and future prospects. Identify all now opportunitios and throats.
- *Think action.* It's too easy to do nothing.
- *Stick to priorities.* Provide clear decisions, bold policies, and stay with your grand theme.
- *Strategic partnerships and strategic deals seldom pan out as planned.* The problem is that the projected synergy used to justify the strategic partnership is often overestimated. Amazingly, this overestimation seems to grow in deals that will not work without the "synergy."
- *Bad information makes for bad decisions,* and at least 80 percent of management is decision-making. Insist on good (verified), "no doubt about it," "take it to the bank" information.

- *Cut bait on a bad deal,* abandon mistakes, and jettison errors in judgment. If the first responsibility of a CEO is to select the right business, a key part of this responsibility is the capacity to be the one to walk away when necessary.
- *Limit the scope of your mission statement* to that of establishing a target. Its purpose is to define success so that everyone in your company will be striving for the same goal. Your mission statement should be a clear and concise call to action that expresses your company's contribution to its customers. The core competencies necessary to deliver the contribution should at least be implicit in the statement. If needed, use a separate document to communicate your values, strategies, tactics, and fundamental principles. Including your business philosophy and your personal ideology in your mission statement may be good public relations, but this clouds its ability to define direction and promote focus.
- *Strategy, in business as in war, is about putting your company in position to fight and win the battle.* Tactics are related to the face-to-face, day-to-day actions required to win the battles.
- *The army with the most soldiers wins.* The company with the most resources wins. In a battle, the winning general figures out how to have more soldiers at a particular site and time than does his opponent. This is what strategy is all about.
- *Never buy meteor insurance.* You cannot mitigate or eliminate all risk. Risk is a part of business and a part of that for which you get paid. Major risks must be recognized, assessed, and managed, but there is not enough money or time to address every possible risk. So when your banker or board of directors asks you to eliminate all risks, remind them about the fallacy of meteor insurance.
- *Understand your competitive position* by answering these questions:
  1. Why should a customer buy (use) my product (service) as opposed to any other?

2. Who are my customers?
3. Who are not my customers, i.e., who buys from my competitors and why?

Money and Numbers

- *Everyone underestimates cash requirements* for startup operations.
- *Do not confuse numbers people with numbers people* just because they know accounting. Many in your company are skilled in the use of numbers, but there are big differences in their specific capabilities. Bookkeepers do not necessarily know credit. Credit people do not necessarily know finance. Finance people do not necessarily know about acquisition analysis. Acquisition analysis people do not necessarily know about budgeting. Budget people do not necessarily know about investments.
- *Never blame the accountants,* they are just accountants. Their purpose is only to audit the battlefield and restab the wounded after the battle is over.
- *Demand unfiltered information.* Get important information firsthand.
- *Nothing costs more than equity.* Debt, for example, is much less expensive than equity.
- *Do not make "corporate" a burden.* Be cautious with administrative fees, so-called "market rate" rents, opportunity costs of money, and charges for corporate personnel visits to divisions. These charges, when overdone, divert the attention of operating managers from customers, employees, growth, and profitability, and direct them towards corporate. They cause resentment, and give managers a scapegoat for their lack of performance. Excessive "corporate fees" can also hide the true cost of corporate. These fees and transfer charges can make corporate the most profitable division in the company, even when "corporate" has no customers and no revenues.

- *Do not get fooled by the accounting.* Accountants categorize transactions according to Generally Accepted Accounting Principles (GAAP) or Certified Public Accounting (CPA) rules. These principles and rules rarely reflect reality. According to accounting rules, trained employees and key managers have no asset value. Profits do not equal cash, and some forms of borrowing—like off balance sheet leasing—reflect no assets and no liabilities on the books. Fixed costs are not always fixed. Liquidity ratios do not always reflect liquidity. Look beyond the numbers to the fundamentals.

Experts and Consultants

- *Avoid consultants like the plague.* If a consultant provides a benefit at all, he does so only when you dedicate company resources to his project at the rate of three hours of company to one hour of consultant. Build your own team with strong players instead.
- *Never pay anyone to aggravate you.* You can get it done for less.
- *A lawyer's purpose is to create legal meltdown.* A lawyer puts your money and your adversary's money in a big pile and then proceeds to melt it down.
- *Do not let lawyers go to school on your ticket.* If they profess to be experts, they should not charge for legal research.
- *Lawyers have been known to negotiate on their prices.* You do not always have to pay those stupid fee-per-hour invoices.
- *Do not put lawyers on staff.* You will just pay them to hire more lawyers. There will be jurisdictional reasons, time-frame reasons, and specialty reasons for their (and subsequently your) hiring of other lawyers. Staff lawyers build their own empires. People in your company will run documents past them that previously were never even read over, much less checked for legality.

Business—Never As Usual

- *Satisfied customers* are the ultimate source of all continuing cash flow.

- *Never respond in anger.* Do not write, talk, or make decisions while angry.
- *A closed mouth gathers no feet.* Consider this as career advice.
- *Face bad news squarely.* Develop the capacity to take the rough with the smooth.
- *Old founders never go away, they just die.* If they have not died, they will stay there. No matter how often they talk about succession or retirement, they will not leave the company until death takes them. Plan accordingly.
- *Hire well, manage little.* Always put a premium on successful experience.
- *Avoid bureaucracy.* Develop a disdain for committees (by any name) that are purely advisory in nature.
- *Save 90 days' more energy.* When you think a big deal or difficult transition is nearing completion, do not bet on the timing. Prepare yourself and your team for an additional 90 days of effort. This will help avoid the emotional roller coaster of deals that appear to be closing but continue on and on.
- *Delivered quality* is measured by the degree of customer satisfaction with the product or service.
- *Produced quality* is achieved by meeting the customer's expectations and specifications on the first attempt to do so. Degree of produced quality can be calculated by measuring the costs of "unquality" (i.e., rework, scrap, warranty, and lost business). Improvements in produced quality will not be realized until the behavior of those doing the work is changed.
- *Customers will not tell you how to design a product.* They will tell you what they like and do not like, but you have to guess what they are willing to pay for and the best way to address their needs.
- *For 2,000 years, it has been unkind to kill the messenger.* If you react poorly to bad news, pretty soon bad news will be withheld from you. Your news will end up like Russian roulette: It will not be really "bad" news until it's "really" bad news.

- *Never buy from panhandlers.* Do not buy it if you did not know you needed it before they called.
- *Live by the sword, die by the sword.* If you take credit for the company's good fortune and your great management during a rising market, what will you say when the market falls?
- *There is no such thing as an endless boom market.* It only seems that way when times are good.
- *Repetition is the goal of production.* Resist the temptation to cross-train everyone by constantly moving them from job to job. Most production organizations need only between 15 and 30 percent of their production force cross-trained. The rest require repetition to take advantage of learning curve efficiencies.
- *Set artificial but firm deadlines.* Everyone knows the payroll must be calculated and input by Wednesday, so it can print on Thursday and be delivered on Friday. These deadlines make it clear that "payroll" is legitimate and must be handled promptly and correctly. The secret to managing what might be called "softer" items, such as training and planning, is absolute (serious consequences if you do not meet them) deadlines.
- *When your only tool is a hammer, every problem looks like a nail.* Go to a surgeon and he will recommend an operation. Go to a chiropractor and he will crack your back. Go to a psychologist and he will ask you about your childhood. No doubt, you get the picture.
- *Training is tough.* It is often as hard to teach a new dog old tricks as it is to teach an old dog new tricks.
- *Any deal that does not allow for all the players to win is a bad deal.* Structure every deal so that all the partners are wearing the same colored jerseys. Things that make you feel good or bad should affect your partners in the same fashion.
- *No sustainable competitive edge means no sustainable profits.* End of story!

- *No bluffs*. Not with customers, suppliers, employees, or shareholders. Play them only when you have them. A bluffer is soon found out. Let your word be your bond.
- *Markets determine prices*. Cost tells you if you can afford to be in this business. Price to create the largest market demand, not just to cover cost or create margin.
- *Do not give it away*. When you first start a business, there is a tendency to prematurely give away too much stock; after all, it is "really" not worth anything in the beginning.
- *Underpromise and overdeliver* in customer service. It starts with the promise. If you promise too much, you may never catch up. Make conservative promises and liberal deliveries.
- *If you can only measure three things*, measure customer satisfaction, employee satisfaction, and cash flow.
- *There are teams and there are committees*. Teams have a goal, a responsibility, and a method of performance measurement for *each* team member. Committees have only group goals, responsibilities, and performance measurements.
- *Use the multiple operations advantage*. Whenever a company has similar multiple operations—like a chain of retail stores—the potential for this particular advantage comes into play. If you have a franchise system with 50 or more outlets, undoubtedly one is setting the pace for all of the others. All you have to do is find it and copy it. There is no need to reinvent the wheel.
- *Focus most of your resources on tomorrow's opportunities* versus yesterday's problems.
- *Do not condemn the judgment of another* just because it differs from your own. You may both be wrong.
- *The purpose of management is to make decisions and to lead*. Cut back positions and de-layer the organization whenever you find managers or layers that do not make decisions or do not lead.
- *Choose the bolder route* when faced with equally viable courses of action.
- *Beware of books giving (business) counsel.*

Chapter 14

Final Thoughts: Simple Truths from Great Complexities

Difficulties mastered are opportunities won.
—Winston Churchill

Sir Winston Leonard Spencer Churchill (1874-1965) was Great Britain's greatest 20th-century leader and statesman. Although he is widely renowned for his leadership as Britain's Prime Minister during World War II, it's less common knowledge that he achieved this great status in spite of early difficulties with academics, political defeats, and World War I naval and battle campaign failures. In addition, his inability to manage his personal finances was chronic. Many who read early drafts of this book have suggested that this lack of financial prowess might dictate quotes from a difference source, at least in the sections dealing with numbers or money.

But I chose the quotations from Winston Churchill not in spite of his shortcomings and defeats, but in part because of them. When reading about Churchill, you encounter a vigorous, tenacious, and principled man. He understood that leadership begins with a mind-set. His ability to conceptualize clearly his role, his work, and himself gave him the strength to follow through on his convictions. And he managed to gain this reputation for the integrity of his convictions even though he switched from the Conservative to the Liberal and back to the Conservative Party over the course of his career. He had the courage to fight for his beliefs, the intellectual honesty to change his position in the face of new facts, and the grace to forgive his political opponents. Churchill was a man who accepted responsibility for failures, even when the fault was not his alone. He was decisive with a bias toward action, but he also knew when not to decide an issue. He was a clear and highly organized thinker and could attend to detail while keeping focused on the central issues. He understood risk and was calm under stress. His patriotism was unchallenged and his optimism unrivaled. His persistence and his ability to leverage his unique strengths helped make him the right leader at the right time. He had his imperfections, as we all do, but he compensated for them and achieved greatness by using his strengths to pursue a noble cause. Through it all, he was able to provide a guiding light for his country and perhaps the world. His is a model of true leadership, writ large.

The whole of Churchill, shortcomings and successes together, demonstrates that leadership is not dictated by *every* aspect of a person's behavior. It comes from an energy derived from an individual's passion. All effective leaders find their own energy source by discovering their passions and then identifying and leveraging their own personal strengths. Winston Churchill may not have found his strengths early in life. Perhaps he had to wait for time and circumstance to provide the right opportunity to apply them. But he knew his passions and his principles; when World War II came along, Churchill was ready to take on the noble cause of a nation.

So the reasons for the Churchill quotations are simple. The quotations remind us to discover our own passions and to find and leverage our own personal strengths. They show us the importance of overcoming our disappointments and shortfalls and of applying our strengths to a noble cause. And they demonstrate that clear thinking about the fundamentals, when combined with a personal sense of ethics, a clear vision of the future, positive communication, and focused energy, can provide extraordinary results.

Leveraging Your Own Strengths

As an ordinary individual, you possess the power to leverage your own personal strengths to generate the energy of extraordinary leadership. When you apply that energy to a cause you consider to be noble and let integrity and character guide all of your actions, you will not only succeed but also allow the many who join you to prosper.

Only you can supply the energy that comes from clarity of passion; the methods and disciplines of *CEO Logic*, however, will help you to convert that passion to consistent and focused results. These are the secrets, not only of clear-thinking CEOs, but to managerial success at all levels of business. CEOs develop valid business philosophies consisting of fundamental business principles, their own personal management philosophy, and insights into a particular opportunity, and convert them into core operating values. They then use these core operating values to communicate and educate their management teams, to validate their vision of the future, to develop a specific operating strategy, and to guide their efforts at management execution.

If you follow this model and learn to think like a CEO before you become one, you'll be more than ready for the position. If you never become a CEO, your approach to your work will be sounder and you'll have a stronger grasp of the fundamentals that drive business behavior. Wherever you are in your career, let the practice of *CEO Logic* become the hallmark of your own personal philosophy and the foundation of your own extraordinary success.

The Sources of Clear Thinking

As you begin the journey of discovering and documenting your own valid business philosophy, let me share with you the baseline principles and practices that have served as my own sources for clear thinking throughout my career. These core principles and habits have been the touchstones for success that have carried me up through the ranks.

The principles behind all other principles

Your ethics and your word are your bond. Being successful in business never requires you to compromise your values or to behave in unethical ways. Remember that business, unlike God, neither forgives nor forgets a breach in ethics. As the saying goes, "Money comes and goes, but reputation lasts forever." A good business plan attempts to create new wealth, not to take it from others.

Keep your eye on your core competency and competitive edge. As I've discussed, all successful business strategy flows from two fundamental, inviolable principles:

1. Strengthen and leverage your core competencies.

2. Extend and sustain your competitive edge by allocating your resources to exploit opportunities and/or defend against threats.

Jeff Haines, CEO of Royce Medical Company, a very successful manufacturing and distribution business, is a master of these principles. His competitive edge stems from his twofold core competencies, in this case in research and development of proprietary patented products and cost-efficient selling through telemarketing.

His overall strategy to grow the business consists of continuous improvement of all elements in his business, particularly research and development and telemarketing. He realizes that applying resources in a focused way to specific projects will provide long-term payback *only* in proportion to their positive impact on product development and cost-efficient selling. This is truly thinking like a CEO—focused on the fundamentals but keenly aware of the big picture.

13 Habits of Highly Effective CEOs and Managers

1. Feel your passions like a CEO and allow them to energize your vision for the organization.
2. Select the right business.
3. Measure the right issues.
4. Gain leverage by focusing limited resources on core opportunities.
5. Make continuous improvement a permanent goal.
6. Use the insights you gain by thinking through the true purpose of each resource.
7. Communicate your core operating values and personal management philosophy clearly and often.
8. Align operations with strategy.
9. Allocate and apply separate resources to the three basic business strategies: manage today's operations; improve today's methods; prepare for tomorrow's business.
10. Design business systems that accommodate ordinary people.

11. Devise and operate by a value system that provides good consequences for good performance and bad consequences for bad performance.
12. Hire the best and deal with people as they exist, not as you would prefer them to be.
13. Manage daily cash flow separately from profit and loss issues.

Prepare for the Management Journey Ahead

The free enterprise system offers virtually unlimited opportunities, but with these opportunities come nearly unlimited challenges. The more successful you become, the more visible you are to competitors. The more visible you are, the more challenges you will receive. The discipline of *CEO Logic* can ground you in the balance you need to meet these challenges: a balance between change and order. Change is needed to improve today's business and to prepare for tomorrow. Order is needed to be successful today.

And if there is a single key to balancing change and order, it is to develop a valid business philosophy and to interpret each operating principle in a way that makes sense for your particular circumstances, your personal management style, and your particular company. There are very few absolutes. Everything from your vision for the organization, to your strategy, to your execution must be continually monitored, reviewed, and modified as circumstances dictate. Having the insight and judgment to know when to change and when to stay the course separates the great managers from all others. In the end, insight, judgment, honor, ethics, and courage are the only absolutes.

Remember that simple truths are often hidden beneath the great complexities that will mark your management journey. Make clear thought—the logic practiced by the successful CEO—your central habit of mind. *What you think affects what you do, and it's what you do that determines your success.* Master the discipline of applying *CEO Logic* to the fundamentals, and think your way through to extraordinary business success.

Bibliography

Adizes, Ichak. *Mastering Change*. Adizes Institute Publications, 1991.

Alford, Steve. *Playing for Knight*. Fireside, 1990.

Drucker, Peter. *Management: Tasks, Responsibilities, Practices*. Harper and Row, 1973.

Drucker, Peter. *Drucker on Asia*. Butterworth-Heinemann, 1997.

Drucker, Peter. *Managing in a Time of Great Change*. Truman Talley, 1996.

Hamel, Gary, and C. K. Prahalad. *Competing for the Future*. Harvard Business School Press, 1994.

Mintzberg, Henry. *The Rise and Fall of Strategic Planning*. Prentice Hall, 1994.

Nelson, Bob. *1,001 Ways to Reward Employees*. Workman Publishing, 1994.

Ohmae, Kenichi. *The Mind of the Strategist*. Penguin, 1982.

Porter, Michael. *Competitive Advantage*. Free Press, 1985.

Porter, Michael. *Competitive Strategy*. Free Press, 1980.

Index